Theodora Ioannidou

The Holocaust of the Pontian Greeks
still an open wound

The Holocaust of the Pontian Greeks
still an open wound

Theodora Ioannidou
e-mail: dora_ioannidou@hotmail.com

Author / Publisher: Theodora Ioannidou
Translation editor: Katerina Garagouni
Cover: Mediterra Books
Production supervisor: Platon Malliagkas - mediterrabooks.com
© 2016 Theodora Ioannidou
ISBN 978-960-93-8443-8

Photo on front cover: Pontian children in the bread line
Photo on back cover: Pontian refugees from Fatsa, waiting to board a ship to Greece

He who loves the truth must also find the strength to endure it. Furthermore, any effort to lessen the harsh impression created would be a distortion of the facts. The individuals whose stories are told herein are not an exception but the rule in the Pontian drama.

Contents

Acknowledgements

The compilation and confirmation of facts and information brought me in contact with people who were often complete strangers. Nevertheless, the distinct Pontian element that I hurried to convey over the wire in the countless phone calls I made to them, both in and outside Greece, transformed even the slightest hesitation on the part of these strangers into sincere eagerness to support the project. With some I compared facts, with others I consulted on details of the Pontian language, with yet others I exchanged photographs. Every word herein that concerns our Pontian past, our common ancestral pain, was written with their invaluable advice. They are not mentioned here by name because there are truly far too many. They all know, however, how grateful I am to them.

Thanks are also due to the Pontian Fellowship of Melissia, as well as the towns of Drapetsona and Amfiali, in whose libraries I located important information. The contributions of photographs by the War Museum, the Greek Red Cross, The National Television and Radio Stations (ERT), the Historical and Literary Archives of Kavala and Mrs. Anna Theophylactou were invaluable. There is no way to adequately thank the Center for Asia Minor Studies or the Committee for Pontian Studies for their tremendous assistance. My practical way of thanking everyone is simply the publication, with the consent of the owners, of all the materials that reached me, including handwritten testimony, audio recordings and rare photographs.

Two other sources of photographic material must be mentioned, first, Oberlin College, for whose substantial contribution from their archives I am grateful, and second, the book *Certain Samaritans*, by Esther Pohl Lovejoy. My gratitude to this author and activist should be regarded as representative of that which every Pontian feels to her, as well as to all the American women, in particular Theda Phelps and Olga Stastny, who voluntarily and whole-heartedly aided my ancestors during their persecution by the Young Turks and Kemal. They traveled thousands of miles from home to help total strangers, and were not afraid to give public voice to their horror when they witnessed the genocide of the Christian peoples of Asia Minor, rather than silently condone such atrocities.

My fervent thanks also go to the highly capable graphic designer, Lia Vanidou, for her work on pagination, photo editing, and the overall layout of the book. Regarding the English translation, the support and advice I received from Joel and Katerina Shields, Dimitrios Garagounis and Rosemary Yeagle has been invaluable, and can only be described as a blessing. It was their patient, devoted effort in revising version after version in accordance with my whims that served to strengthen my conviction that the Pontian issue is not merely of interest to the wider, ethnic Greek community around the world, but to all nations and individuals everywhere.

Finally, I am deeply indebted to two staunch advocates of the Pontian cause: Michalis Charalampides, who, among other things, laid the foundation for the mission of seeking vindication for the Pontians, and Professor Konstantinos Fotiades, who waded through hoards of testimony and organized it all with indefatigable patience. I dedicate this work to both of them. They honored me with their friendship. They supported me with their advice. I will be at their side in our common struggle.

Preface

by Konstantinos Fotiades
Professor of History, University of Western Macedonia

History as a remembrance of past human actions has come to an end. Now History has to be understood as the forerunner of human actions to come. When the past is recounted in our day and age, it is recounted with a view to the shape of things aimed for in a future state, a state that concerns not a portion of the world, not one country or another, but the whole world. History is now written and taught from the perspective of globalism, so that it may contribute to the construction of a homogeneous world community: ONE world for the ONE human race.

In this forward-looking perspective of globalization, History cannot be the thorough remembrance of things past, but has to be the selective forgetfulness of the past, an edited version of the totality of human actions and omissions that have produced the present. History can no longer provide descriptive services to humanity, because it now has a prescriptive mission: it has to play a very constructive role in the politicoreligious program of world governance and ecumenical conciliation. Past actions which elevate one people or one religion to grandeur and splendor or lower another to barbarity and baseness inescapably contribute to the heightening of a strong sense of national and religious identity. Concomitantly national and religious divisions deepen and the one-world agenda is disrupted. Understandably, therefore, such practices of patriotic History must be expunged.

History now smoothes over its rough spots, silences past enmities, and renames catastrophes. Past acts of heroism and acts of atrocity, human suffering and human cruelty, ambition and cowardice, patriotism and betrayal, need to be toned down, discolored, recharacterized. What was once vitally real in human life, the actual way people went about exercising their freedom and their self-determination, in war or peace, always through their understanding of tribal, national or religious identity, now has to be abstracted from. Real lives and real deaths, oddly enough, need to become irrelevant to History.

The book you are now holding in your hands, *The Holocaust of the Pontian Greeks*, does precisely the opposite. It stays close to the particular, the concrete and the patriotic, and it does so in reference to the exceedingly painful historical events of the Pontian Genocide, 1916-1924. The Pontian Genocide is not merely a highly charged issue that makes a particular nation uncomfortable when talked about, but a historical reality of the most inhumane character, a reality brought about by certain elements of the Ottoman empire in collaboration with dignified World Powers and with the toleration of the so-called «international community».

The *Holocaust of the Pontian Greeks* is not just a J'accuse by Theodora Ioannidou, aimed at those responsible for one of the major gruesome historical crimes that took place in the 20th century. It is not merely a moral and psychological condemnation of those nations and men in power who brought about the Pontian Genocide. It is a dramatic account of a handful of living human beings that suffered man's capacity for evil and sought to prevail in the face of it. It is this inhuman and rather demonic capacity for evil, which is woven as a definite diachronic strain in the human fiber and which repeatedly manifests itself throughout time with equal heartlessness, that stands as the main theme of this book. Man's capacity to dehumanize and annihilate his fellow man is what stands stigmatized.

The historical accounts presented here in the literary style of a most gripping novel, though not «politically correct», are definitely most actually correct, derived from first-hand sources that bear the indisputable wounds of personal witness. And rather than abstracting from the particular in order to fit the current mold of anaemic History-writing, they focus expressly on the particular. Only World-historical personages and

History-making personalities, such as politicians, diplomats and generals, are treated abstractly in this book. The narration, in fact, could not get more concrete or closer to reality, unless it were to become as gruesome as some of the omitted data actually reveal.

The historical accounts presented here pertain to ordinary people caught in the mill of history: men, women and children, whose lot it was to live under conditions of war and peace that others determined. It is their particular circumstances that are here wrested from oblivion and brought back to living memory. The historical narrative unfolding in the following pages is so concrete that it fills your nostrils with the smell of fire and smoke, of sweat and blood, while making your heart and mind palpitate with the agony and hope, the despair and the courage of people who had been masters of their lives, lost everything, and sought to regain a foothold amidst inauspicious historical conditions.

The reader is invited and treated to a vivid experience of historical injustice and human resilience that is profoundly moving. The author, however, is left to ponder the more profound question of what in God's inscrutable providence makes historical injustice just.

Translators' Preface

It has been an honor to participate in this project to foster worldwide awareness of the reality of the Pontian Genocide, in all its scope and long-term consequences. A few remarks on the specific challenges of this translation would seem to be in order.

While it is always difficult to render an exact translation from one language to another, on account of the deeper connotations which even the simplest words may carry for the native speaker and which are inevitably lost on the foreigner, «translating» from past to present can be problematic even within the same language, as usage, fashions, customs and everyday items become obsolete over time. In this case, Mrs. Ioannidou had the additional task of elucidating the Pontian dialect for non-Pontian Greek readers. Thus, in order to retain an element of the original mood and culture being written about, we have often resorted to leaving a word or phrase in its Pontian Greek form, though transliterated for readers of English, giving its meaning in a footnote. This decision, of course, led to the further difficulty of transposing the Greek alphabet into Latin characters. It must be confessed that we followed no hard and fast rules, but for the most part endeavored to convey the Greek pronunciation as accurately as possible for English readers. On the other hand, we occasionally adhered to the traditional rendition of a name if we felt that it was recognizable, such as Giorgos for George, though the pronunciation would be more like Yorgos. Further, we chose to represent the very common suffix -ης found on many first and last names with -es because we like the way it looks, whereas -is would more likely be pronounced closer to the original Greek. It should also be noted that place names have been kept in a more or less Greek version, though all of them have quite a different name in modern-day Turkish and would not be found in their old form on a contemporary map. Finally, we chose to represent the name of the region, Pontus, as the Pontus, against common practice and standard grammar rules, in order to retain the Greek sense of its being not just another place name but larger than life, an integral part of their very existence.

One part of this work in which we feel we have not achieved the best possible result was the rendering of Panayotes Spyrantes' lengthy verbal testimony in Chapter 4. Expressions which were vivid and effective in the original spoken Greek sounded choppy and awkward when rendered into precise translation. We were thus forced, in places, to use a more formal tone and join sentences together for a more natural flow in English, at the cost of losing the flavor of the oral account.

As anyone who has spent a large part of their life in each of two different cultures knows, there are certain aspects of the one which are only indirectly translatable into the language of the other. Implicit in a single word are basic elements of the culture which are so unique that the translator must either resort to an explanatory footnote, or ignore these nuances and use the next-best synonym available in the target language. Such a word is «βάσανα» and its derivatives, «βασανίζω» and «βασανισμένος». The closest synonyms in English are «torture» and «torment», yet the Greek people, and perhaps more so the Pontian Greeks, have been so tortured and tormented for so many hundreds of years that the very weight of the word is different for them than for anyone from an English-speaking background.

An American or a Briton who hears the word «torture» will immediately think of prisons, dungeons, or torture chambers, or the more modern methods employed nowadays by «intelligence» services around the world. For the Greek, however, the images and associations that are evoked by the word «βάσανα» are based on their own extensive daily experience of the varieties of torture, torment and suffering which may exist: the βάσανα of extreme poverty and all its ramifications, the βάσανα of war-torn villages and cities, the βάσανα of living for 400 years under a foreign power whose faith is radically opposed to one's own, and the struggle to keep Christian Orthodoxy alive during all that time, the βάσανα of having the boundaries of one's «emancipated» country drawn by the rulers of other superior powers, of being used as pawns in the greater scheme of things, the βάσανα of civil war instigated by external powers, of brother fighting against brother, the βάσανα of dictatorship, the βάσανα of the endless cycle of loan debt and the corresponding stranglehold measures taken by an enlightened Europe to combat it...

The list goes on and on. A people which has suffered so deeply, so permanently, as it would seem, inevitably shapes its language to express this suffering, and that is not easily managed by the language of another culture which has not undergone such prolonged pain. On the other hand, the events portrayed in this book speak for themselves, even if the translation does not perfectly convey each word or phrase in its full linguistic and connotative value.

Every effort has been made to adequately impress upon the reader the stark reality of the unprecedented persecution these people went through, and the amazing strength of character and faith which not only brought them to mainland Greece with their minds and souls intact, though badly battered, but also preserved for future generations that self-same resilience.

We can only applaud the efforts of Mrs. Ioannidou and others like her to finally heal the still gaping wound of the Pontian Genocide, and thank her for the opportunity to contribute what little we could.

Introduction

«May the shades forgive me for reviving all this.»
Alexandros Papadiamantes

When I decided to research my family tree a few years back, my aim was simply to inform myself. I was of the belief that my daughters ought to know their roots, since not only their present but their future itself was already bearing the inevitable marks of globalization. I did not want them to become estranged from their past. Thus, I decided to learn so that they might learn as well. Totally unprepared for both the volume and the type of material I was to unearth, I began. Quite playfully I scribbled on a blank page the imperial title «Bourbons» and on another the equally pompous «Hapsburgs» for the families of my father and mother, respectively. I filled in all the names I knew and so did all the relatives drafted for the same purpose. Gradually, forgotten ancestors began to emerge and take their place in my «imperial» rosters–ancestors called out of the quiet, the oblivion they had secured for themselves by their death.

The self-deprecatory titles I had chosen were amusing: family trees are usually the aspirations of prominent families, not those of insignificant ones like mine. At the same time this conjured-up device served to defuse the audacity of my enterprise, namely that of attempting to break into those tightly-sealed, buried lives. In other words, I was no longer forbidden entry for lack of titular nobility.

The gradual accumulation of names eventually broadened into a web right before my eyes. The tree began to grow branches and offshoots: uncles, aunts, endless cousins, unknown siblings of grandparents' and various other figures began to claim space in my notes, but also in my everyday life. They silently took shape in the midst of my hectic daily pursuits and with their discreet presence, my family assemblage advanced. The challenge of the project to delve as far back in time as possible, resulting in ever denser foliage in the genealogical tree and involving individuals who hearkened back to the beginning of the previous century, held a curious charm for me.

Before long, however, the superficial list of names ceased to be the primary objective. The clarification of our degree of kinship was no longer the focus, for other things were of more gravity. Hidden behind the names were tormented souls and bodies, a fact that could not long be ignored. They were human beings. Hesitantly, I began to ask how they had lived and died and what circumstances had determined their destiny. I learned of the unexpected reversals in their lives and the catalytic role of the historical moment in their turbulent paths. It was at that point that things took another turn for me. All frivolity ceased: what lay before me was utterly chilling. The initial surprise was succeeded by a string of queries: was my own existence grounded in such dramatic events? What determines how merciless life will be for each of us? Why, in the school of pain, are some of us permitted to take easy lessons while others must take extremely difficult ones?

I am Pontian Greek, a third-generation refugee, descended from grandparents all born in the Pontus. I was born and raised in Athens, where I studied, married, and still live today. As a young student in the fifties and sixties, I was taught nothing about my forefathers' homeland. Not one line regarding the Hellenism of the Black Sea region was to be found in our schoolbooks. We Pontians were present... yet absent. The Pontian issue was entirely ignored, as if we had never been exiled from lands that amounted to half the size of present-day Greece. Once again, silence was kept regarding true history in order to serve political aims. The Pontus was treated both historically and nationally as if it was insignificant, like a hangnail that had simply been cut off.

The ostensible excuse was, of course, that such a catastrophic defeat necessitated the avoidance of any reference to the subject. That may be true in part, but defeat, too, can teach a valuable lesson. All ordinary people at a personal level, but also whole nations at a broader level, derive benefit, when we find the courage to face the reality and make use of its didactic message. After all, what is the commemoration of 1940 but the celebration of a heroic defeat for the Greeks? We lost, yet without being defeated. The historical dignity of a people is based, first and foremost, on its fighting spirit rather than on the positive or negative outcome of events.

My parents, second-generation refugees, though actively involved in the establishment of the Pontian Fellowship of Melissia and its various functions, avoided any reference to recollections of refugee experiences, so that they were of little use in teaching us what the education system did not. Only a few times did they refer to their past, and then they spoke mainly of the German Occupation, of deprivation and of orphanhood. Of course, they would *kalatsevan*[1] in the Pontian dialect, especially when they did not want to make us, the *chatala*[2], privy to their exchanges. But they lived in the Attica Basin, the basin of proscriptions, far removed from the villages of Macedonia which were the main strongholds where Pontian traditions were revered and preserved. In the capital the desire for a better life prevailed, which was reflected in the craze for whatever was foreign, along the lines of Danish furnishings and La Cumparsita[3]. The people wanted to advance, without understanding that theirs was the one country in the world that could only go forward by looking back[4]. Of course, there were political struggles, and rallies over events in Cyprus. Yet the British gallows which were wiping out the youth of Cyprus obscured the Turkish gallows, so that the Pontian refugee population was forgotten in the various corners of Athens. Living in such an environment, my parents struggled mainly to provide us children with whatever

---

1. A Pontian word which means «discussed».
2. Pontian for «children», from the Ancient Greek word, *atalos*: young one, child.
3. A grand tango from Uruguay then very much in fashion.
4. This was the opinion of the prolific author and newspaper editor Demetrius Kampouroglou (1852-1942), who throughout his extensive writings endeavored to demonstrate the unbroken continuation of Hellenism from ancient Greece to modern times.

they had been deprived of in their own childhood, and the homeland of their ancestors gradually became of secondary importance in their lives. Nevertheless, to this day, my mother's joyful voice and that of my aunt's still echo in my ears, calling to each other in our then sparsely-inhabited neighborhood when they happened to hear Pontian music playing on the radio: «Despoina, Pontian songs!» «Ourania, Pontian songs!» They could not hide their excitement.

But there were others, too. There was that ever-so-tormented first generation of refugees, who, like my grandmother Chrysoula, had been born *'s sin patrida*[5]. It was they who were crowded into the quarantine stations and the refugee shacks. It was they who were slowly kneaded together with the soil of the tobacco fields they tended in northern Greece. And it was they who had been met with suspicion or outright hostility by the locals and were derided as «aout-ides» because, in their near-Homeric dialect, they still pronounced the pronoun *outos* (he) as «aoutos».

They had been driven out of lands uninterruptedly Greek ever since the 8th century B.C., and which even in prehistoric times were imbued with the spirit embodied by Phrixus and Helle, Prometheus, Hercules, Iphigenia, the Amazons and countless other figures in Greek mythology. They were uprooted by tribes that first made their appearance from the depths of Asia in the 11th century A.D. They had arrived in rags, starved and pushed to the limits of human endurance. Every one of them had family members that were either dead or missing, and often they themselves were the only survivors. Upon their re-settlement on the Greek mainland, they worked very hard to become self-sufficient, exemplary models of dignity and pride. Naturally, they had their share of human weaknesses. But as the snow had blanketed mountains, homes, and trees when many of them were fleeing to escape slaughter, so their personal Calvary covered any human shortcomings.

It was them that I set out to write about. They are already dead, to the great relief of Turkey and all those who have assumed the onerous role

---

5. Pontian for «in the homeland».

of the erasure of history, and who, unfortunately, are often Greeks. They are still at work today, toiling undisguised, unabashedly broadening the ranks of those employed in this task of painting over reality. They can certainly say with vindication: «They're dead at last», in accordance with Kemal's historic pronouncement: «We have finally eradicated them». And yet, for more and more third-generation Pontians such as myself, the determination to obtain justice gains strength daily. Times change. The venerable elderly faces among whom I sauntered as an unsuspecting little girl are for me both an impetus and a cause: an impetus to delineate the boundaries of bestiality innate in the human being; a cause so that we can finally close the accounts of our patrimonial debts in a Greece that, as Makrygiannis so aptly lamented «is breathing its last» though having given birth to «the parents of all mankind».

The stance of the first-generation refugees was silence. They realized that any description would not only be painful but utterly inadequate in comparison to the reality of their all-powerful experiences. They were jammed by the thousands for months in ports and boats on the way to Greece, and when they finally arrived, the Pontian dialect was unknown to the local people. They neither understood their mainland hosts nor were they understood by them. Their speech was hushed and some of their voices were barely audible at all. Even at moments of joy their smile remained frozen, like that of an ancient statue and nothing more. Time for them seemed to have come to a halt, balanced on the boundary between a happy "before" and a tragic "after". Precisely there on that boundary, their days ended, on the incision of the wound, which remained unhealed up until their dying day. They may indeed have sung and danced, always to the strains of the Pontian lyre. As a rule, however, they were silent. That is how they were etched in my youthful memory: mute, distant and irrevocably embittered. They are those who never laughed, the inconsolable. And the wound is still open.

GENEALOGICAL TREE
Included here are only those family members directly
connected with the figures whose life stories are told
and whose names are indicated in bold print.

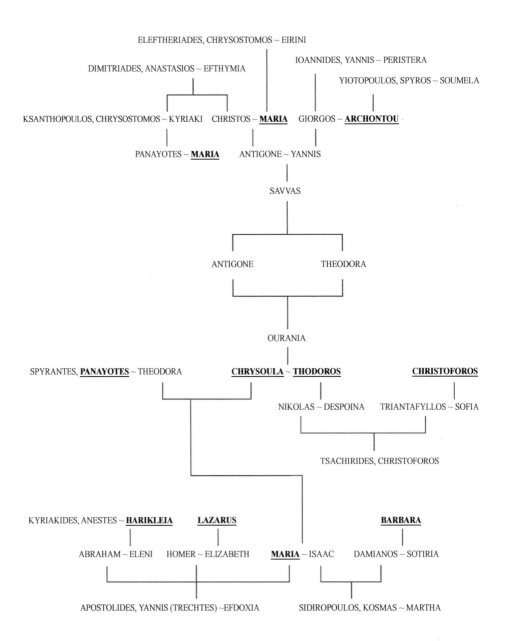

«NOT ONE COUPLE WAS LEFT INTACT»

MARIA DIMITRIADOU
[1875-1949]

«Anastoro ta palaia ki e karda m' pharmakoutai;
krougne 's so nou m' ta meria moun ki e goula m' pa gomoutai.»

(I recount the past, and my heart is poisoned;
the old places come to mind and the tears choke me.)

Maria Dimitriadou was my father's grandmother. Her daughter Antigone was his mother. She was born in the seaport of Oinoe, which together with a string of other cities adorned the Asia Minor coast of the Black Sea. This area was inhabited at the time of Alexander the Great, by settlers who had come from Oinoe, Greece, a township which still exists on the slopes of Mount Kithairona in Attica. Following the sea trail of the Argonauts, they crossed the Aegean and entered the Black Sea. When they reached the spot where six rivers all flowed into the sea, they decided to stay put. Amongst these abundant waters, three rivers on the east and three on the west, they would build their homes. There they would dwell. This was the beginning of Oinoe.

Some historians believe that this migration took place even earlier, at the end of the 5th century B.C. In that case, one wonders whether the Spartan raids on Attica at the beginning of the Peloponnesian Wars played a role in the transition, or perhaps the great famine that beset Athens. Still, regardless of any supposition or theorizing, we can say with certainty that the ancient Greek desire for wider horizons led to the conquest of the Pontus hundreds of years before Christ.

My great-grandmother Maria had already died by the time I was born, so I knew her only from photographs, in which she appeared stern and distant. In fact, looking at her, I wondered if she could ever have shared any joy. Her look was cold, and she seemed to be gazing into nothingness. Aren't all the grandmothers in the world kind and smiling? Aren't they the ones who give encouragement and spread optimism? Yet this grandmother appeared irrevocably embittered and remote. She looked as if she believed that any protest she might make would not be heard, or that if it was heard, it would make no difference to her. She was a fossilized grandmother. Why?

All of us, young and old, knew that she was a woman of faith and deeply religious. When at the age of seven my father's legs had been paralyzed for six months due to a serious infection, his parents were terrified by the great likelihood that their child would never walk again. The only one who believed he would get well was his grandmother Maria. She herself carried him in her arms all the way from their home in Kavala to worship the relics of Saint Gregory in Karvali[1]. At the church, she prayed for a miracle. Up until that time, my father could only get around by scooting along in a sitting position, but the moment he venerated the relics he felt that he could stand. He tried to stand up and he succeeded. Those of the congregation who were present were moved to tears of joy, and cried out in amazement: «The little boy walked! A miracle! A miracle!» It was a scene little Savvas would remember for the rest of his life. How was it possible, after such a stirring experience, that his grandmother, that black-clad shadow in the photograph, who had been justified in hoping for a miracle, no longer seemed to have hope in anything? What had happened to make her look as though she felt death was her only hope?

My great-grandmother's parents had a typically large family, with one son and five daughters. The girls married soon and well. Maria found her match in Christos Dimitriades, a hard-working, clever young man, who besides being of an imposing appearance had a dynamic character. He was a merchant who dealt in dried nuts and beverages, and his store was located right on the harbor of the city. His business grew year by year, and even expanded abroad. Loads of his goods traveled from the port of Oinoe, not only to Constantinople but all the way to France as well. Their life seemed to be going smoothly. Nothing of a very alarming nature was afoot at the beginning of the 1900s.

At the beginning of the twentieth century Oinoe retained a significant amount of its past splendor, despite having suffered for years, as had

---

1. A town in the Kavala area which was founded in 1924 by refugees from Karvali, Cappadochia. In their flight, they brought the relics of St. Gregory to their new home.

the wider region, from the violent practices of the *derempeides*[2] and the looting raids of the Ottomanized Laz pirates. A great part of it had, of course, burned down during the terrible fire of 1887, its merchant fleet had declined and many residents had emigrated, but business enterprises and social activities were once more on the rise. The surrounding hills were richly planted with beans, grains, filbert trees, hemp, rice, and all kinds of fruits, products which provided more than enough to meet local needs and were also exported to foreign markets. The residents, though perhaps a little too fond of wine, did not easily pass up an opportunity to make a profit.

The wealthier citizens often traveled on business, but also for pleasure. Indeed, it was common practice to take a pilgrimage to the Holy Land, as they were devout Christians. The journey, which usually lasted from the beginning of December until the Sunday after Easter, the Sunday of Saint Thomas, was a sea voyage by way of Constantinople. A group of pilgrims would spend months preparing enormous amounts of supplies, ranging from food and cooking utensils to mattresses and bedclothes. Several members of Maria's family had completed that trip, or in Pontian Greek, *edevan 's so hatziliki*[3], hence, the prefix *Hatzi-* on quite a few of their names. Apart from the change to Hatzimaria, there was Soultana who became Hatzisoulti, Eleni Hatzelengo, Eirini Hatzeirini and so on.

An echo of the urban lifestyle of Oinoe reached all the way to us, as we came to know some of our kin who hailed from the seaports, people with richer social experience and broader horizons. While this background resulted in a somewhat looser adherence to the Pontian traditions, at the same time it granted an abundant warmth and cordiality to their interactions. In contrast, our relatives from the mountainous regions, with their

---

2. From *dere beyler,* which means «lord of the valley». They were Ottoman officers with unrestricted claims on the lives and property of Christians, due to the relative sultan's edict of 1665. They instigated violent mass conversions to Islam, burnings, lootings, evictions, killings. It was enough, in some cases, for a child to speak Greek for them to cut out his parents' tongues.

3. «They have been to the Holy Land.»

rather peculiar behavior, adhered unwaveringly, perhaps obsessively, to the Pontian ethic and customs. It makes one wonder just how many and what combinations of spiritual, psychological and biological influences determine who we are.

Hatzimaria and Christos Dimitriades lived in a two-storey stone house in Kourkouletza, one of the six wealthy Greek neighborhoods of the city, which was bustling with activity. They lived near the church dedicated to the Dormition of Our Lady and the cemetery. In the adjacent Greek neighborhood of Periyiali, apart from the many coffee shops, bakeries and numerous retail shops, there was, more importantly, a Greek book-shop with its own reading room, a proof of cultural sophistication and a means of preserving Greek ethnicity.

They had five children and set out to raise them in the best way pos-sible. The last pregnancy, that of the «uninvited» Chrysostomos, had ini-tially startled my great-grandmother unpleasantly, as she had thought she was through with having babies. She already had three girls and a boy. Would she have to start all over again? It was most distressing. Then a friend tried to comfort her, saying that life may bring it about so that this, her youngest child, would be the one to look after her in her old age. A primitively optimistic remark, which, however, seemed to have a sooth-ing effect on the troubled mother, who in any case would have rejected any other option on principle. In this way, my grandmother Antigone's little brother Chrysostomos was born.

Naturally, they raised their children with dreams of seeing them healthy and happy: their three daughters should marry well and their two sons carry on the family business and raise nice families of their own. Such ideal images of life, those expectations for prudent, happy home-building, sometimes become reality. In those days, however, at the time of the First World War, such plans could not possibly succeed. The war had the first word and nothing was certain. Turkey belonged to a differ-ent coalition of powers than did Greece. Not only for their family but for all of Oinoe, for all the Pontian Greeks, the reversals followed rapidly one upon the other. Already by 1914, Talaat pasha[4] had commanded that the Christians be transferred to the inhospitable interior of Asia Minor.

In March 1916 the situation grew much worse when an economic embargo was declared against all Greeks. Shopping in their stores was forbidden and fines were imposed on offenders. Still other measures were implemented to intensify the persecution. Nothing was so pernicious, however, as the new deportations. In October the urban population was ordered to move to the Turkish villages of the Oinoe area, while the eleven Greek villages were burnt to the ground. It was a matter of course that before they burnt them, they made sure to loot all the residents' property and seize their livestock. They slaughtered the frail, the ill and the elderly, while as many women as they came in contact with they either raped, killed, or both. Many of the younger women were lost in the slave bargaining which had been organized especially for the *tsetes*[5]. Every kind of social scum had the option of choosing whichever young girl he wanted for his debauchery[6]. They were dignified, honorable Greek women, fed like meat to human devils. I remember as a child hearing some rare mention of such subjects, one in particular referring to an aunt by marriage. She was spoken of in low murmurs, instead of being crowned with the wreath of a martyr. They kept silence in order for life to continue.

---

4. Mehmet Talaat was Minister of the Interior (1913-17) and Grand Vizier (1917-18), a leader of the Young Turks and a merciless implementer of the genocidal scheme against the Armenians and the Greeks. He was murdered by an Armenian fugitive in Berlin, where he had taken refuge after the Turkish defeat in WWI. One of his decrees to the prefecture of Chalepos, dated September 13, 1915, stated typically: «Without the slightest discretion towards women, children or the weak, no matter how tragic the method of extermination, and having silenced the voice of conscience, their existence must be completely wiped out» (*Military History of Modern Greece*, published by the General Army Command, 1980, page 138). Indeed, in a confidential document dated May 14, 1914, whose content was later leaked in the newspaper *Le Temps* (6.24.1914), he explicitly commanded that the exiled citizens sign affirmations that they were willingly leaving their homes.

5. Tsetes (from the Turkish word *cete*, which means «band of robbers») were armed Turks who formed mobs and exerted unchecked savagery against the Christians. Their actions were condoned and protected by the official Turkish government. The members of such groups were usually uneducated, outcasts from society and criminals who had been released from prison.

6. Published in the Parisian newspaper *Journal*, 6. 9. 1916.

From 1916 to 1918 the entire western Pontus was undergoing unprecedentedly fierce tribulations, which were continued later on under Kemal's[7] orders, whereas during the same period the eastern Pontus breathed freely, protected by the Russian troops who occupied the area.

The first deportation from Oinoe to the interior took place on a freezing Friday, January 17, 1917, in the dead of winter. Ordered by Rachmes Osman, it involved mainly the male population and included approximately sixty male Pontian Greeks who were among the most educated and most affluent in town. Forty armed guards on horseback accompanied them on their agonizing trek[8]. My great-grandfather Christos Dimitriades and the husband of Maria's sister Hatzisoulti were among the exiled. Neither one returned. The husband of a third sister had already been killed when the Turks attacked him in his fishing boat off the coast of Samsunta, leaving her with three small children to care for. Only the fourth and fifth sisters' husbands managed to escape death because they had taken their families to Romania and Russia some time earlier. The three sisters were alone with their children, without even one man to protect them. Hatzisoulti ran after the procession of exiles with an infant in her arms, crying and begging them to let her husband go, or to let her go with them. A *tsantarmas*[9] chased her away, swearing at her and hitting her with his gun. She started back. What expression did her face wear as she returned to their empty home with the baby in her arms? With what effort did she drag her steps away from the procession that was depriving her of her protector, her companion, and the father of her child? Only a great cinematic work could possibly capture the magnitude of her tragedy.

---

7. Mustafa Kemal Atatürk was the founder and first president of the Republic of Turkey. Born in 1881 in Thessaloniki, he was sent to military school at the age of 12, and then to the military academy in Istanbul, graduating in 1905. He made his military reputation repelling the Allied invasion at the Dardanelles in 1915. In May 1919 Kemal began a nationalist revolution in Anatolia, organising resistance to the peace settlement imposed on Turkey by the victorious Allies. In 1921 he established a provisional government in Ankara, and in 1923 Turkey became a secular republic, with Kemal as its president. In 1935, when surnames were introduced in Turkey, he was given the name Atatürk, meaning «Father of the Turks». He died on November 10, 1938.

8. From the Pontian newspaper *Epoche*, April 18, 1919.

9. Derived from the French *gendarme*, a guard or armed policeman.

They transferred the exiles on foot from the coastal area to the rough interior of central Asia Minor. Marching inexorably, they passed town after town and were abused unceasingly. On the way they stopped at miserable inns which could house very few, while the rest stayed outside in the freezing cold. Eventually, they reached Amaseia[10]. Half of the men had already died in the first ten days of the trek. They kept them there for twenty-five days, and perhaps the most optimistic among them believed that they would finally rest. They hoped in vain, however. Neither Amaseia nor any other place was their final stopping point, for their destination was death itself. They forced them to bathe outdoors in the middle of winter and to march without food or water under all kinds of weather conditions. The guards' heartlessness towards the weak and the sick, their demand for superhuman strength and the continuous beatings of the healthy were standard annihilation practices. Their orders, but also their ingrained character, left no room for human kindness: «*Yiourounouz!*»[11] shouted the Turks, who were often criminals convicted for robbery or murder and who had been released with the explicit order that they should exterminate the indigenous peoples.

Up until his death as a national martyr at the young age of 32, Nikos Kapetanides[12] continued to publish his newspaper *Epoche*, in which the following article was written regarding the exile of the people of Tripoli[13] from their hometown, near Oinoe:

---

10. Contemporary Amysa. Home of Strabo, the geographer, and seat of the Mythridates, founders of the Pontian kingdom.

11. «Move on!»

12. Journalist and publisher in Trapezunta until his patriotic death in September 1921 in Amaseia, where the infamous Courts of Independence hanged him and 177 other select Greeks who were leaders of the Pontian intellectual and economic communities. Having been charged with seeking Pontian independence, at the trial he interrupted to emphasize that he was struggling not only for independence but also for union with Metropolitan Greece. He died crying: «Long live Greece!» The Kemalists realized how fatal a blow it would be for Pontian Hellenism to be left without such leaders.

13. The residents of Tripoli were exiled in November 1916 and nearly 80% were decimated. Noteworthy is the fact that, although the ostensible reason for exiling the indigenous was the presence of Russian troops in Trapezunta as early as April 1916, the first deportation was intentionally delayed until the heavy winter had set in.

«Towards the evening of December 30 (1916), the great procession of exiles from Tripoli of the Pontus reached a plateau just an hour's distance from the village for which they were heading. At which point, the gendarme in charge announced indifferently that they had to spend the night there, in the snow, as there was no more suitable spot nearby. The peasants, all mountain people and knowing full well of the historic blizzards in the whole region of Mount Ermez, at 2,300 meters' altitude, in terror tried frantically to persuade the man to move on, but it was impossible. They timidly observed that the village was only an hour away, but in vain. The snow was growing denser. They spread their blankets and placed the children and the ill on them. The men and the stronger women would be compelled to stand guard all night, in spite of the extreme cold. «It was a starry night and a bitter north wind was raging. Around midnight, however, the wind stopped. Black clouds and thick fog covered the area. Soon a ferocious blizzard began. What hours of agony the unfortunate ones passed will never be known. The certainty is that the gendarmes, sensing that the blizzard was coming, rushed down to the village without a word of warning to the Greek exiles. Around dawn they arrested six men just outside the village, the only ones who had managed to escape the disaster. With them they climbed up to the plateau, ostensibly in search of the exiles. They scanned the vast, smooth stretch of the plateau, but to no avail. Not a trace could be seen, not a soul, not a body. Everything had been buried under the snow.»

Major Yowell, director of the American Near East Relief Committee in Harput[14], wrote in a report to his administrative superior in the U.S. regarding the exiles of 1922: «...The sufferings of the Greeks deported from the districts behind the battlefront are terrible and still continue. These deportees began to reach Harput before my arrival in October. Of the 30,000 who

---

14. A place of exile for the ethnic Greeks where there was an American relief station, due to which a great deal of testimony was recorded regarding the conditions that prevailed. The city stands on a hill in a plain to the east of the Euphrates River.

left Sivas[15] 5,000 died before reaching Harput. One of the American relief workers saw 1,500 bodies on the roads. Two thousand died on the roads east of Harput. ...All along the route the Turks are permitted to visit the refugee groups and select women and girls whom they desire for any purpose. ...Their whole route today is strewn with the bodies of dead, being consumed by dogs, wolves and vultures. The Turks make no effort to bury these dead and the deportees are not permitted to do so.»

He added, in a personal comment to his superiors: «In the rear of the processions Turkish officers and soldiers committed unheard-of acts of rape on women and virgins, whom they abandoned half dead on the roads and left to die. They wouldn't allow us to take the orphans of the Greeks who died along the way. I harbor no prejudice against any religion. I am not a missionary. The cynicism of the Turks is beyond any description. From the flock of the displaced exiles they arrest the women, lead them unhindered to the harems, and then seek their relatives, to whom they announce this in order to extort ransoms. Many terminally ill Greeks were grabbed from the hospitals and thrown into the streets to die 'like dogs', as the Turks put it. In spite of our efforts, most infants died on the way because we had nowhere to place them for treatment.»[16]

This shocking eyewitness report proves beyond all doubt the parameters of feminicide and infanticide, both of which are encompassed in the term *genocide*[17]. Among the 25,000 people who were lost out of the

---

15. Sevasteia, a city in central Turkey built on the banks of the Euphrates River. The foundations of the modern Turkish Republic were laid at the Sivas Congress which assembled there on September 4, 1919.

16. From an article in the *New York Times* dated May 6, 1922, entitled «Killing by Turks Has Been Renewed».

17. According to the United Nations Declaration of Human Rights this is a precise term, referring to violent crimes committed against a group with the intent to destroy its very existence. Under this definition, the first genocide, i.e., the systematic and violent extermination of a race or a part of it, in the 20th century occurred at a German concentration camp in Namibia, Africa, from 1904 to 1907. Due to abuse and malnutrition 100,000 indigenous died. Thus, candidacy for primacy in the perpetration of this unconscionable practice goes not only to the Turks but also to the Germans.

30,000 exiles in this single deportation, there were hundreds of weak women and innumerable terrified children–defenseless mothers, wives, sisters, unprotected little Greek children–in the hands of callous brutes. Countless are the times such treatment was suffered by ethnic Greek women and children in Turkey.

In 1921 another procession of exiles from Oinoe was decimated. When decisions are made with demonic inspiration it is easy for the world to become a hell. That is exactly the kind of inspiration that entered the head of the German advisor to the Young Turks, Liman von Sanders[18], when he created the perfect plan for genocide: methodical extermination, with no shred of humanity or inhibition of any sort. Did it succeed? Certainly it did, so well that several years later it was used against the Jews by Hitler.

From the numerous accounts of a similar kind, it seems that the more sophisticated Germans who conceived of this white slaughter had advised the untrained Turks superbly. The educated and conceited Ivan Karamazov effectively guided the murderous hand of the untrained Smerdyakov, with the difference that Dostoevsky's hero, Ivan, urged the perpetrator without conscious criminal intent, whereas the Germans knew quite well what they were urging.

---

18. German general who served as an adviser and military commander to the Ottoman Empire during WWI. He was the one who decided on the deportation of virtually all the Greeks from the coast to the inland areas, in other words, the one who inspired the white slaughter: «I assure you that the frost and cold of wintertime, rain and great humidity, sun and extreme summer heat, diseases of typhoid fever and cholera, as well as hardship and starvation, will bring the same result as you are planning, that is, to get rid of them by means of slaughter». He continues his argument as follows: «With the system I am suggesting, their death is certain. Furthermore, their women will no longer give birth and in that way you will have solved your demographic problem, while the ignominious and hateful breed of Greeks will be wiped out and vanish forever within a generation and you will have gained your uniform Turkish homogeneity» (Sasarides, Aggelos, *The Genocide of the Pontian Greeks*, Logos kai Praxe, issue 57, Athens 1994). After the war ended he was arrested in Malta in February 1919 on charges of having committed war crimes, but he was released six months later. He retired from the German army that year.

A more «civilized» variation was used again in 1943 against 1,229 Greek, Armenian and Jewish citizens of Constantinople. Successful business-men for the most part, but not having the means to pay the unjust, huge taxes which had been levied, they were sent to open a road to Erzerum[19] in the snow, hungry, beaten, and jeered at as tax evaders, while their property was being sold at auction. Turkish wealth was begotten by brigands, despite the fact that today its business community enjoys international respect. The Turkish press ironically and impudently criticized the supposedly heartless Greek profiteers, while wealthy Turkish citizens from Constantinople were found to buy their possessions, indifferent to the fact that they had been seized unjustly and shamefully. On the outskirts of Baipurt[20], repeatedly drenched with the blood and tears of exiled Christians, once again sighs were heard and innocent souls were lost. According to valid sources, in the same place of exile a group of missing Greeks were martyred after the Turkish invasion of Cyprus[21]. The 1916-1924 genocide of the Greeks of Pontus, the exiles of 1943, the terrible hooliganism of 1955 in Constantinople[22] and the 1974 invasion of Cyprus are the basis for the well-earned, infamous reputation for acts of horrific oppression and sheer terrorism, without the slightest twinge of conscience. Failure to punish gives rise to further offense, experience to audacity, and effectiveness to statistical guarantee.

---

19. Probably ancient Gymnias (see Xenophon, *Anavasis*).

20. The Byzantine city of Vaiverdon. It was visited by Marco Polo.

21. Petros Kasimates, *Missing: Top Secret*, A. A. Livani, Athens 2009.

22. In September 1955 fanatic Turks destroyed churches, looted property and raped women and children, actions prompted by the trumped-up charge that Greeks had planted the bomb which exploded in a house touted to be the birthplace of Kemal in Thessaloniki. Typical of the persecutions, referred to as «uncontrollable» though they were tolerated by the authorities, is the following event, according to eyewitness reporter G. Karagiorga: A 7-year-old girl found herself in the middle of a mob, who handed her over to a man of gigantic proportions, a porter by trade, nicknamed «Gorilla». The child was raped in front of the crowd, and the monster yelled «That's what happens to infidels!»

Now and then a telegram from my great-grandfather would arrive at their home in Oinoe. Hatzimaria would send him money, which he usually did not collect, because in the meantime they had moved the exiles. At other times the banks would be instructed not to accept the money orders which the exiles tried to cash. At some point all news from Christos Dimitriades ceased. In vain they asked for news of him, in vain they waited for him. They achieved nothing. What was his last thought, as he felt he was departing from this world, leaving his wife and five children? Did anyone happen to be nearby to moisten his lips, gently close his eyes at the final moment, or toss a handful of dirt over his dead body? Was he torn to pieces by a jackal on the very spot where he had collapsed or had he been thrown into some ditch? No one ever found out. What is certain is that a hard-working, industrious family man, like thousands at the time, perished as if dispossessed, completely alone and far from home and family. Instead of spending his last moments surrounded by the love and care he deserved, my great-grandfather died in utter desolation. In the deep of winter, in the inhospitable mountainous regions where they were exiled, it is highly doubtful that he was buried. The Turks allowed only the face of the dead to be covered with a handkerchief, nothing more. In this modern tragedy the ancient tradition of burial, the sacred duty of Sophocles' Antigone, was unlikely to have been fulfilled.

Hatzimaria was 42 years old when she lost her husband. Her possessions, her land, the shop and the house, all the fruits of their labor, in only a short while had turned into inanimate evidence of a vast futility. Wealth is a visitor. Her elder son, Anastases, had deserted the army and was in hiding. Only the women were left, with little Chrysostomos. When they learned that the butcher Topal Osman[23] was heading for Oinoe, Maria

---

23. Topal Osman was a bloodthirsty former boatman and tobacco smuggler, who was left lame due to an injury he sustained in the Balkan Wars (*Topal* means «lame»). Kemal found in his person the ideal cohort, and granted him power over the lives and deaths of all the Greeks who lived in the coastal zone of the Pontus. With 4,000 tsetes at his command, he spread mayhem with unprecedented ruthlessness, advancing the cause of the Asia Minor Catastrophe.

was paralyzed with fear for the boy's life, because it was known that underage children were the main target of that particular criminal. Many children were drowned on his orders, having been loaded onto barges which were taken out to the open sea and sunk–innocent babies, whose cries disturbed the already restless sleep of the Christians on dry land. In yet another case, between Poulatzaki and Kerasunta, many unprotected little children of the exiles were thrown in fury over the steep cliffs at the shore and died a martyr's death[24]. Apparently, the pleasure derived from this method was more intense in comparison to that of drowning them.

Hatzimaria's little son was saved by Armenian rebels. They were men who had escaped the slaughter of their people in 1915 and were hiding on my great-grandfather's farm, on the hills of Oinoe. They came secretly to the city one night and took him away under cover of the dark. In that place, Chrysos and Anastases met again by coincidence, without either brother knowing beforehand that they were so close to each other. They underwent baptism by fire when the rebels were set upon by 500 armed Turks. The renowned Greek leader Basil agas[25], with only 35 men at the foot of the Hill of Our Lady, and the Armenian Agop Tsartsampales with his men on the peak, managed to defeat them, battling bravely against the numberless enemy. The conflict lasted from morning till night. In a coordinated movement they were able to surround the Turks and shouted at them in their own language: *«Meshesini siktiyim, asker nernte kour-toulsachlar siniz? Allah yia size berir, yia pize berir. Houcoum arkantas-lar, houcoum dort taraftan!»* That is: «Damn your faith, how will your soldiers escape? God will help either you or us. Attack, comrades, attack from all sides!»

The claim to divine favor doubtless reminds us of a Homeric battle,

---

24. Archive of the Greek Ministry of the Interior, A/5/VI, protocol number 576, Athens (6.15.1922).

25. Basileios Anthopoulos, an architect by profession, was a rebel captain also known as Basil Oustas. He fought in vain to save the western Pontus after reaching an agreement with the Russians, who nonetheless failed to keep their promise to come to that region. He was later killed in an ambush in Constantinople.

only that the horror of this particular conflict is unfit for poetic verse. The battle was fierce and victory was granted only after long hours of intense struggle. There were rabid exchanges of gunfire, murderous hand to hand combat, injuries, and death, followed by revenge: 23 captive Turks were beheaded. Chrysostomos averted his eyes so as not to see, but Agop, the leader of the rebels, had other ideas. It was time he became a man, he said, and he forced the little boy to look the horror in the face. When Kemal later gave amnesty to the Armenians so that he could deal with the Greeks in Asia Minor without distractions, the two brothers returned to their home in secrecy.

It was in April of 1923 when the town crier announced that they had to leave urgently for Greece, on a ship which would soon arrive in the harbor for that express reason. Under the institutionalized injustice of the so-called population exchange, later ratified at Lausanne[26], their uprooting took on a legal façade.

But the persecutions continued. Two young Turks approached Chrysostomos near the wall of the cemetery, and before he could ask them what they wanted he saw that one of them was aiming his pistol at him. The other held in his hand a piece of paper which he insisted Chrysostomos should sign. It was a property transfer that would cede them the house and lands. The little boy was terrified and tried to escape by jumping over the wall. He was found in the cemetery with a severe wound to the head. It may sound absurd to extort an underage child's signature in order to seize property, but it happened. His frantic mother ran to him and gathered her little boy up in her arms. The wound was bleeding,

---

26. The Treaty of Lausanne was a peace treaty signed in Lausanne, Switzerland on July 24, 1923, which ended the conflict and defined the borders of the modern Turkish Republic. It provided for the independence of the Republic of Turkey but also for the protection of the Greek Orthodox Christian minority in Turkey and the Muslim minority in Greece. However, most of the Christian population of Turkey and the Turkish population of Greece had already been deported under the earlier Convention Concerning the Exchange of Greek and Turkish Populations signed by Greece and Turkey on January 30, 1923. Only the Greeks of Constantinople, Imvros and Tenedos were excluded and the Muslim population of Western Thrace.

and no medicine was to be had. She bound his head with a clean cloth, having first collected mold from the spidery, long disused basement of their home and applied it to the wound, because she had heard that it was beneficial. The little one got well. Another five years would pass before Fleming would scientifically ascertain the therapeutic value of green mold for infections.

Anastases stayed in hiding, for he would be arrested if he dared show himself in an attempt to leave with them. Hatzimaria, with her three daughters and Chrysostomos, took a few bundles of whatever had not been sold and went down to Skala, to the port. From there they were transported in boats to the ship which would take them to Constantinople, and from that point they would eventually travel to Greece on another ship. They abandoned their home, which had already been emptied of furniture, clothing and anything of the slightest value. They abandoned their neighborhoods, the churches with their demolished bell towers, the streets, the squares, the mountains that had swallowed their father. They abandoned a piece of their souls. Also travelling with them to the home-land was Maria's brother, a widower with four children (one of whom was lost to typhoid during the long voyage), as well as the sister whose husband had been murdered off Samsunta and her three orphans. Not one couple had been left intact.

The ship they were on was owned by a Turk named Katir bey but was fly-ing a French flag. There were about 45 crew members and two captains, a Russian and a Turk named Nazim, the latter of whom showed interest in my lovely grandmother Antigone so that they were obliged to hide her. The ship, arriving with refugees from Trapezunta, took 362 passen-gers on board at Oinoe and about 300 more at Samsunta. They departed, deeply fatigued and weak, while the lands that had given them birth all too soon disappeared from sight. They thought only of saving their lives —nothing else concerned them anymore. Yet their hope was once again dashed. As soon as they had left the port far enough behind, the Turkish crew members locked all the children in the hold. Chrysostomos was among them. The reason? They were demanding that half-fare be paid for them, though originally they had made no such stipulation. The fear

40

that they would drown the children if the ransom were not paid loomed like a nightmare before the mothers, relatives and friends, who all began to search for *panganotes*[27], selling whatever they could, or borrowing.

This extortion ended only when the Turks achieved the financial blood-letting they sought. Then the terrorized children were freed. It was not enough that they had uprooted them, not enough that they had taken their belongings. They were not satisfied with having condemned them to widowhood and orphanhood. No! They had to seize everything, even that which they did not have! The thought that the grandchildren of these heartless individuals are now Turkish citizens makes one shiver. They may not be to blame themselves, but is it not essential that they know what their grandparents did to ours, especially given that the so-called exchange was supposed to take place within a legal framework? Still, it is difficult for someone to admit that his good grandfather once behaved like a common murderer.

After the imprisonment of the children there followed a new machination. The Russian captain confided in the Greeks that, according to information he had from the American captain of a warship which had been at Samsunta, tsetes were waiting at the Gerze harbor, near Sinope, to rob them and afterwards kill them. Under the pretext of refueling, the ship would approach and when it reached the port the tsetes would board with the help of their fellow conspirators, members of the crew. What insatiable predation!

The Greeks decided to defend themselves. Thus, at dawn on April 27, 1923, as the ship changed course the signal was given, three whistles from the ship, and they moved like lightning. Katir bey and his men were taken by surprise. They tried to stop the Greeks–their cohorts at Gerze were waiting, everything had been planned so perfectly–but to no avail. One heroic lad climbed the mast and attacked the man at the helm. He seized the tiller and while the others were putting the Turks

---

27. Banknotes. Turkish pounds in the form of paper bills. Three banknotes were worth one gold pound.

out of commission, he changed course again. They killed him. His name was Andreas Karabases. In vain did his unfortunate sister search for him among the passengers at Constantinople, where she had arrived earlier. The furor lasted about ten minutes. The shouts, the hand to hand combat, the chaos of the conflict and the injuries froze the blood of all those who had time to realize what was happening. The Russians took the side of the Greeks, risking death themselves. At last, the Turks were captured and locked in the hold.

They may have avoided death, but the reality of events remained terrifying to my relatives and the other refugees. How would they manage to continue their journey? Thirsty, hungry and worn out, they reached Constantinople, then under the administration of the Entente Powers, only after having burnt everything they could. Whatever was made of wood–doors, stairs and floors–had become fuel, since at all costs they had to keep away from ports. The remains of the ship looked like a giant fishbone, according to Great-Uncle Chrysostomos' account of their adventure. They handed over the imprisoned Turks to the French Commission in Constantinople. The captain and the ship owner were tried and executed in Marseilles.

For 54 days they stayed in quarantine, gazing longingly at Constantinople but unable to disembark. On land all the Greek buildings which had been conscripted to house the refugees, chiefly schools and churches, not only in the city but also in the suburb of St. Stephen and the wider vicinity, were full to the point of suffocation. They bought food from boats that came to the ship, since they were given only one loaf of bread per person which was supposed to last for seven days. When they were finally put off at the Selimie barracks[28] in the Asia Minor section of Constantinople, conditions were even more desperate there. The Greek Red Cross had seen to it that at least the semblance of an infrastructure was in place for nutrition and medical care, though it was substandard. The

---

28. Today this building houses the headquarters of the First Army of the Turkish Land Forces. Of the 20,000 Pontians who were in quarantine there in 1923, only 9,000 came out alive. The victims died of hunger, contaminated water, or diseases. A number of refugees committed suicide by jumping to their death from the upper storeys.

epidemics were mowing them down, however, because the water mains had been contaminated and their lives were once more in danger.

Hatzimaria had another worry during all this misery–she would not be able to buy tickets for Greece when they were finally released, as there was no money left. So Chrysos and a friend absconded and went to look for work. At first he sold matches on the Galatas Bridge. How did the darling child of the Dimitrades family manage in those times? Did the mother and daughters have any recourse other than patience? Were they able to stop worrying even one night with their little boy on the streets? That little boy with the matches had suddenly and prematurely become the protector of four women. They were counting on him to get them to Greece.

Fortunately, Chrysos was especially gifted. Indeed, indicative of his resourcefulness and boldness is the fact that in the city he endeavored to learn a craft. After his first effort at breadwinning on the Galatas Bridge, he went to a barber and was allowed to brush the hairs off the customers' clothes for tips. There the idea occurred to him to learn his boss's trade in order to improve his situation. But who would sit still to be shaved by a beardless boy under 15 years old? Chrysos persuaded poor laborers to let him pay them a small sum so that he could perfect his bloody practice on them. Eventually, his savings were enough to enable the family to set off for Greece, on the ship *Ocean Androu*. Selimie, that Golgotha, would now be seen only in their nightmares. They had endured its horrors from June 13 to August 13, 1923, long enough for them to never forget it.

On August 16 they arrived in Kalamaria, a suburb of Thessaloniki[29], where they found Anastases by means of the Red Cross notices. He had also managed to get to Thessaloniki. From there they were sent to a vil-

---

29. Thessaloniki is the second-largest city in Greece and the capital of Greek Macedonia. It was founded in 315 BC by Cassander of Macedon and was named after Phillip II's daughter, half-sister to Alexander the Great. An important metropolis by the Roman period, Thessaloniki was the second largest and wealthiest city of the Byzantine Empire.

lage in Drama, where the impoverished Greek government gave them fields and animals. However, they knew nothing either of raising animals or of agriculture, since they were from a coastal area. They moved again, this time to Kavala, where they established a home in the settlement of Souyiolou. In this place two of the girls married Oinoeans, while Anastases married and went to a village near Kavala. Soon grandchildren were born and the extended family grew.

Despite Hatzimaria's great sorrow over her deceased husband and generally for the losses they had suffered, not to mention the privation they continued to experience, her life took a new direction. Besides, when everyone around has suffered in similar ways and the environment is one of misery, it is easier to be patient. The collective tragedy is shared and collective consolation alleviates the pain. Unfortunately, her wounds did not have time to heal. Life was merciless. In the space of fifteen years, she lost four children one after the other: Anastases when he was about 30, and her three daughters between the ages of 25 and 32. Each died of a different cause, but the main factor was poverty. They had no medical care, they lived in destitution, and conditions were bleak. They had escaped the Turks and Selimie, only to perish in Greece. Only Chrysostomos was left, her fifth child, the one who had been granted by her unexpected and unplanned pregnancy. That «extra» baby would be her support until she died. Life plays its own games. She lived with him and the family he raised with his Pontian wife, an exceptionally patient, kind woman from Samsunta, an aunt especially tranquil and noble, of that touching type that after some time is regarded as a blood relation by the husband's kinfolk. They had four children.

Hatzimaria could no longer bear living in Kavala, however, because «it had taken her children», as she expressed it. She asked her son to leave, so they eventually moved near Athens, in the vicinity of the Old Slaughterhouses. In any case, wherever they went everyone was poor. In order to make a living, Chrysostomos took whatever odd jobs he could find. He made the rounds of the neighborhoods selling shoes from a cart, was an itinerant photographer, barber and ice-cream vendor, leeched anyone who had high blood pressure, fixed watches, removed and replaced teeth (according to what he had learned from a dentist in Kavala for whom he had once worked) and, in general, never missed an opportunity to do whatever he could to earn money to support his family. At the same time, once he had opened a barber shop next to their house he began to take private lessons in math and grammar, while continuing the violin lessons he had started in Kavala, until he reached the final level and received a diploma in music. In some ways there was a most uncanny family likeness among my relatives. I remember him being absolutely determined to suck the marrow out of life, which in his childhood had subjected him to such trials, and he enjoyed all decent pleasures to the fullest: the Turkish bath, song and wine. Actually, many refugees took refuge in drinking wine, seeking its consolation often, though for the most part without becoming alcoholics. Of course, I do not know if his neighbors agreed with his taste in music, when he regularly tuned in to a Turkish radio station and played whining Eastern love songs which could be heard all along the street. Decades after their uprooting he still longed for the sounds of his childhood years. The entire form of whatever entertainment he enjoyed was always dictated by the strains of Eastern music.

Hatzimaria was the typical Pontian mother-in-law, who had the first say in her son's house, and his wife was the typical Pontian daughter-in-law, who had no say at all. It is well-known that Pontian society did not rest on equality within the family, especially not equality for daughters-in-law. The limits defining their relationships, however, did secure peace and stability in the home. Chrysos's weakness for his mother was perhaps extreme, but it was amply justified by the dire trials they had shared and which shaped their peculiar relationship.

Be that as it may, there were constant and welcome visitors to their home near the slaughterhouses, mainly Hatzimaria's grandchildren. Among them was my father, Antigone's son, the apple of his uncle's eye. There he found the love and care he had been deprived of at 12 years old, when his mother had died. There, many of his youthful dreams found a home, and his grandmother, though distant, did her best to take the place of her especially tender daughter, my grandmother. Chrysos, though very strict regarding the upbringing of his own two boys, believed my father could do no wrong, being the son of his favorite sister. I do not remember him ever calling him Savvas. He always called him *«anepse»*, that is «nephew», pronouncing the «s» in that special Pontian way which resembles the French. The choice of addressing him in terms of their family relationship instead of by name was the best way to express the partiality he felt for this good-natured orphan of his sister Antigone's.

In 1953 Chrysos, by then quite a mature man, travelled to Oinoe. Thirty years had passed since he had left and he felt a fervent longing to visit it. He went all alone, and against the advice of a Greek friend from Constantinople that they would «devour him». The authorities greeted him with particular honor, and made him an honorary citizen, as he was the first Greek to visit the city since the Catastrophe. On the first day he was visited by three Turks, for an almost incredible reason. They paid him a sum of money that their father had owed to his father, Christos Dimitriades. Their father's dying wish was that they repay him at the earliest opportunity. Integrity has no country and honorable people are found everywhere, even among peoples whose behavior has been largely reprehensible in the past. The ethic of the debtor, not his death, determines who owes whom. The sacrifice of a cock which Socrates owed had to be offered, despite the fact that he was dying[30].

After spending a month in Oinoe, Chrysos returned to Greece without having paid a penny, even for the hotel where he stayed. The friends and acquaintances of his parents had paid for everything. Certainly, the superiority of the victimizer over his victims gives rise to justified puzzlement. Did they treat him that way only out of respect towards his family? Or did they feel guilty over what their countrymen had done? Did they perhaps feel the need to arrange for their life after death? Or had they realized how different the place would be if the Greeks still lived there? There is no way of knowing. Perhaps the apology which the Turkish state denies they owe was actually made unofficially by those

---

30. Socrates' last words were: *«Criton, we owe a cock to Asclepius. Don't neglect to make the offering.»*

anonymous Oinoeans who gave hospitality to my uncle. Although it was politically ineffective, an act of small scope, it completely exonerated those who offered it, and it would be a lucky thing if today's Turkish citizens showed a similar sensibility. If, that is, propaganda left room for the injustice, which the politicians stubbornly refuse to admit took place, to be compensated for by corresponding actions. Private relations among Greeks, Armenians, Assyrians and Kurds offer an opportunity for at least a small taste of national self-awareness on the part of the Turks, and eventual exculpation.

Hatzimaria was less fortunate than her husband, who died without experiencing the death of his children, the plight of a refugee, or poverty. His exile and death were a type of redemption that can only be understood with hindsight. His wife was the one who escaped, only to suffer worse things. One year before she also died, she met with her sister Hatzi-soulti, who after many years of effort had managed to reach Greece from Romania. She and her family had also suffered, though from different hardships. The greatest difference was that they had been through an additional emigration, while the greatest similarity was that they had arrived without any property. The two women cried and sobbed over the life which had scattered them wherever the wind blew, over their count-less sufferings. This sister's history was also full of difficulties, although it followed a different orbit.

When she was left alone with her child because her husband was lost in exile, she headed for Romania. After some time she married a widower from Trapezunta. Both of them had suffered losses. This man, despite his persistent efforts, was unable to locate his two children, who had disap-peared when he was exiled. They had four children together, and gave the name of one of the missing boys to the first. When years later they were informed that the boys were alive and were to be found in an orphanage in Thessaloniki, they took them back to Romania. Both Hatzisoulti and her husband were overjoyed: the family now had seven children, two of whom, in fact, had the same name, Lefterakes. A delightful consequence, in spite of the likely mix-ups that would occur on a daily basis.

In other cases, however, things worked out much differently and refugees reached the extremes of utter psychological depredation, that is, when the supposedly dead relative who was later found to be alive had been a spouse rather than a child. Often the longing to unite the family, the joy of discovering that one's spouse was alive, was succeeded by horror. One or both of them had remarried. How many «resurrected» refugees were forced to choose between the old life and the new beginning they had made, I wonder. How many separations took place, and how many dreams were demolished? Or could they reconcile the irreconcilable through lies? How did the children who may have been born feel? The variations of woe were endless.

In the refugee shack at the Old Slaughterhouses of Kallithea, the dignified lady of Oinoe, Maria Dimitriadou, spent the last years of her life permanently unsmiling. In its small, poor rooms, she mulled over the memories which tormented her. How she started her life, how everything was overturned, how many losses she had experienced, how much sorrow she had tasted. «Do not consider anyone blessed before the end.»[31] At nights when she could not sleep, she heard the waters of the Ilisos beside her, barely flowing. The river was running dry, as were her eyes. Only when her biblical figure made its own exodus was she relieved forever of all the kinds of slaughter she had known.

31. Words of Solon, the Wise: *«Midena pro tou telous makarize.»*

View of Oinoe, early 20th century (archive of Anna Theophylactou).

The church of the Dormition of Our Lady in 1930.

Christos and Maria Dimitriades' house in Oinoe.

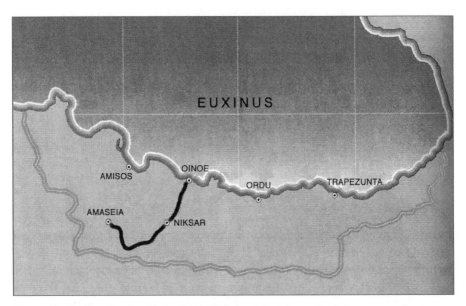

The path of exile taken by Christos Dimitriades. Near Amaseia all traces were lost.

Argana Maden. Pontians in exile in 1921 (archive of the Committee for Pontian Studies).

Human bones, the remains of some unknown victim of the genocide (archive of Oberlin College).

An inn in Sevasteia. Such tiny, ramshackle buildings were designated to house the exiles, who were arriving by the hundreds (archive of Oberlin College).

Cartoon from a Turkish newspaper. On the huge box it says: «the rising cost of living» and on the small bag: «property taxes». The wealthy, fat Greek man is saying to the little man: «Quit complaining! See, I'm burdened, too!» This was the ironic contribution of the press in response to the seizure of Greek property in Constantinople (from the book *Diary of Exile. Erzerum 1943,* published by Estia Bookstores).

The flowers of exile. The Constantinopolitan Kiourtsoglou with a fellow exile in Erzerum in 1943 (from the book *In exile. Erzerum Askale*, published by the Greek Foundation for Historical Studies).

Trekking through the snow, at the same time their belongings are being sold at auction in Constantinople. The continuation of Turkey's methodical extermination of the Greeks (from the book *Diary of Exile. Erzerum 1943*, published by Estia Bookstores).

Skeletal figures of the Herero tribe in Namibia at the beginning of the 20th century. Tens of thousands were worked or starved to death because they rose up against German colonial rule.

Nikos Kapetanides with friends wearing martial uniforms (*zipkes*). He is in the middle among those standing (the Kapetanides family archive).

Pontian rebel captain Basil agas, in a family photo. This architect and contractor of public works became the protector of the unarmed Pontians and a persecutor of Topal Osman's hordes (the Anthopoulos family archive).

The Greek delegation to the negotiations in Lausanne. Calamity imposed by political expediency. Center, Eleftherios Venizelos. A few years later he would nominate Kemal for the Nobel Peace Prize, a tactic that found imitators among Greek politicians, who continued laying a wreath on his monument (archive of the library of the Greek parliament).

Vaccination of refugees by a nurse from the Greek Red Cross in the Pontus (photo archive of the Greek Red Cross).

«Exchangeable» Pontians at the harbor of Fatsa, which neighbored Oinoe, waiting to get in the boats which will transfer them to a ship heading for Greece (photo archive of the Greek Red Cross).

Uprooted Pontian women at St. Stephen's, a suburb of Constantinople (archive of the Committee for Pontian Studies).

The Galatas Bridge at the beginning of the 20th century. This is where Chrysos sold matches.

Anastases, center, Chrysos, right, in Kavala.

...she lived with the family of the child granted her by the unexpected pregnancy.

...her especially tender child, my grand-mother Antigone.

Hatzisoulti and her husband, center, in Romania with several of their children. Far left, Big Lefterakis, and in his mother's arms, Little Lefterakis.

Chrysos in Oinoe. In the background can be seen the bell tower of a Greek church, the Dormition of Our Lady in the Greek neighborhood of Kourkouletza.

The Ilisos River in the 1950s. The houses are clearly in better condition than the refugee shanties were. The river is very low, as before.

Chrysos' family, along with my grandmother Antigone and her three children.
The oldest boy is my father, Savvas. The
older woman in black is Hatzimaria.

Hatzimaria's sister who was in Romania,
with her daughter and husband. He was
the only one of the sisters' husbands who
escaped death because he went abroad.

Pontians in exile (archive of the Committee for Pontian Studies).

«THE CHERRIES OF DEATH»

ARCHONTOU IOANNIDOU
[1874-1966]

«Ekei kerin 'ki afketai, thymiaman 'ki kaiei,
mnimosynon 'ki 'inetai, stavron 'ki steroutai.»

(There no candle is lit, no incense burns,
no memorial service is held, no cross stands.)

Archontou was my father's other grandmother. Her son Yannis was his father. She, too, was born and raised in the city of Oinoe. Like Maria Dimitriadou, she was a *Niotissa*.

Her parents had five daughters and one son. The Pontian middle class to which they belonged was industrious and thriving, so they lived comfortably. Despite the fact that the city had fallen from its past splendor since the great fire which had destroyed its renowned shipyards in 1887, Oinoe continued to offer opportunities for progress and advancement to those who were determined to succeed.

She married Giorgos Ioannides, who was a tanner. Their characters were very different: he was far from generous in any respect, while she was boundlessly ready to make any sacrifice, and embraced everyone with open arms. Did she love him, or were they brought together by a matchmaker? No one knows. What difference would knowing the answer make anyway, when what ensued in life leveled the differences in their beginnings? Whether it had been love or a compromise, the past lost all its significance before the unyielding reality they would soon face.

The tanneries of that time operated with primitive methods. My great-grandfather would stretch the fresh animal skins over rods made of hazel wood and leave them in the sun to dry. When they were dry, he sold them mainly to shoemakers. The *tsarouchi*[1] was in its heyday then, and few people wore the more modern-style European shoes. Giorgos made enough for them to live on without lack and, given that Archontou particularly loved good food and was very generous with it, there was no shortage of small pleasures in her daily life. She did not need wealth. She was content with simple things, such as a culinary success–perhaps her stuffed vine leaves turned out well, or her ground meat pies. They had two sons and

---

1. A hand-sewn leather shoe.

two daughters. As the boys began to grow up, they joined their father in the tannery to learn the craft, for it would one day become theirs. The girls stayed home to prepare for the sole occupation their traditional community intended for young women, that is, marriage. Indeed my grandfather Yannis's sisters became exceptional housekeepers, as did most Niotisses.

That was until calamity struck, and split their life forever into before and after. Suddenly, and completely unjustly, everything in their lives changed with the murder of their seventeen-year-old elder son. All human happiness is transient, of course, but it was the way he died that struck them the hardest. He was in the habit of returning home every day, to fetch lunch for his father at work. One day he was passing a field where some Turkish farmers were picking cherries. They had set some aside to be sold to passersby. Savvas decided to buy some, but then he made his fatal mistake: he took a large sum of money out of his pocket, which he happened to have with him in order to pay a bill for the tannery. He paid for the cherries and left, little suspecting what a temptation the money was. Just down the road, a band of Turks lay in wait. Either they had seen him paying, or the farmers had informed them that he was carrying a lot of money. They waylaid him, stoned him to death, and robbed him. A trial was never held and the case was hushed up. The life of a Pontian Greek was already of little worth in Turkey around 1915. The murderers went unpunished and my great-grandmother Archontou wore mourning for the rest of her life.

Meanwhile, conditions for the Pontian Greeks were worsening by the day. It was not only the fact that trade between the Turks and the Greeks was forbidden by law and punished with heavy fines, but at the same time, fierce persecution of draft-dodgers was unleashed. These young men would take to the mountains, while in reprisal their families were dragged into detention and violently beaten. Yet military service in the infamous *Amele Tampourou*[2], the labor battalions of the Turkish army,

---

2. These special battalions were created in 1914 by the Young Turks, the ruling political party at the time.

was tantamount to torture or even death. That was the original concept behind their creation. It was part of the insidious white slaughter which was resorted to after the international outcry against the blood-drenched Armenian genocide.

The central square of Oinoe, with its huge plane tree, the Kavlani, became a place of martyrdom. There, beneath the imposing palaces of the Komnenoi[3], the gallows were set up. The heads of three *katsakides*[4] who had been publicly hanged were nailed onto long poles and paraded through the streets of the Greek neighborhoods to intimidate the people. Another three Christians were thrown alive down the smokestacks and into the boiler of a ship at sea. At that moment, on the deck of the ship stood Kemal's notorious agent, Topal Osman, mayor of Kerasunta[5], the man who gave the orders for such heinous crimes and who derived such exquisite pleasure from them. Oinoe and the entire Pontus were summarily transformed into a genuine hell.

Such terrorism led inevitably to the Pontian resistance movement. The mountains filled with deserters and unarmed civilians, who took refuge in the rebel hideouts for protection. They were hidden and provided food by relatives and friends, as well as by quite a number of Turks who realized the injustice that was being perpetrated against their Greek neighbors. When the army arrived, however, the situation rapidly deteriorated, for fierce fighting broke out and many villages were set on

---

3. Several weeks before the occupation of Constantinople by crusaders in 1204, one branch of the Komnenoi continued the Byzantine Empire in exile in the Trapezuntian heartlands of Asia Minor. These emperors, the «Minor Komnenoi» as they were known, ruled in Trapezunta for over 250 years, until 1461, when the last Roman emperor was assassinated by an Ottoman usurper.

4. Draft-dodgers or deserters.

5. Typical of the persecutions in that town of martyrs is the night of Christmas 1916. A large number of the residents were shut in the church of St. George of Patlama, where they spent Christmas night imprisoned. Many lost their minds, so that they actually tried to eat the leather parts of their shoes, sitting on top of the bodies of those who had already died, while next to them was their excrement. The Turks would not allow their relatives to help them, and neither would they give them water from right outside the church. They gathered their children and drowned them in the sea, and burnt down the church with the residents inside.

fire. Added to the terror was the torture of hunger. The heroism of the Pontians was undaunted, though their supplies were unbelievably short. Both the guns and the bullets were limited. Yet, despite the fact that they were up against numerous very well-supplied army units and were themselves underfed and exhausted, they refused to back down. The unarmed civilians were beaten, robbed, raped or killed, while their orphaned children were left unprotected in the roads and forests. The rebels continued to resist. Did they have any other choice? Of course they did, only that they preferred death rather than submission to the Turks and forced conversion to Islam.

Topal Osman was a man utterly without moral inhibitions and was unchecked by anyone. Characteristic of his cold-heartedness was the order for tsetes to surround the exodus of inhabitants fleeing the siege of Kerasunta, so that not only would no one escape the slaughter, but neither would anyone be able to go in search of food. The entire city was hostage. Such tactics, of course, were already familiar in the history of mankind, for example, on the night of Saint Bartholomew[6], only that there, a few thousand were butchered rather than tens of thousands, and the bloodbath lasted only a few weeks, not whole years. History often uses different criteria to measure the comparative gravity of events. Thus, the countless «nights of St. Bartholomew» which the Pontians underwent have been left in the margins of history.

«I'll offer up such 'incense' to the Greeks of the Pontus that they will choke like wasps in caves!»[7] boasted the murderous butcher Topal Osman. He did not mean in even-sided battles, of course, but mainly cowardly burnings of the hideouts of the terrified, unarmed Christians –women, children and the elderly. He forbade the Greeks to enter the sea, and they were fiercely beaten on the slightest provocation, for instance,

---

6. The St. Bartholomew's Day Massacre in 1572, which has gone down in history as the epitome of rampant violence, began with a targeted group of assassinations and resulted in a wave of Catholic mob violence, directed against the Huguenots (French Calvinist Protestants) during the French Wars of Religion.

7. Sener Cemal, *Topal Osman Olayi*, Istanbul 1992.

when they were caught fishing or grinding wheat. The streets of Koula Kagia still resound from the drama of the Pontians, who were used as pack animals in the Turkish army for months on end. Underfed, thirsty, ill, their clothes in rags, they were forced to carry loads of war supplies on their backs for twelve hours a day, whether it was raining, snowing, or scorching hot from a heat wave. Anyone who could not endure it was left by the roadside to die, alone and helpless, in order not to waste the bullet that would have ended their suffering. The Turkish harbor-master of Trapezunta, a certain Kiaxias, indignant over the crimes committed against the innocent, tried to save some of the Greeks. Topal Osman had him killed in an ambush without a second thought.

Some of the Niotisses, unable to face what they knew lay ahead–seizure, rape, exile, or forced conversion to Islam–threw themselves over the cliffs of Oinoe, many of them holding their babies in their arms, and drowned[8]. Was it in recourse to despair, or in quest of salvation? Probably both at once.

A valorous act on a par with that of the renowned women of Zalongo[9], Greece, who refused to submit to the Turks during the war for independence from the Ottoman Empire, this tragic event was repeated many times in the tormented Pontus. This was the case in Pafra and Simikli, in Kerasunta, where a group of Pontian women who were being chased threw themselves in the river to drown, and in Kounaka, in the area of Vazelonas, where 26 young women did the same thing after the horrifying events which were played out at the monastery there[10].

---

8. Archive of Greek Ministry of Foreign Affairs, 1922, A/5/VI, protocol number 576, Athens (15.6.1922).

9. During the Souliote War in December 1803, 50 Souliote women and their children were trapped by Ali Pasha's troops in the mountains of Zalongo in Epirus. In order to avoid capture and enslavement, the women threw their children first and then themselves off a steep cliff, committing suicide. The event quickly became known throughout Europe.

10. St John Vazelonas. The oldest monastery of the Pontus, it is said to have removed from the Zaboulon mountain in Matcka where it was first established in 270 AD. There, in April 1916, 22-year-old Kyriaki Tsironidou was chased through the woods where she had been hiding and was raped by 9 tsetes, in front of small children. She was beheaded while the ninth was still defiling her body. Before the evacuation of the monastery, 14 young girls who had taken refuge there were also raped, had their breasts slit, and were then beheaded.

The testimony of Lambros Mavrides[11], from Tepekioi of Poulatzaki, stands witness to the torture and persecution inflicted on the Pontians: «Topal Osman arrived at dawn and surrounded the village with his tsetes. They rounded up the villagers, one by one, and forced them into a house, near the church. Men, women, children, the elderly, infants. They set the house on fire and burnt them alive. First they had singled out four or five young women and kept them for themselves. Then they poured ten cans of diesel fuel inside and all around the house, and threw in a hand grenade. The house belonged to Kota Kontou. The horror lasted ten or twenty minutes, during which they were all screaming. The women's voices *'s son ouranon evgainan*[12].

»The house blew up amidst the flames, and buried everyone. One girl managed to jump out the window and escape the fire by running away. The tsetes sent bullets after her, but it was downhill and she got away... The five women who had been selected for rape by the Turks realized what was to happen to them, so when they saw the fire and heard the screams, they jumped in, shouting: "Blessed be the Lord's name". They threw themselves into the fire and were burnt to death along with the others. All the villages around Samsunta were reduced to ashes. The virgins and the young boys were raped and led away to the mountains. Many of the latter, in order to avoid being dishonored at the hands of the Turks, killed themselves. For the same reason, many parents killed their daughters and sons.»

Topal Osman's abominable life ended as he was being hunted by a contingent of Turkish soldiers. This pursuit was with the consent of Kemal, who by then was far more concerned with establishing an impeccable posthumous reputation for the future history books. Once his guiding role as the mastermind behind the crimes against the Pontians had produced such highly satisfactory results, he began to distance himself from the wicked boatman who had executed his commands. Thus abandoned by the moral

---

11. Verbal testimony, Oct. 31, 1964, by Lambros Mavrides from the village of Anatole, Ioannina. Archive of the Center for Asia Minor Studies.

12. «pierced the heavens».

perpetrator of the genocide, Topal Osman and a few of his faithful tsetes barricaded themselves in a house near Ankara to escape the soldiers. Osman was fatally wounded in an exchange of fire. Neither the rivers of Christian blood he had set flowing nor the crates of looted goods from wealthy Pontian homes which he had sent to Ankara for safekeeping were able to save him. Not the lire, the silver plate, or the gold jewelry. His final disillusionment was indeed dramatic.

Was such an ignominious end sufficient vindication for the countless victims who lost their lives on his account? Were the few minutes of agony before he died enough to compensate for the heartbreak and tragedy he had caused? Why does it concern us? What do the armies of Pontian new-martyrs have to do with revenge? By far the majority of Greeks do not stoop to such a thing. It is not in our moral make-up to seek it. The outstanding moral issue which has not been addressed, however, regards the presence of the monument in honor of Osman which to this day blights Kerasunta. The Germans have no statue of Eichmann. Why do the Turks believe they must honor this criminal? Was it, perhaps, erected to mask his crimes, as if it were a marble verdict of «not guilty»? Whatever the political intent to deceive might have been, the yashmak concealing so many crimes should long ago have been removed. It is demeaning and humiliating for the Turkish people themselves to look upon the monument and realize that Topal Osman belonged to their nation.

In the terrible September of 1921, the greater part of the male population of Oinoe was slaughtered, while many women and children were exiled. Great-grandmother Archontou's second son, my grandfather Yannis, was a draft-dodger during this black period. He had to go into hiding, or the Amele Tampourou would probably leave his mother with no son at all. The Turks set fire to the forest in order to either burn the deserters or force them to show themselves. Like phantoms in a tale they wandered, haunting rivers and caves, starving and ragged. Countless were those who lost their lives as they were pursued in such hunts, either by way of the harsh conditions or the Turkish bullets. Fortunately for my great-grandmother, Grandfather Yannis was not among them. Sometimes she would receive news of him, sometimes she heard nothing. Thus she waited, patiently, and lived in the hope that she would not be deprived of her second son.

In the meantime, she was trying to survive with her daughters and husband, in an Oinoe where not only terrorism prevailed but also great poverty. The thriving businesses of the Christians had passed into the hands of Turkish partners, whom the government had imposed on them by law. This is what happened to my great-grandfather's tannery, which was now operated by a Turk. Their terrible poverty could not be mitigated even by selling some of their property, as any divestment of Greek assets had also been forbidden by law. Their elder daughter had married, but she was unprotected because her husband was in hiding. And in addition to their fears, hunger began to torment them as well. Although my great-grandfather was not dismissed from the tannery, due to his disabled leg, it is certain that he was unable to satisfy his family's hunger. In the cities, but also in the fire-stricken villages, skeletal figures searched for anything they could find to eat. There are cases in which starving persons went mad and entirely lost control of their actions. Prodromos Iliades[13] writes in his memoirs that in the village of Koultsouchour in the western Pontus, he saw a dead woman lying facedown on the ground with her mouth full of wild greens. No longer having the strength to pull the greens with her hands, she had tried to graze like a wild animal, but at that very moment she perished.

That was how the year 1923 came in. That was when the cold-blooded bartering of human beings was designated by the name «population exchange». The Christians were ordered to leave. Giorgos and Archontou abandoned the graves of their parents and their unjustly killed son, left behind the fruits of their labor, their house and the tannery in Oinoe, and arrived by ship in Kavala. They were exhausted, or, in their own words, they were *amon sourountzakia*[14]. The coastal city of Kavala resembles those of the Pontus like no other in Greece, the way it is built in the shape of an amphi-

---

13. Andreades, Georgios, *Memoirs of Father Prodromos Iliades (Fourtuna Htan)*, Erodios, Thessaloniki 2002.

14. An Oinoean colloquialism which means «like trash».

theater overlooking the sea. They disembarked at the inlet of Keramoti in Chrysoupoli and settled in Souyiolou, a neighborhood where they were later given a refugee house.

My grandfather Yannis did not leave Oinoe with them, as he was in danger of being arrested as a draft-dodger. He arrived in Kavala after three months, travelling the vast distance entirely on foot. He walked as far as Constantinople and then pushed on to Thrace and Macedonia. He hid in the daytime and walked at night, for, in spite of the Treaty of Lausanne, the Turks were still maniacally pursuing the deserters.

Grandfather had come across the I.D. card of a dead man who happened to have the same last name as his, Ioannides, but a different first name. It was Christos. I.D. cards were essential for anyone leaving Turkey but they were not issued to draft-dodgers, so he managed to get out under this false name. He slept wherever he could, ate whatever he found, and reached his family in such a weakened condition that they did not even recognize him. He had very long hair and a long beard, his face had darkened and he was as thin as a skeleton. He was so exhausted he could hardly speak. Years later, as a child, I was hard-pressed to figure out why, while we all called Grandfather Yannis, on my father's official papers his paternal name was declared as Christos.

Great-grandmother Archontou's two unmarried children started families in Kavala, while her elder daughter settled in Thessaloniki with her husband. Grandfather Yannis married Maria Dimitriadou's daughter Antigone, who as a child had had everything she wanted, and whom he had even serenaded with love songs back in Oinoe. Her younger daughter married a kind but sickly Oinoean, and worked as a nurse in the Kavala Municipal Hospital. Eight grandchildren were born. Although there was a large potential labor force in the area due to the number of refugees who lived there, the opportunities for work were few, and my grandfather did not find a job easily. Kavala was flooded with the unemployed poor. Occasionally, he earned a few days' wages working for his wife's uncle, who was constructing the army barracks and other refugee buildings in Kavala. Great-grandfather Giorgos opened a small cobbler's shop, but as this did not provide a sufficient source of income, he moved to Thessaloniki to live with his other daughter. Thus, everyone depended fundamentally on Grandmother

Archontou, who bent her back to the task of earning a living. For years she worked as a cleaning lady at the Kavala Hospital for Infectious Diseases. She stayed there round the clock, sleeping in a corner they allowed her to use. The patients were women with venereal diseases. Fortunately she had excellent health and was able to survive in such an environment, unlike one of her sisters, who died quite young, shortly after the exodus from Oinoe. She earned the equivalent of three peoples' wages, washing, ironing and running errands for the women of loose morals, who, fortunately, often turn out to be generous. Waiting on them, she scraped together as much as she could to support her children and grandchildren.

But how could she fill the stomachs of so many in the middle of such widespread privation? Like an angel her figure would appear in the door-way of her penniless son's humble home. Every Friday she went by the local grocery store. She had arranged with the shopkeeper for them to pick up whatever they needed during the week, and she would pay for it with her week's wages, which barely reached her pocket before they were spent.

Her daughter-in-law was a person of pride and nobility, having been born in a wealthy home in Oinoe, and thus did her best to hide their straitened circumstances. When her mother-in-law dropped by one evening to see how they were getting along, she found my eight-year-old father and his siblings sipping plain tea for supper. In order to sweeten it Antigone had put a piece of candy in each cup, for she had no sugar. Archontou was indignant, and raged at her daughter-in-law: «Oh, you Turkish woman, you! Didn't I tell you to get whatever you want from the grocery store for the children to eat?»

Outside there was snow. She rushed out, leaving them all dumbfounded. They had never heard her speak like that to Antigone, let alone call her a Turk. The word insinuated hardness of character, baseness and a lack of sympathy, none of which were qualities of my grandmother's. In a short time she was back, loaded with groceries: salami, butter, cheese, bread, honey. A real feast for her grandchildren! The memory was permanently engraved on their minds and especially on that of the eldest, my father, Savvas.

In those hard times, during which they became all too well acquainted with the privations of refugee life, the only thing that warmed them was the hope that the future would bring something better.

Unfortunately, it brought worse. Archontou's younger daughter became a widow and was left unprotected with her three children. Soon the elder daughter became a widow as well, and was left alone with another two children. And then the worst blow fell. My grandmother Antigone died in 1939, completing the cycle of widowhood for Archontou's children in the most tragic way. While the folk wisdom of the time may have philosophized: «Son-in-law and daughter-in-law I've lost, but my two children I still have,» the fact is that the whole place was filled with orphans. The death of her 32-year-old daughter-in-law embittered Archontou far more than the loss of her two sons-in-law. She was actually fonder of her than she was even of her own son.

«My little bird, children are orphaned only from their mother,» she often told my father, to show him how much more she sympathized with him than with her daughters' children, who still had their mothers.

Grandfather Yannis, just over thirty years old, devastated by the loss of his wife and with his youngest child only four years old, asked his mother to live with them so that she could look after the children. Of course this was impossible, though not because she did not care for them. She simply had to continue working at the hospital, as it was the only dependable source of money for all of them. Otherwise, they would not be able to survive.

Finding a woman to take the place of my grandmother Antigone was thought to be a better solution. The new wife was also from Oinoe and now worked in a tobacco factory. Her first husband had divorced her because they had no children. She had unjustly borne the stigma of being the infertile one of the couple, whereas she soon gave birth to a son and a daughter, my father's youngest siblings. The girl became a nun, ending her relatively short life at a monastery in the Drama area. It is an honor and a blessing for our family to have a blood relative of such humility, faith and pure soul, who dedicated herself to monasticism.

When the Bulgarians entered Kavala in 1941, my fourteen-year-old father sobbed inconsolably, hidden behind a clump of bushes. Savvas had lost his mother quite recently, and the city where he was born was filling up with the enemy. He was choked with grief. The magnificent Bulgarian Navy, wearing trousers made out of gunny sacks and shoes made of pig leather, had come to conquer the Aegean in their obsolete old ships like covered wagons sporting smokestacks.

The Bulgarian invaders surpassed the Germans in savagery. In 1942, when the Great Famine set in, my grandfather was sent to the Bulgarian forced labor camps from April to October. He belonged to the euphemistically called *skapaneis*, or «diggers», more commonly known as the *dourdouvakia* (the Greek version of the Bulgarian epithet for soldiers in forced labor). Though for the Bulgarians it was a term of derision, to the Greeks it became a title of honor, for they were the young men who refused to submit to the Bulgarians.

In the middle of summer, with their heads clean-shaven and exposed to the scorching sun, their job was to spread the tarmac on the roads which were being opened in Philippoupoli. The food was meager and barely edible. They were rationed water every two hours in the amount of fifty drams –about one hundred sixty grams– which was not even a cupful. My grandfather was afflicted with a cataract. Was it from an injury, an infection, or from the intense sun that beat down on them? I do not know. He was taken to be operated on at the Municipal Hospital of Kavala, which the Bulgarians had since taken over. After that he became completely blind in one eye and could see very little with the other.

My father, in the meantime, had become well acquainted with the brutality of the Occupation. He paid for a single whisper in Greek with a rough slap across the face and was ordered by the Bulgarian who overheard him: «*Balgarski tagovoris!*»[15]

Yet hunger was his worst trial. Hunger gnawed at his vitals, just as it did to everyone. His stepmother, left without her husband but with three children and a newborn, could not make ends meet. Grandmother Archontou was living with her second daughter at the time. The Bulgarians had

---

15. «You'll speak Bulgarian!»

dismissed both of them from their positions at the hospitals. For days on end, this daughter made the rounds of the villages administering injections, and in this way secured enough to feed her own children and her mother. Archontou, however, endeavored to feed her son's children too, for they were perpetually hungry when they crossed her doorstep.

Finding themselves desperate, my father and his twelve-year-old sister decided to trade something of their mother's. They took her coat and the hand-embroidered bedskirts that she had sewn in Oinoe while dreaming of her bridal bed. She had carefully guarded them in the quarantine station at Selimie in Constantinople, then had decorated the refugee shack with them, only to have them traded off by her starving children in the end.

Outside the city, Savvas and his sister reached the sheepfolds belonging to some Sarakatsanoi[16]. The shepherds who lived there deceived the innocent children, giving them a lamb which had died on them but which they pretended was freshly slaughtered meat. The children loaded it on their backs and set off, believing they would at last satisfy their hunger. A Bulgarian whom they met along the way demanded to know what had happened and, when he got to the bottom of things, went back to the sheepfolds with the children, returned the rotten meat, and insisted they be given back their mother's things. The children then went on to the villages around Kavala and were able to exchange the goods for a little corn and wheat. Their joy at the prospect of feeding everyone at home was the perfect antidote to the trouble they had been through and to the bitterness they felt at parting with their mother's mementos. In high excitement, they started back. It had been a good exchange, despite the upset. Just before they reached their own door, however, they ran into a Bulgarian road block. They froze in their tracks and turned pale. The provisions were confiscated and they were left empty-handed. What sheer frustration!

Again they made the rounds of the villages to find something to eat. His sister had holes in her shoes and was crying from the cold. My father decided to steal a pair of shoes he had seen outside the door of a house. After a while, my aunt's wet feet began to warm up. Was it unethical to

---

16. A Greek tribe who generally got their living as shepherds.

74

steal them? Who can judge? Another time my aunt stole a squash and they managed to assuage their hunger a bit. Though it was squash, not bread, my aunt was certainly another Jean Valjean. During this period my great-grandmother was not able to help much, as she no longer worked at the hospital. However, she still managed to scrimp and set aside a little food for her son's children from that which her daughter had provided for her.

They finally saw better days when my father became the regular assistant of a priest, a simple man who served at the cemetery of Kavala. My father spent all his time next to graves, which were continually being filled and emptied, holding the censer, the candles, and whatever else was necessary at a funeral or memorial service. True, he slept and woke alongside the dead, but, at long last, he was able to eat his fill and sometimes feed his stepmother and the other children as well. The priest's wife would send her word whenever there was leftover *kollyva*[17] or olive oil and she would come and get them.

Bulgarian terrorist rule and lack of employment forced my grandfather, once he had returned from the labor camps, to try to reach German-occupied Thessaloniki. From Karvali he and his daughter would be transferred secretly in a small boat, and when they had escaped, they would see to bringing the others as well. Unfortunately, the Bulgarians caught them, took them to a detention center and fiercely beat my grandfather before the eyes of his terrified daughter, who wept silently. They let them go, but under certain restrictions. From then on, their life was continually under threat. They tried again, and eventually were able to escape. The welfare service in Thessaloniki gave them a place to live.

Great-grandmother Archontou, all this time, was unable to fill her grandchildren's stomachs. All she could do was take the edge off their hunger. The good eating she had known in Oinoe was now a bitter memory in the face of the hungry, deprived little ones around her. As soon as her son sent the necessary funds, she, her daughter, her daughter-in-law and the children all went to Thessaloniki. Only my father stayed behind, with

---

17. Boiled and sweetened wheat used as an offering in memorial services.

the priest. He would depart at a later point. When that time came, however, things did not go as well as expected.

At Imaret, the imposing Venetian castle which overlooks Kavala, many Greeks suffered greatly at the hands of the Bulgarians during the Occupation. My teenage father was among them. Just as he was hiding in the boat that would take him to German-occupied Thessaloniki, he was betrayed. They tortured him by repeatedly beating the soles of his feet, hoping he would reveal his helpers, and his feet swelled up from the beating. They beat him so mercilessly that he was practically unconscious when they told him to leave. The boatman who would have taken him from Bulgarian-occupied territory to that of the German occupation was also badly beaten. The Greek who had betrayed my father was later hanged by the Bulgarians themselves.

Eventually, my father managed to get away in a fishing boat and reached Chalkidiki. The fishermen let him off while still at sea so that they would not come close to shore and be recognized. He began to swim, heading for the Greek Red Cross facility. All alone, he battled the waves. He was a young teenager with a will to live. After a great struggle he made it, though he nearly drowned on the way. The Red Cross took him in and clothed him. When he eventually found his family in Thessaloniki, he was completely exhausted. His grandmother, Archontou, nursed him tenderly until he grew stronger. He was able to rest for a while. But the times were hard, and the needs great. He would have to start working as soon as possible.

He began by selling fruit in the streets from a pushcart. The flavor of those fabulous tangerines from the island of Kalymnos, the most delicious of his merchandise, would remain unforgettable for him. He always appreciated fine tastes, taking after his grandmother Archontou. Beside him on the sidewalk was a young girl who was also selling fruit. Days passed before he learned that she was actually his first cousin, the daughter of his mother's dead brother. She had become an orphan in Serres, and the Bulgarian occupation had cast her into Thessaloniki as well. They were two suffering young refugees, laboring on the same sidewalk, sharing the same blood in their veins and the same poverty, yet strangers to each other; scattered little souls who had been thrown into life's struggle in the wake of the tempest their parents were fighting to survive.

During that harsh period, Grandmother Archontou's only brother, Savvas Yiotopoulos, died. He passed away in Athens, where he had gone to work in a tannery. What desperation he must have reached, to have believed that the poverty-stricken, occupied capital could accommodate his hunger along with everyone else's!

His life is yet another refugee tragedy. When in 1921 he was sent into exile, he had already become a widower. Holding one of his little boys by the hand and carrying the other on his shoulders, he set out on the march in the dead of winter. Conditions were extremely rugged and after several hours of walking the two little children begged him to leave them somewhere. At first he refused to even think of such a nightmare, but the pleading soon turned into crying, and eventually he was forced to give in. He left the older one in a populated area, where he hoped some kind-hearted Turk would save him. With one child, perhaps he could make it. After a while, however, the not quite five-year-old child began to beg him to stop. They had not gone far from where he had left the boy's brother. So he left this one too, in the hope that the two children would meet each other and stay together. How much can a single hope diminish one's anguish? To both of them he had repeated over and over that he would come back to find them, and that they should never forget their name or that they were Greeks and Christians.

When he returned from exile he tried to find them, but in vain. His two little boys were nowhere to be found. Five years later, he summoned the courage to start another family. With his second wife he had a little girl, but he was again widowed. With the newborn, he joined the exodus from Oinoe and came to Greece, only to die, lost among the hordes in sorely tried Athens. Is there room for a «why» among so much suffering? What determines the measure of one life's trials? How do we people endure? Did Savvas Yiotopoulos's little boys survive? Could it be that I have third cousins in Turkey today?

Among my great-grandmother's long-suffering relatives there was another tragic figure, the daughter of one of Archontou's sisters. She was widowed and left with two little children on April 22, 1943, at the age of twenty-eight. The Germans executed her forty-year-old husband, also an Oinoean, at the Police Academy in Athens, along with another seventeen resistance fighters, in retaliation for the death of their own soldiers at the hands of the rebels. He had been arrested a few months earlier when a Greek collaborator with the invaders betrayed him. His activity in the EAM[18] was truly heroic. Besides organizing the National Solidarity soup kitchens in Renti, he had also set up an illegal printing press. Inside the well which was in his yard, he had managed to dig out a little room in the walls. He had a mimeograph in there, and spent the nights printing copies of proclamations and notices. His wife would haul him up in the morning using the winch, and handled their distribution herself. She would hide the notices in large bags full of collard greens and would deliver them to his comrades. After her husband's execution, she left the Renti area and moved to another place, because the man who had betrayed him assaulted her with an indecent purpose in mind. He was chasing her maniacally at the factory where she worked and nearly caught her. Where this heroic woman found the strength to resist such a monster is a wonder. She hit him with a brick in order to escape his grip and coworkers let her out a small side door, from where she and her two orphans abandoned their house immediately and moved away. She was brave and dignified, and never let anyone take her husband's place to the end of her life.

My great-grandmother Archontou never returned to Kavala again. She stayed in Thessaloniki until her death, near her daughters, who worked as nurses at the Hospital for Infectious Diseases while she looked after their children. Most of these, after they grew up, married and lived their life in Thessaloniki. Her house was next to the Church of St. Dimitrios. She rarely missed the services that were held there, only ten steps away

---

18. The National Liberation Front (EAM) was founded on September 27, 1941. It was the main movement of the Greek Resistance during the Axis occupation of Greece during World War II. Its driving force was the Communist Party of Greece (KKE), but its membership throughout the Occupation period included several other leftist and republican groups. Its military counterpart was the Greek People's Liberation Army (ELAS).

from her doorstep. From them she drew strength and solace for her soul, which was just as tired out as her body.

Her palms were wide like shovels and she had calluses on her knuckles from all the washing, badges of her daily labor. If Mother Earth were to be personified, she would certainly look like my great-grandmother, Archontou.

I wish I had realized, those few times she spent at our house in Melissia, how much care and affection that little old woman had given in her life, though she drove us deaf with the liturgy playing at full blast on the radio every Sunday at daybreak, and for whom I had to sleep on a trunk so that she would have a bed. I wish I had understood that the *tsimeni*, the spicy pastrami skin–her favorite treat–which my father would bring home to please her, was his way of repaying in part the lifelong debt he had incurred when she brought the bread and other treats that winter night to accompany the plain tea of his poverty-stricken childhood. It took me a very long time to perceive what a warrior in life my great-grandmother had been, and how much she had endured.

I can still hear the blessing that she often gave to my father, who bore the name of her wrongfully killed son, Savvas. Half in Turkish and half in Greek, she would say, «God, many are your blessings» together with «May even the dirt that you touch turn into gold.»[19] Though I only learned quite recently what those odd words meant, I had always felt that their harsh sounds held a great deal of love.

My great-grandmother's sisters all lived to a ripe old age in refugee rooms in Renti. She would crowd in there herself when, in spite of her advancing years, she mustered the strength to visit them and reminisce over the place that had given them birth, now-distant Oinoe, and the food that they used to enjoy–the pies dripping in butter which they loved so much and which they never again got their fill of. I remember one of them in the hospital, shortly before she died, scolding the nurse who was urging her not to tire

---

19. The first sentence was in Turkish: *«Allah, tsok artounsoun»* and the second in Greek: *«To choma na pianeis kai flouri na ginetai.»*

herself out: «Oh, get out of here. Are you out of your mind? I don't want to lie down. Let me fall. So what? I'm tired. Let me die and be done.»[20]

My great-grandmother had reconciled herself with death in the same unconditional way. She passed away naturally, tranquilly, and simply, at the advanced age of ninety-two, her days having been filled with every form of trial. Of ultimate certainty to her faithful soul must have been the meeting after death with her son Savvas, the lad whose murder was the reason that never, during any of the many springs she saw in life, did she taste a single cherry.

---

20. *«Ame strampiou. Tsanepses? 'Ki thelo na ksaploumai. As rouzo afka. Tiden 'k' en'. Epougalefta. As apothano ki as teleno.»* 'Strampiou' was an Oinoean colloquialism approximating «get lost!», or more literally «go with the lightning» (from the Greek *astrapi*, which means lightning).

View of Oinoe, early 20th century. A small boat dock can be seen.

The funeral of heroic Kyrkas (Kyriakos) Giarenis, a relative of my great-grandmother's. He was executed by Topal Osman himself at the port of Oinoe, according to the testimony of Chrysostomos Kerasides to G. Lampsides, included in his book *Topal Osman* (the Giarenis family archive).

Boats transfer «exchangeable» Pontians to the refugee ship, located at sea off Samsunta (photo archive of the Greek Red Cross).

The monument to Topal Osman which stands in Kerasunta. An equivalent distortion of historical fact would be for the Germans to have erected a monument to Hitler in Munich.

Refugees at Selimie with a nurse from the Greek Red Cross (photo archive of the Greek Red Cross).

Kerasunta, a typical Pontian city at the beginning of the 20th century. On the hill the church of Saint Pandeleimon can be seen.

Port of Kavala, similar to the ports of Pontus (Historical and Literary Archive of Kavala).

Kavala before WWII. Archontou's sisters, children and grandchildren. The smiling little boy in front is my father, Savvas.

Kavala before WWII. Pontian refugees from Oinoe. Among them are relatives of mine.

Archontou's daughter-in-law Antigone with her 3 children. She died shortly after this photo was taken.

View of the old city of Kavala. In the background, Imaret, the Ottomanized Venetian fort (Historical and Literary Archive of Kavala).

Army base for the dourdouvakia in Bulgaria (archive of Theodora Ioannidou).

Dourdouvakia taking a break. Darkened by their labor in the sun and unsmiling, except for the Bulgarian guard, front center (archive of Theodora Ioannidou).

Bulgarians in Kavala. A far worse occupying force than the Germans (archive of Theodora Ioannidou).

Archontou with her great-grand-
daughter Antigone.

My grandfather Yan-
nis, also called Christos.

The tragic Savvas Yiotopoulos. Are
his great-grandchildren, my would-be
third cousins, living in Turkey today?
Will they ever find out that they have
relatives in Greece?

Mother Earth.

«NO LAND BELONGS TO US;
WE ALL BELONG TO IT»

MARIA KSANTHOPOULOU
[1892-1986]

«Thelo as 's son topo m' anthropon,
ki as 's sin avlitsa m' choman ki as si kyrou m' tin pachtsan,
enan sachan' milopa.»

(I want someone from my own land,
and from my little yard some soil, and from my father's garden
a panful of little apples.)

Maria was my father's aunt and godmother. She was an only daughter with four brothers, and her happy childhood years in Oinoe seemed to destine her for a carefree and serene future. She was indeed fortunate to be the daughter of Nikos Geleklides!

He was the richest merchant in the city, and the entire village of Keris as well as a large part of another one in the vicinity were included in his enormous estate. The yield from his hazelnut crop was most impressive. From his groves the nuts would be taken to the local port, where they were sent to Constantinople and on to other markets abroad. But that was not all. He also exported eggs to Massalia -now called Marseilles but still known to the Greeks, to this day, by the name of the ancient colony settled there by their ancestors from Phocaea, Asia Minor. Yet another business enterprise of his was trading in raw materials for manufacturing, such as timber for barrel-making, and many other such goods. His right-hand man in all this was his eldest son, Hatzigiorges, a highly intelligent and industrious young person. True, the 1912 ban which forbade Greek ships to make port in the Pontus, imposed by the Young Turks in retaliation for the union of Crete with mainland Greece, dealt them a heavy financial blow. Nevertheless, they continued to be the most powerful family among the ethnic Greeks of Oinoe.

When Maria reached marrying age, the afflictions of the Christians had already begun. In 1911 legislation was passed which obliged the Christians to undergo compulsory service in the Turkish army. On the surface this would seem to be a reasonable amendment to the laws, but in actual essence it was designed with the basest of cunning, given that very few of the enlisted managed to survive. It was one more stage in the extermination process known as white slaughter. The virulent living conditions they faced, serving in the labor battalions which were specially created for them in 1914, i.e., the notorious Amele Tampourou, and the inhumane treatment the recruits received often rendered enlistment tantamount to sheer suicide. A typical case of such treatment was the hanging of a Christian soldier because he had shown up at the base exactly one hour late.

Such were the circumstances when Maria, nicknamed *Guzel*[1] for her beauty, was ready to start a family. The beloved of her heart was Panayotes Ksanthopoulos. He was hardworking and handsome, but he was also poor. When Geleklides' only daughter announced to her parents that she loved him, the huge gap in their financial situations, which would ordinarily have made such a match impossible, was bridged in their eyes by the fact that he was exempt from the army because he was an only son and had three sisters. For this reason his life would be safe, and Maria would not have to endure any of the suffering which had become all too common for Pontian wives and mothers.

And so they were married. Their lovely new house was in the district of Kayades. Built on rocks overlooking the sea, its foundations were lapped by the waves. Her husband worked in the family egg export business and they lived comfortably and happily. One by one, four children came into the world. In their home they had all the prerequisites for a happy life, but outside the atmosphere was growing heavy. It was not long before the storm broke, and catastrophe was in the making. In 1914 Turkey's decision to ally itself with Germany in WWI gave rise to conflict in the breast of every enlisted Pontian, for they would be forced to fight against their mainland Greek brothers on the side of the Western allies. Consequently, the mountains filled with draft-dodgers and deserters, and the persecutions intensified.

As the days passed, nothing of their familiar life was left standing. A dramatic equalization was imposed on them, methodically, insidiously, without the slightest pretext of being a fair redistribution of wealth. It was a predatory seizure of the fruits of their labor and long experience as merchants. The ruination did not discriminate. Just as they razed homes,

---

1. Turkish for «pretty, beautiful».

churches and schools all over the Pontus, so they leveled all differences among the Greeks. Rich or poor, male or female, educated or illiterate, healthy or frail, they were all equally exposed in the face of death.

The edifice of the new Turkey was being built on this lopsided system of justice: a Turkey for the Turks, and only for them. When the Russians entered Trapezunta in 1916, the persecutions in Oinoe and the surrounding area took on even more dramatic dimensions. Propaganda exploited the religious faith of the Islamic masses, who were thus fanatically enraged against the «infidels». Their looting, dislodgement and terrorism served in turn to reinforce the nuclei of Pontian self-defense. The hills around Oinoe filled with draft-dodgers and Greek rebels, as well as Armenian rebels who had survived the 1915 slaughter of their people.

In October 1916 the Turkish army, having first taken hostage the inhabitants of the smaller Greek villages in the area, moved on to the larger village of Keris to do battle with the rebels.

According to I. Saltses: «An entire Turkish division was mobilized against them. They rounded up the elders of the eleven Greek villages and took them hostage. Then they moved on to Keris, one of those villages, part of the estate of Nikolaos Geleklides, a landowner and merchant from Oinoe and one of the elders of the community, where the rebels had assembled for the fortification of the area. The conflict with the division that had brought its artillery against them lasted 24 hours. The rebels' supplies were running out. They managed to break through the division and escape.

»Nikolaos Geleklides and his son were taken to the top of a hill outside the village, to St. John's, and a court martial was held. They were acquitted. However, upon the demand of the Turkish *agades* and the military leaders in Oinoe, they were executed. Along with them the 520 villagers who had been held hostage were slaughtered. The account was closed with the burning of all eleven villages and the displacement-white slaughter, i.e., the exile, of the entire male population of Oinoe, up to 70 years of age, to the interior.»[2]

---

2. Saltses, Ioachim, *Oinoe*, in the journal *Pontiaki Estia*, Thessaloniki 1950.

The rebels who had gathered on the vast property of Geleklides were mainly Armenians, with Zilovanes as their leader. They fought heroically against the considerably greater Turkish forces, but were unable to defeat them. Aunt Maria's father and her brother, Hatzigiorges, were regarded as inciters. They were arrested along with the village teacher, the priest and several workers, and were killed. Various empty promises on the part of the Turks to free them had preceded the event, but the only result was the emptying of the house of all valuables such as jewelry, watches, and gold plate. In the midst of such calamity, were theft and deceit necessary? Apparently they were, in order for us to grasp the financial parameter of the Pontian tragedy, which was so cunningly disguised behind the Turks' nationalist insecurity complex.

First they shot Hatzigiorges, before the eyes of his father. Then they commanded him to pick up his dead son. He braced himself and advanced, barely able to keep from collapsing. The formerly powerful leader of the Oinoean community, completely devastated by his loss, lifted his son onto his shoulder and turned to go. At that moment he received the bullet that killed him too[3].The seizure of the Geleklides estate which had begun was now reaching the final stage. On the very land that had given so many laborers a job, on the land that had granted them such abundant gifts, there they shot them. The same ground that they had watered in order to give forth fruit, they now watered with their own blood. No land belongs to us; we all belong to it.

Was this incident an isolated case of hatred? Even if the executions are considered justified, was there any excuse for such a ritual to take place? What macabre pleasure excited those who watched the father pick up the son who had just been shot before his eyes? What false illusion of might and power infused them when they shot the father as well? Were they perhaps murderously jealous of their victims' wealth? Or was such spite provoked by propaganda? It could be one or many of these things. At any rate, it is a shame that any similar dealing becomes a study in human

---

3. However, according to the Pontian newspaper *Epoche*, they were decapitated (4.18.1919).

vagabondage, whereas the Pontian drama has been largely ignored on the world stage.

From the time of the violent religious conversions in Asia Minor when the Christians were tortured in order to adopt the Muslim faith, an inexhaustible ingenuity on the part of the Turks to inflict pain was already evident. Many exceptions exist, of course, but they do not suffice to cancel the rule. Nor can the touching assistance given to some Christians by many Muslims wipe out the Turkish abomination, for they salvaged a few isolated souls, their own. No individual action, however extreme, can erase the shame of an entire nation. Even if it is a minister of Parliament, as in the case of Salachatin, who would later state: «Is it perhaps the desire of the national assembly to wipe out every person who is not a Muslim? To exile and exterminate them until not one of them is left? In that case, how can we live before the world? Will we be able to stand?»[4]

Superficially, they may have stood. Even their friends, however, know of examples such as the following:

Maria Tilikidou, from Skalita, Matsouka, who was forced to pay the cost of the bullets with which her rebel husband was executed in the village square.

Ioannes Antavaloglou, a banker and great benefactor of Samsunta, who was led along with his son to the gallows at Amaseia in September 1921, though in June they had already murdered another son of his. As they were putting the noose around his son's neck, the father begged that they hang him first, in exchange for three bushels of gold lire. It was not enough that they became ironic with him, gloating that the money was already theirs. They shoved the boy's chair out from under his feet with emphatic determination before they kicked his own away. In an obscure corner of Athens, the third son of this tormented family quietly lived and died.

The many other similar cases of boundless hatred and cold-blooded revenge are too numerous to report. A recounting of the aftermath of the

---

4. *Minutes from the Secret Sessions of the Grand National Assembly of Turkey*, vol. 3, page 720, Ankara 1985.

battle at Keris may suffice to illustrate the point. Initially, the executions concerned males over 15 years old. The place filled up with dead bodies. Then it was the animals: cattle, oxen, goats. And at night, brutal transgression against the women began. They raped them one after another, though they were wailing and grieving. From the extreme violence, some of them died because their spine was broken. In one attack, the victim was being pulled from both sides, by the Turkish soldier and by the women beside her. She was saved from rape only when the braids were torn from her skull. A Turkish deserter, Emilach, who had lived among the Greeks for years and was completely trusted by them, betrayed them utterly. As soon as the Turkish army arrived, he betrayed, murdered and choked with his own hands the very people who had regarded him as one of themselves.

After the murder of Nikolaos and his son Hatzigiorges, the Geleklides women and children were left completely unprotected. Aunt Maria's brothers were all absent: One of them was in Constantinople, another one in Batumi, and the third, along with her husband, had gone into hiding. Turkish partners took over the family businesses, and soon appropriated everything. On such dishonorable practices is the success of Turkish capitalism based. The creation of an urban capitalist establishment is due to the exploitation of the hard work of foreigners.

Their mourning was heavy. The family had been hit from every angle. And that was not all. Two of Maria's children died during that period, a boy and a girl. More losses, more sorrow.

When in 1921 the women and children of Oinoe were once again ordered to be exiled, Maria was alone. Her husband was still in hiding because they had started to murder the remaining male population. She, too, hid for a few days, taking shelter in a shed. Along with her were her own two children and a neighbor's child. The hiding place belonged to a Turk. Did she pay him? Did he feel sorry for her? We do not know. What is certain is that, thanks to him, she did not have to go into exile. The little food that they were provided she paid for by selling off household items for whatever she could get.

In 1923 they boarded a refugee ship as members of the «exchangeable» population. They experienced the horror of the barracks at Selimie, in sight of Constantinople, where so many thousands of Pontians were deprived of their lives. The account of Sophia Mentesidou gives a typical description: «When they took us to Selimie, they put us in the wards. There was not enough room for all of us and we were jammed on top of each other. Many people caught typhoid. We caught typhoid and my mother died, even while the baby at her breast was still nursing. Every day the municipal authority gathered the dead and dragged them away on carts, heaped like logs. So many people lost their lives in Selimie that by the time we left, there was one person at one end of the ward and one at the other.»[5]

The *Manchester Guardian* reported on April 6, 1923: «100 dead were counted at Selimie, two-thirds of whom remained among the living for days. 50 died in one room alone. Of the 20,000 inmates, only 9,000 survived. Hunger, thirst, exanthematus typhoid, smallpox. Some of the refugees threw themselves off the fifth floor of the barracks and committed suicide. They could not bury the dead fast enough and the stench was awful. The refugees who had been burdened with the duty of burying the dead, the only people who were allowed to leave the barracks, turned away in disgust and fled.»

From Selimie, they were taken by ship to Makronissos for quarantine. More trials there. The water was contaminated, the food minimal. When they were at last given permission, they departed for northern Greece. Their move to a village in the prefecture of Drama put them in an awkward position. What did those urban dwellers from Oinoe know of tobacco cultivation or raising farm animals? So they picked up their meager belongings and moved to Kavala. They were given a house formerly occupied by Muslims to live in. It was utterly dilapidated. There, in 1925, another child was born, the youngest son of Maria and Panayotes Ksanthopoulos.

---

5. «Otan egane mas 's so Selimie, esevame 's sa thalamous. O einas ekeitoun apan' 'son allon 'k' ehorname. Polloi eperan ton typhon. Eperamen ton typhon, e mana epethanen kai to moron 's son korfon ats evizanen. Kathan emeran e demarchia emazeve t'apothaments k' ysterna amon kouria esyrnan' ats apan' 's sa kara. Atoson polloi epethanan 's so Selimie apes, pou ontes efygame o einas eton s' enan tin akran ki allos s'allon tin akran te thalamonos.» Verbal testimony, June 22, 1958, by Sophia Mentesidou from the village of Agios Dimitrios, Kozani. Archive of the Center for Asia Minor Studies.

They did their best to get by. A few mats to sleep on the floor and one pan for cooking were their only belongings. But though they were prepared to struggle for survival even under such circumstances, fate was against them. A snake had managed to get in amongst the baby's blankets. That was the last straw. Their courage left them and they broke down. They resolved to move immediately to the city of Drama.

Aunt Maria's brothers lived there with their families, in an inn they had bought with the compensation they had been given by the state and the funds my aunt's younger brother brought with him from Russia. He was a teacher, and had deserted from the Turkish army after his father and brother were murdered. He escaped to Batumi, travelling all the way on foot, having faced hunger, forests full of snakes and wild animals, gorges and torrential waters. He worked tirelessly there for several years, and managed to put aside a substantial sum before he was deported by the Stalinist government and reached Greece with hope for a new start in life.

The trip from Kavala to Drama took four hours using the transport available in those days, so that they nearly collapsed from hunger on the way and were forced to beg. As soon as they got settled in Drama, they searched for ways to make a living without delay. The two older boys of the family became shoeshine boys. With their box of supplies resting on the sidewalk, they polished the shoes of the residents of Drama and did their best to help the household. The older of the two was a child of out-standing mathematical ability. His customers were often astonished by the lightning rapidity with which he solved the problems they brought him. The papers flew beside the brushes and the polish and the bright little refugee was much loved. It was evident even then that after the sidewalk, university was in store for him.

Panayotes opened a greengrocery. From the massive egg export busi-ness which he had operated with his brothers-in-law he was now reduced to dealing in a kilo of potatoes or a half kilo of onions. At that time he also began to chant at the church of the Holy Trinity. That was when the pre-fix *Hatzi* was added to his name. They started calling him Hatzi-Panika. Was it an invention which would permit him to chant, with whatever that entailed regarding their living circumstances? Was it a misunderstanding based on the fact that his brothers-in-law had visited the Holy Land? One thing was certain, that he himself had never been there. That was a trip only for the wealthy, and he was unable to live affluently for a long time. Most likely, he acquired and presented false papers, simply for the sake of supporting his family. Not that he was not a devout person. Quite the opposite. At one point, in fact, he considered becoming a priest, though it did not happen. That was something which required his wife's consent, and she was not eager to give it.

The struggle to make a living in Drama left the old life in Oinoe farther behind every day, the wealth permanently lost, and the happy childhood years a distant memory: those days when they would swim in the cave of Feka, between Tepe and Fanari or Floko. Instead of the *hamamitsa*, the small Byzantine bath, which no Pontian Greek ever took delight in again, they had to be consoled by the springs of St. Barbara in Drama. In Oinoe, other small children have enjoyed these natural beauties up until today, oblivious to the vicious uprooting which took place in order to establish the Turkey of Kemal's vision. Innocent and uninformed, until the education they receive regarding their neighbor misinforms them... They will never be taught that countless Oinoeans perished in Sevasteia[6], Amaseia, and Malateia[7] or that the railroad between Sevasteia and Ankara was built by Pontian Greeks, whose corpses, when they inevitably died working there, were used by Turkish medical students to learn anatomy. They will never be told that Turkey is literally built on the bodies of dead Pontians.

The Geleklides home became a military hospital. When it was originally built, around the year 1900, they could have designed it in an impressive style worthy of the architecture seen in the wealthy homes

---

6. Sevasteia, modern-day Sivas, has existed since ancient times. When the Greeks of the Pontus were being exterminated by the Young Turks starting in 1916, Sivas was often the destination for those who were being «resettled», or in effect being sent on death marches.

7. Ancient Meletini, according to Strabo, now capital of the prefecture of Malateia in southeastern Turkey. The city has been a human settlement for thousands of years. Malateia was the scene of anti-Armenian violence during the late nineteenth and early twentieth centuries and a destination for exiled Greeks of the Pontus.

of Trapezunta. They did not choose to, however, perhaps because they were practical landowning producers and merchants rather than bankers or members of some other highly educated profession. They built quite a large edifice, with a huge basement, stables and sheds, as well as adjacent accommodations for the workers who would stay there from time to time. This functional group of buildings burnt down in 1950. The only thing that was left, until quite recently, to remind someone of its history was the name of the street, *«chastachane sokak»*[8], which replaced the original name of *«Geleklidoglou sokak»*.

The orphaned daughters of the unjustly murdered Hatzigiorges Geleklides lived in Athens. One of them had taken on the position of concierge at an apartment building located on Ioulianos Street. Which one among the tenants who encountered the sisters, aloof and somber, could possibly comprehend what reversals had occurred in their lives? And even if someone were aware of what they had gone through, could that person feel what they felt? It was not the loss of great wealth that troubled them, though they now lived an austere life. They could live without counting their riches. But how could they live, counting the number of deaths they had seen? A great deal of silent pain has «walked» alongside us. Many brave souls have lived quietly among us. Many were true heroes of the Pontian struggle, swept unnoticed into the whirlpool of anonymity. Countless are the invisible unsung heroes of the Pontus, who either were mercilessly persecuted or fought without thought for themselves and yet received no recognition in Greece, whose only alleviation of their pain was the post-war misery and the failure of the Greeks to acknowledge the magnitude of the Pontian struggle.

The years passed. The family of Maria and Panayotes Ksanthopoulos was not subdued by poverty. Although they experienced privation, their life began to improve daily. They were especially pleased in 1933 when their eldest boy entered the School of Mathematics as one of the top students.

---

8. «Street of the ill».

However, when in 1940 the Germans occupied Greece and the Bulgarians entered the city of Drama, their daily circumstances became unbearable. Whatever household items were of any value were sold for a pittance at Liberty Square by the miserable residents of the city and the surrounding villages. They were starving. Foodstuffs disappeared. The merchants were forced to take on Bulgarian partners and use of only the Bulgarian language was compulsory. Even the components of the water system were sent to Bulgaria by the occupiers. So great was the hatred and the savagery of the invaders that anyone who could, left the area. Unable to choose freedom, our unfortunate people chose a different Occupation. They went to the areas that were occupied by the Germans, west of the Strymonas River. All the passages, however, were guarded, which made the attempt terribly difficult. With the aid of their eldest son, then a university student in German-occupied Thessaloniki, the Ksanthopoulos family managed to join him there. They crossed the river by clinging to a cable, in order not to be swept away by the strong current. Maria, being quite short, nearly drowned as she stretched her legs to reach the river bed.

Their new start brought new difficulties. Maria worked in a tobacco factory in order to support the family, as her husband was unable to work. He was already suffering from the disease which would prove fatal to him. Hatzipanikas eventually died of tuberculosis and Maria lived nearly 50 years as a widow.

When they began their life together in Oinoe, they could not have imagined the deprivation and losses which life held in store for them. The genuine lire in Aunt Maria's *kentarliki*[9], a symbol of prosperity in the Pontian community, were sold off to cover their daily wants, though, in any case, Aunt Maria had lost all interest in adorning herself early on. Fortunes change hands, people change places, while souls endure and continue life's passage.

Her family's case is a typical example of the adventures of the urban dwellers of the Pontus, who prospered, advanced, were educated, and strengthened the foundation of Greek supremacy in the Black Sea area.

---

9. A necklace made of gold lire worn by wealthy Pontian women.

Wrongly, unjustly, and ignorantly, the ethnic Greeks who came to Greece from the Pontus were identified as Pontian villagers only. It was not only the farmers, shepherds, metal-workers and other small craftsmen who came to Greece as refugees. The urban dwellers, with their high social status, wide cultural experience, and intellectual pursuits, also contributed dynamic members to the downtrodden hordes of Pontians who took refuge in Greece. The College of Trapezunta[10] was founded in 1682, and its students formed the intellectual nucleus among Pontian thinkers, both male and female. Soon other educational institutions were created, and along with the large monasteries, they offered the community well-rounded, creative personalities for long decades. Until, of course, the persecutions began and these same individuals became the main target, in order to leave the ethnic Greeks without leaders to guide them. The wrong impression which mainland Greeks formed of the nature of the Pontian population was largely due to the fact that they all arrived destitute, coupled with the fact that the Pontian dialect sounded to them like broken, illiterate Greek. However, the gradual comeback and advancement of Pontians in all fields in their new homeland must unquestionably be attributed to individuals who derived from the cultivated urban dwellers, educated professionals and businessmen of the Pontus.

Aunt Maria lived peacefully to an old age, looked after by her children, though simultaneously she assisted in raising their children as well. Around 80 years old she suffered another blow: her eldest son died. She lived the rest of her life with her younger son's family.

---

10. Known as the Frontistirio of Trapezus, it was a Greek educational institution which operated from 1682 to 1921 in Trapezunta and provided a major impetus for the rapid expansion of Greek education throughout the Pontus region. Initially housed at the Panagia Soumela Monastery, its main goal was the cultivation of the national and religious identity of the local Greek communities. It was supported by generous donations granted by wealthy Greek families. In 1902 it was re-housed in a new, imposing building, which remains today as the most impressive Pontian Greek monument in modern-day Trabzon. The school closed in November 1921, as the Greeks were being forced out of the region. Today the building functions as a prestigious Turkish high school.

Near the end of her life she suffered from delusions. In her mind she was attending to the storage of supplies for the winter at her childhood home, and looking after the stables and the horses. It was a merciful intervention. In that way she escaped her lifelong sorrow. Not, of course, for lost wealth, not for the comforts of life nor for glory, but the simple fact that her brother's life, at least, had not been not spared.

Ultimately, no truth about humanity is valid if one ignores the evil side within us, the stores of darkness which are curtailed by proper moral guidance but which, given the appropriate ideological camouflage, can be unleashed uncontrollably and wreak havoc on the world. It is just as the English pastor Frew, head of the British Relief Fund, said as early as 1918, referring to the unfolding events: «Even if devils themselves were in control of things, I doubt whether they would have done any worse.»[11]

---

11. *The Morning Post*, London, 12. 6. 1918.

Kastros, one of the Greek districts of Oinoe, indicative of the prosperity and cultivation of the ethnic Greeks in Pontian cities. The houses, lordly and well-built, literally sit on the water (from the book *Those Who The Wind Lashes*).

One of few Greek homes which remain in the district of Periyali today (the Giarenis family archive).

View of Maria Ksanthopoulou's childhood home, when it was being used as a military hospital. The Turkish flag can be seen, top left.

The mansion of the tragic Antavaloglou family. Reason enough for the father and his two sons to be murdered (from the book by the Association of Pontian ladies, *Living memories of Pontos*).

The mansion that once belonged to the Porloglou family (from the book by the Association of Pontian ladies, *Living memories of Pontos*).

Nikos Geleklides during the glory years of Oinoe, his wife and three of their children. He and the oldest son, Hatzigiorges, center, were executed by the Turks. Aunt Maria is the baby on her mother's lap.

Maria on her wedding day, young and wealthy, wearing the traditional *kentarliki*.

The handsome Hatzipanikas, with the typical large, thick moustache of the householder.

Harvesting hazelnuts in the Pontus (postcard from the beginning of the 20th century).

Hazelnut growers in the Pontus (archive of the Committee for Pontian Studies).

Women sorting figs at the beginning of the 20th century (archive of A. Mailes).

Ioannis and Sophocles Antavaloglou, tragic father and son, bankers and businessmen of Samsunta, hanged on Sept. 21, 1921, by the infamous courts of independence in Amaseia.

The monument of disgrace in Amaseia. Kemal and his comrades are honored at the place where 177 ethnic Greek magnates were hanged.

Pontian women at Selimie with the director of the Greek Red Cross, Mr. Kouyioumtzoglou (archive of the Committee for Pontian Studies).

Refugees leaving the barracks of Selimie. These ones managed to survive (from the book *Certain Samaritans*).

The barracks of Selimie today. A place of martyrdom for the Pontian Greeks.

Kavala at the beginning of the 20th century, soon to be inundated by the downtrodden (Historical and Literary Archive of Kavala).

Drama during the Bulgarian occupation. The Greek language was scratched out and written over in Bulgarian, not only in the shops but also on the icons in the churches (postcard during the Bulgarian occupation).

Maria with her husband and three children in Drama.

Hatzipanikas seated, left. The ladies, left to right: my grandmother Antigone's two sisters, Maria Ksanthopoulou, third, and Antigone.

Maria Ksanthopoulou in her old age in Thessaloniki.

«THE MAN-KILLER
KOP-TAGOU»

PANAYOTES SPYRANTES
[1901-1975]

«E kardia m' en' geralin, sychna pychna matoutai.
Amon ti lampas to ghyalin, an krous ato tsakoutai.»

(My heart is fragile; it often bleeds profusely.
Like the globe of a lamp, if you knock it, it shatters.)

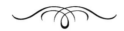

Panayotes Spyrantes was my mother's uncle, married to one of my maternal grandmother Chrysoula's sisters. He was born in the village of Tantourlouch, near Argyroupoli[1], within the eastern Pontus prefecture of Chaldia.

When he was very young, his father died in the forced labor camps of the Turkish army. Under the pretext of improving the infrastructure of the Turkish Empire, the aim of these camps was to eradicate the Christians by submitting them to severe living and working conditions, with the result that many a family was left without sons or fathers. In this way, Uncle Panayotes was likewise orphaned and lived with his mother and his paternal grandfather.

He was from the family of *Spyrant*. According to the Pontian custom of name-giving, the suffix *-ant* signified a forefather, some Spyros, in Uncle's case. In other cases the same ending could refer to one's place of origin. Thus, from *Ypsilant-*, which means «hailing from Ypsala», a village in the Pontus, we have the renowned family of the Ypsilantes, who sacrificed four of their five sons for the sake of their country. Best known were Alexandros and Dimitrios, the former of whom, as the leader of the *Filiki Eteria* (The Society of Friends), laid the plan for the 1821 revolution against the centuries-long Ottoman Occupation of Greece, while the latter successfully led, among many others, the last battle in the struggle for independence, in Petra of Boeotia in 1829.

---

1. A town located 80 km south of Trapezunta. The city was established around 700 BC by Ionian Greeks, who first discovered silver in the region. As for the name of the city during the Ottoman period, the Greek-speaking population also used the name *Gümüşhane* (place of silver) but, in the first decades of the 19th century, the hellenized form *Argyroupolis* was established.

When in 1916 Russian troops entered Trapezunta, the Greeks were overjoyed. The Armenian slaughter the year before had utterly terrified them, mind and soul. The welcome presence of people who shared the Christian faith gave birth to the hope that all further persecutions would be averted. From now on, the youthful Panayotes, or Patzos, like all the non-Muslim young men, would no longer be in danger of losing his life in the way his father had.

Unfortunately, however, they only breathed the air of freedom for about two years. The Russians were ordered by their new government to withdraw. The consequences were tragic for the Greeks, even though they were the ones who for two years had protected their Turkish neighbors from reprisals by the Armenians who were serving in the Russian Occupation army. Who would remember the solidarity, the concern, or the friendly support? Who would dare to hide, defend, or feed the Greeks who had once succored them?

The situation quickly grew out of control. Gangs of unruly, fanaticized Turks, incited by propaganda, surged against the Christians. The moment the Russian troops would abandon an area, these gangs would rush in and spread havoc. Before long they reached the remote little Byzantine villages around Tantourlouch. Their appearance and their cries left no doubt as to their intentions. In January 1918, on the morning of the Christian Epiphany, they surrounded Tantourlouch.

Uncle Patzos' account, documented by researchers from the Center for Asia Minor Studies, constitutes an invaluable record of the conditions they faced during the exodus from Tantourlouch:

«On the evening of January 5, we were gathered in the school. We had just come back from singing the Epiphany carols around the village and our teachers were distributing the food people had given us children as we went from home to home. The money they had given us would be kept to be used by the school council and the church. We had brought the lyre with us and were dancing. At daybreak, Turkish tsetes surrounded the village. The Russians were leaving our parts and right behind them would come the Turkish tsetes.

»They entered the village and rounded up the men first and then the women. They gathered them in two spots. Along with them came Turks

117

from nearby villages and the looting of our homes began, and lasted until evening. Around three in the afternoon we got up and left, taking whatever we could carry in our arms. But what could you take? They had confiscated all our livestock.

»Forty or forty-five families, the whole village, picked up and went to the neighboring Turkish village of Demiroren. The people there were more sober and prudent. Before the Russians came, that was where we had gone and stayed for six months. And when the Russians came, we kept them from leaving and protected them.»

Uncle Panayotes's grandfather, a man of gigantic stature, was the only one who was determined to resist when the rest of the villagers were frantically departing for the unknown. Where were they headed? To a place near their homes or farther away? Would they come back, and when? Would they be able to endure the freezing cold of the outdoors?

He preferred to act like lightning. There, all alone. He had a gun, as did all the Greeks, for it was the only way to prevent constant theft by the Turks. He chose to fight, regardless of the risk to his life. He barricaded himself in his home and took on countless rebels. He must have realized how futile this gunfight was. The village was already going up in flames and the looting was carrying on non-stop. Yet he refused to budge from his decision to defend his home, his land, his village, his life. He had to get even with those who had done away with his son. His accounts would be balanced once and for all, then and there. No more retreating, no more tolerance. He was a giant in spirit as well. Of course he was killed. But was he defeated?

From a purely rational perspective, his stand-off was futile; one might consider it sheer madness. Nevertheless, from a spiritual point of view it is profoundly reminiscent of certain other Greeks, ages past, who also refused to take even a single step backwards and were determined to sacrifice themselves, in that narrow strip of ground called Thermopylae[2].

---

2. The Battle of Thermopylae was fought between Greeks and Persians during the second Persian invasion of Greece, in 480 BC. A mere 300 warriors held the narrow coastal pass of Thermopylae for 3 days, against over 100,000 Persians. Both ancient and modern writers have used this battle as paradigmatic of the power of a patriotic army defending its native soil.

The tsetes cut the nose, ears and genitals off his grandfather's dead body. They then stuffed them in his mouth and tossed him on a pile of manure along the escape route of the other villagers. In this way, they not only gained revenge for his resistance, but also derived the monstrous pleasure of inflicting absolute terror on the others.

Uncle Patzos continues: «We reached Demiroren in the middle of the snow, around ten or eleven at night. The snow and the illnesses seemed endless. The snow was two or three meters deep. We couldn't make any headway. The roads were blocked. The distance was short, but there was no way through the snow. At last we arrived. We went and stayed at the home of Tsolach bey. He was a good bey. He was the one who invited us there. He invited the whole village. He distributed us among three or four houses. We stayed two days. At the end of the second day the tsetes came looking for us. 1,500 tsetes had gathered in the area and were demanding to slaughter us. Meanwhile, half of the Turkish residents wanted to hand us over to be slaughtered, while the other half wanted to let us leave. We got wind of this debate, so at midnight we sent some of our people to Baipurt on foot, trekking from mountain to mountain. In the middle of winter, in all that snow, these people set out on a hike of ten hours.

»There in Baipurt, after the Russians pulled out the Armenians took the upper hand, and they wanted to set up resistance and fight for autonomy. The villagers we had sent found some of our fellow villagers who were already there and together they went to Arsak pasha (the Armenian leader) and told him of our situation. He goes to a Turkish hodja[3] and writes a letter in Turkish. He gives the letter to the hodja and tells him to take it to Demiroren and give it to Tsolach bey. The letter said: "If you don't turn over the Greeks to us here in Baipurt in 24 hours, I'll send 500,000 troops to burn you down."

»The hodja arrives with the letter at 5 o'clock. He gives it to the bey, who reads it. We caught on pretty quick. Soon they tell us to get ready to leave. They shove us out of our homes, at night, in the snow, under

---

3. Muezzin, i.e., a Muslim cleric.

the bright moonlight, on their own horses and with 100 armed men from the village to escort us. They took us to the village of Chatrach[4]. It was a mixed village (it had a hundred families–fifty Greek and fifty Turkish). When the Russians were on their way to our region back in 1916, these Turks exiled the Greeks to Sebaz and no one ever came back. Five or six families who ended up in Russia made their way to Greece. Chatrach was six hours from Baipurt. We arrived there at dawn. Our people were shouting and wailing because they were afraid they would kill us. The escort kept reassuring us. When we arrived there, they left us and returned to their village. They didn't dare bother us, because the village was on the main road from Baipurt to Erzerum. That's why they were afraid to bother us.

»We thought we would stay in Chatrach three or four days, but they warned us that tsetes were approaching. Right away we picked up and left, and headed for Baipurt. We walked more than six hours through the snow–hungry refugees in flight, plagued by illnesses. When we arrived in Baipurt the place was overrun by refugees. The people in the streets were practically trampling each other.

»As soon as we arrived in the city, Arsak commanded: "All those who can handle a gun should get hold of one, so we can stand and resist." Meanwhile, the Turks were advancing. Nearly all of us took up arms. The Armenian Arsak pasha commanded that we round up the (local) Turks and put them to work shoveling snow, to open a path on Mount Kop-tagou[5] so that the people who had gathered in Baipurt could proceed towards Erzerum. Arsak pasha also committed crimes to avenge the slaughter the Armenians had suffered. He rounded up quite a few Turks, put them in the mosque and burnt them alive inside it. We finally left Baipurt and, opening a path through the snow, we reached Kop-tagou. The women and children had to struggle through the snow; around us there were dead horses, wagons and carts stuck in the snow, and dead

---

4. Also known as Yatrach. About 40 of the 50 Greek families there hailed from Tantourlouch.
5. Kop dag. *Dag* means mountain. In other testimonies it is referred to as Kiop dagi. Located between Baipurt and Erzerum, it has an altitude of 2,868 meters.

bodies. We saw one mother throw her baby down because she couldn't carry it anymore. We picked it up and that night, when we reached the Turkish village Aschala, we gave it to her. How she cried.

»As we slowly traipsed over the mountain, the people lived on dried biscuit and tea which the Russians had left behind in their warehouses. After a thirteen-day trek, we finally reached Ilitse. It took us thirteen days to hike just one hundred kilometers. Sick and barefoot, struggling under extreme conditions and exhausted, we arrived in Ilitse.

»At Ilitse there were hot springs. I remember we had gone to wash. We undressed and got into the cistern. At midnight, the Armenians we were with informed us that the road to Erzerum had been cut off. The tsetes were closing in on us. Armed Armenians, Russians and local Greeks start fighting them. We drop everything once again and get out of there. On the way, those who had guns kept up a little fire and the people marched ahead. It took us from midnight until noon the next day to reach Erzerum. We didn't stop there. We headed straight for Sarikamis[6]. Meanwhile, the Armenians who had stayed in Erzerum rounded up many Turks and burnt them alive.

»Outside Erzerum there was a place, the town of Chasangala. The Russians had brought the railway from Russia up to this point. As soon as we got there, we got into some open-air train cars and headed for Chorontouzou, another large town with a train station. All these places had been abandoned by the Russians and were now held by the Armenians and our own armed men. We arrived in Chorontouzou and stayed the night. They fed us dried biscuit and tea from the Russian warehouses. Our people ate as much as they could and then they burnt the rest, for the tsetes were close behind. We reached Sarikamis. They put us up in storage sheds, in czarist barracks, in schools–there were thousands of us. From the very first day we arrived in Sarikamis, the Greek residents of

---

6. A large town between Erzerum and Kars. In 1900 approximately 500 Greeks lived there. The Russo-Turkish conflict which took place there in 1914 proved decisive in concluding the war in favor of Russia.

Kars[7] and its villages came with *sagkes*[8] and took families to their homes to put them up. The Greeks from Kars had served in the czarist army and some of them were officers. Sizing up the situation, they took up arms again and organized themselves into battalions.

»From every home that was so inclined, in Kars and in the villages, the local residents came to Sarikamis on sleighs and carried five or six families back to their village. The whole refugee population was divided up and housed in the villages. Some went to relatives, others to people from their own home towns who had moved to the Caucasus years before, and several families from our village went to Crimea, where they had relatives. And quite a few stayed in Sarikamis.

»My family went to Moulamoustafa. My grandfather, who had already been in Artachan for years, sent us 150 roubles in Sarikamis for our fare to Artachan. But we didn't go to Artachan because we came down to Kars on sleighs. As soon as we got to Kars from Moulamoustafa, we learned that the Kurds had cut off the road to Artachan, so we couldn't go there. A Greek-Armenian army was organized in Kars, but they fought amongst themselves over the leadership and split up. The Armenians did a lot against the Turks. They killed and burnt Kurdish villagers. That's why they couldn't get along with our people. As soon as our people split from the Armenians, a committee is formed and they decide to open up the road to Artachan, putting up a fight so that the families can be conveyed. There were twenty families from our village that would go there and a lot of people from the other villages of the Pontus.

»In the morning, two hundred and fifty people set off, headed by a priest from Kars. There were armed men, a mobile hospital unit, huge Russian cooking pots–a regular army! We left the families behind, around five hundred of them, on sleighs. Two hundred and fifty of us went to a Kurdish village to do battle. The priest betrayed us and the Kurds ambushed us. Seven men were killed in the battle and five were injured. The priest

---

7. The largest city on the Turkish side of the present-day border with Armenia. Up until 1920, a meritorious Greek community lived in some 70 Greek villages around Kars. The Greeks and Armenians of Kars were deported in 1920.

8. Sleighs.

kept saying to us "Don't shoot, don't shoot!" all the time the Kurds were surrounding us. So the trip to Artachan was called off.

»We went back to Kars, where we stayed for a month. The Turks had occupied Sarikamis and were now advancing on Kars. The Greeks of Kars took over the station, and a steady stream of refugees was taking the train to Russia. Those with money would hire entire train cars. The local Pontians left on their animals. Those without animals or money to hire animals, like us, kept waiting under the overhead shelter at the station, to be given train cars to leave in. We stayed there for fifteen days but finally we didn't get to leave for free. We paid. We all had relatives who had emigrated to Crimea. They collected the funds and sent them to us with two or three people. As soon as they brought us the money, we boarded the train for Tiflida[9]. From Tiflida we went on to Pot[10], where we paid passage on a boat and went to Theodosia[11] because a Turkish destroyer was chasing us between Novorossiysk[12] and Kerch[13] (*see maps, page 132*). So we were forced to go to Theodosia. From there we went to Kerch. We stayed there for two or three days but then we picked up and came on horse carts to Crimea. Then everyone went their own way, to Sudak[14], Theodosia, Sevastopol[15], Yalta[16], wherever we happened to have relatives already settled and who were working, or who had shops and that sort of thing.

---

9. Capital of Georgia.

10. A port city in Georgia located on the eastern coast of the Black Sea, near the site of the ancient Greek colony of Phasis.

11. Still a major coastal town in Crimea, it was first founded as Theodosia by Greek colonists from Miletos in the 6th century BC.

12. Russia's main port on the Black Sea. From August 26, 1918 until March 27, 1920 it was the principal headquarters of the White Army.

13. The Kerch Strait was the Cimmerian Bosporus of the Ancient Greeks, said to be the entrance gate to Hades.

14. A town of regional significance in Crimea, situated 57 km to the west of Theodosia.

15. A coastal city in the southwestern region of Crimea. In the 6th century BC a Greek colony was established in the area of the modern-day city.

16. This town came to worldwide attention in 1945 when the Yalta Conference between the Big Three powers–the Soviet Union, the United States and the United Kingdom– was held there. It is a resort city on the south coast of the Crimean Peninsula.

»We came to Greece in 1922, during the famine, whereas the rest of the villagers from Tantourlouch who had settled in Crimea stayed there only a year and came to Greece on Greek ships in 1919, with the Greek fleet that transported the Greek army to the south coast of Russia and then retreated. Those of us who arrived in 1922 were kept in quarantine for four months, on the islands of Makronissos and St. George.

»We came here from Batumi, on an Italian ship, a freighter. 4,500 of us got on it, but only 1,500 arrived alive. The rest died on board, in quarantine, on Makronissos[17]. After four months in quarantine, on August 14, with the Catastrophe and the withdrawal of the Greek army from Asia Minor, we were allowed to leave. We went to Piraeus and everyone went his own way. I stayed in Drapetsona[18] for five years; the first year we spent in tents but then we built shanties out of shingles and tar paper. Five years later we came here to the Melissia district.»

The above account, in its general outline, requires no commentary. It would serve to heighten our awareness of the conditions under which the exodus took place, however, if we emphasize that the temperatures were far below zero and that the road had entirely disappeared under the snow. They had to keep opening a path unceasingly so that they would not be standing about and literally freeze while waiting. Uncle Patzos and the rest of the youth were up front shoveling the snow so that the women, children and elderly could get through, while other men were protecting the sides to safeguard them from the snow caving in. And what about the old man who had been slaughtered? There was probably no time to ponder his death. The dead could wait peacefully, until the likelihood of the rest of the villagers sharing the same fate had been eliminated.

---

17. Literally *long island*, it lies in the Aegean Sea off the coast of Attica, facing the port of Lavrio. Approximately 40,000 Pontians died in quarantine there in one year (reported in the Greek newspaper *Rizospastis*, 12.8.1923).

18. Municipality on the southwest border of greater Piraeus. Pontian refugees and ethnic Greeks fleeing from other areas of Asia Minor settled there. They lived in flimsy shacks under terrible conditions and worked in the factories of the area.

They faced their worst trial as they made their passage over the man-killer mountain, Kop-tagou. They had been forced to flee Baipurt because the tsetes were after them. The persecution, the hunger, the extreme conditions and the illnesses were not enough; in order for the «faithful» to be rid of the «infidels» once and for all, they had to be annihilated. The refugees loaded the infirm on hired *chouzakia*[19] and set off. But what kind of an imagination would it take to picture the abandonment of a child by its own mother? What horror can be compared to that felt by Sophia Kyriakidou when she discovered that the baby she had tied to her back was frozen? What nightmare can be greater than the one that occurred when a huge avalanche of snow came crashing down on women and children?

Such was the exodus of the ethnic Greeks from Tantourlouch, the Christians from Chaldia. Pursued by gangs of thieves eager to prey on them, with snowstorms raging and deep gorges lying hidden, ready to swallow them up, they pressed on with all their strength, eastward.

Nature, innocent in itself, in this case seemed to be ungrudgingly aiding the persecutors. Little children, the elderly, and women trudged at a snail's pace through unimaginable blizzards. We, the descendants, can grasp very little of all that, for obvious reasons. When the below-zero temperatures are read about but not felt, the parts of the body are not frozen stiff with cold. When the danger of being annihilated is described but has already passed, our breath is not taken away in trepidation. Yet these are the conditions, the harsh reality, which certain people forced others to endure, and all that behind the façade of saving their country from infidels! One reaches the point of wondering whether the impetuous decision of Panayotes' grandfather was not really irrational at all, but may, in fact, have been wise.

And yet, the most significant thing in all this was, and always will be, the truth that the human wrecks of Tantourlouch, together with the overwhelming majority of the Greeks in the Pontus, would have suffered no persecution if they had changed their faith–if they had denounced their ancestral heritage in order to save themselves! But they did not, in spite

---

19. Sleighs.

125

of the terrible toll they paid. They defended their ethnic and religious identity with fortitude. Refusing to exchange it for another, they donned it as armor and fought to the death.

The quality of character of Uncle Patzos, and of the Greeks in general, is readily apparent in their refusal to brook the slaughter of unarmed Turks, which the tragic Armenians had resorted to in retaliation for their own genocide.

After the failed attempt at meeting with the other grandfather, who had been waiting for them in Artachan, there followed their wanderings in Crimea. They finally settled in Sudak where they stayed until 1919, when many of the refugees, including his mother and his future wife's family, decided to come to Greece.

Uncle Patzos remained in Russia to work, while his mother's welfare was assumed by the family of my great-grandmother Maria Sidiropoulou. He lived in great poverty, but just as great was his love for Maria's daughter. He planned to save money and later go to Greece to marry her. At the same time, he would be able to offer a more comfortable life to his worn-out mother.

In 1922 he departed from Batumi[20] to reach Drapetsona, but he fell seriously ill on the way. His journey to the promised land was under wretchedly unsanitary conditions. And, unfortunately, motherland Greece proved to be a place of never-ending happiness only in the refugees' dreams. The water they drank during the voyage decimated them. The epidemics mowed them down, and people lay exhausted, anywhere they could find a spot, jammed against each other, from the ship's hold all the way to the upper deck. The daily dead numbered around seventy, and their lifeless corpses became fuel for the ship's boilers or were thrown overboard. Somehow my uncle managed to survive amidst all this devastation. In fact, whenever his health permitted, he would continue his work as a tinner. He took great care to hide his meager savings,

---

20. Located on the site of the ancient Greek colony called Bathys, derived from the Greek phrase *vathis limin,* meaning deep harbor. From March 1920 until February 1921, tens of thousands of ethnic Greeks were transported in ships from there to Greece, among whom were about 30,000 from Kars.

for they would enable him to start his new life. In the end, though, all his hard work was for naught, as the ship's Italian sailors made off with his savings and once again he was destitute.

An incident that took place during the trip is indicative of just how genteel he was. At some point he met his first cousin, on the deck. She was a young girl herself and had asked him where he was off to with a lit candle in his hands. «Is it any of your business?»[21] he asked. Though his manner was abrupt, it was his discreet way of avoiding telling her that they were about to toss her dead mother's body into the sea and that the candle was lit in supplication for her soul, for the daughter had not yet been informed of the death.

When they finally arrived in Piraeus harbor, they were held in quarantine on the ship. From the first moment there he asked after his family, which essentially consisted of his mother only. He was yearning to see her because he had not seen her for three whole years. The bad news hit him like a bolt of lightning: the day the ship made port was the day of her memorial service. He had arrived forty days too late for one last kiss and embrace. Life did indeed sharpen its teeth on their hearts and souls. The poor woman left this world with neither her husband nor her only son beside her. There, in the shantytown of Drapetsona, she finished her bitter life under the care of my great-grandmother, who soon became the mother-in-law of the desolate Panayotes.

The first quarantine station to receive him was St. George, the small island which lies as if guarding the entrance to the Saronic Gulf, near Salamis (now Salamina). During those tough times on the island, whatever was of value was sold off for next to nothing. A gold watch might buy a single lemon, and a slice of moldy bread could cost a gold pound.

Approximately 2,400 years before that, the Greeks battled heroically against the Persians in those straits and thus saved Western civilization

---

21. *« 'S si goula se errouksen?»* based on the word *goula*, which comes from the Venetian word *gola*, neck and thus, literally «Has it fallen on your neck?».

from Asian barbarianism. In 1922 the Pontian Greeks were fighting in those same straits, this time to survive the hardships brought on them by the barbarianism of another Asian invader. These are situations and events that the West should always take into account when referring to the bulwark of civilization known as Greece.

It may be that paeans are not written when the supreme fight is simply for survival. The struggle to save ourselves does not inspire in the way that saving our homeland does. But this struggle was also valorous, because it, too, concerned people who refused to submit.

They were the people who formed the heroic defense of Hellenism: in the mountains of the Pontus, in exile, in slaughters, and even in quarantine. An age-old civilization was being destroyed and they were fighting without any aid whatsoever from mainland Greece. This was a true tragedy, though no Aeschylus[22] was present to record it.

Panayotes married my grandmother's sister in 1924 and they had four children. His life was marked by honesty, hard work and patience. He made the world a better place with his presence and left vivid memories of his innate discretion, even on us who were only small children at the time. He met with tough trials–the life of an orphan, of a refugee, and of great poverty. Yet the sad, subtle smile on his face always radiated kindness.

Unfortunately, however, one's pain is never quite paid off. Our contributions in tears do not wipe out our inexplicable debts, and no calamity offers surety against the onset of a new one.

Uncle Patzos was widowed at fifty. Thus, he had the mournful opportunity of honoring his wife just as much after her death as he had when she was by his side. Of their children, the only one who was married at the time was their only son. He had started his own family with a Pontian Greek from Russia, who had come to Greece in 1938 at a young age. Her father had perished in exile in Siberia during the Stalin era, as had his brother and the latter's two sons. The annihilation practices used in the

---

22. Aeschylus, known as the father of tragedy, was the author of *The Persians*, whose focus is the defeat of Xerxes' navy at the Battle of Salamis. Some historians believe Aeschylus himself fought there.

extermination of the Pontians were seemingly inexhaustible, carried out by shrewd planning, machinations, and the inventiveness of innumerable agents. The episodes of the Pontian drama unfolded under every kind of bitter cold, designed to freeze the heart.

When his son fell gravely ill, the father bore his suffering in silent anguish. After his wife, this was the second person in the family to be taken ill with an incurable disease. Shortly before the end, he told Uncle Patzos that he knew he was going to die soon. My uncle answered calmly, «I am not giving you my turn.»[23] And indeed, he did not give him his turn. He died in his sleep that same night and did not live to see his 49-year-old son die a few months later.

I do not know if he ever tried to make sense of his trials. But I do know that for some unfathomable reason, on the day of Epiphany in 1918, his life entered the orbit of a future full of trials and torment, leaving behind him the foundations of his traditional past.

It is obvious from his account of the exodus that the long-term inertia in bringing the Pontian tragedy to light is due to a collective shunning of an unbearable reality. Not that the official government is not to blame, but the Pontians themselves avoided going public. They chose to hide their lament behind their songs, and their loss behind their dances. Others, like me, did not even do that. They stubbornly avoided all grief or pain, purposely distancing themselves from it and turning their attention elsewhere, as if we can shield ourselves from the truth forever.

Uncle Patzos, of course, would probably understand nothing of this perhaps extremely amateur psychological analysis. Nor would he need to. People of his kind do not require complex reasoning or explanatory analyses. Besides, the preservation of human dignity that they achieved, walking day and night on Kop-tagou, did not emerge from intellectual dilemmas but from the genuine proclivity of their souls.

They did their duty with the simplicity of the humble chamomile that springs up, raises its stature silently and innocently, then blossoms–and is tried by the wind, the sun, the cold, suffering it all patiently until, in the end, it wilts away.

---

23. *«Ti seira m' 'ki digo se.»*

Tantourlouch, covered in snow. The houses are just as the Greeks left them, except for the tin roofs. When Uncle Patzos saw it for the last time, the snow was over two meters deep. The first building on the right is the Church of St. George, now a mosque. Next to it, behind the electric pole, is the school which Patzos, my grandmother Chrysoula, and all the neighborhood children attended.

The roads we traveled. No signs then. Two meters of snow. The knife at our throats.

Baipurt in a recent photograph (from the guidebook of Pontus-Anatolia, L. Braziotes Editions).

Erzerum today.

Kars today.

131

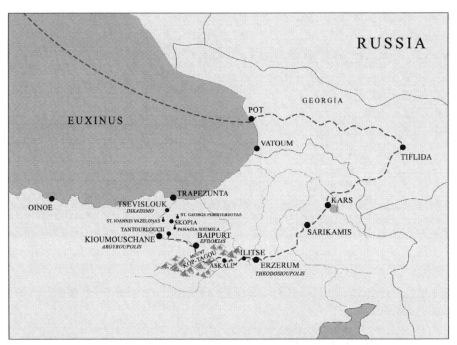

The exodus from Chaldia to Russia ...and from Russia to Greece.

Famine in Ukraine, 1921-23.

Getting water with a *koukoum'* (a copper jug) on the refugee ship. This bare necessity was often a death trap.

The island of St. George. Here, a single slice of bread was worth a gold watch. The buildings shown existed at the time the Pontians arrived there.

A boatload of soldiers heading for the quarantine station on St. George. The tents in the background probably belong to their camp (archive ERT, Poulides collection).

Red Cross nurses overseeing the disinfection of clothes at the St. George quarantine station, 1923 (archive of the Greek Red Cross).

Soldiers posing beside the ovens used for the disinfection of clothes at the St. George quarantine station, 1923 (archive of the Greek Red Cross).

Ship off Makronissos, carrying 4,000 refugees. It is signaling their shortage of food and water, as well as scarlet fever and typhoid (from the book *Certain Samaritans*).

On Makronissos, gazing out to sea. How far away is the Pontus? (from the book *Certain Samaritans*)

Makronissos. Pontian children standing in the bread line (from the book *Certain Samaritans*).

Hopelessness outside a refugee tent (from the book *Refugee Greece*).

Hope looks out from this refugee tent (from the book *Refugee Greece*).

Scene from the daily lives of the refugees (Greek Literature and History Archive, ELIA).

Refugee children outside one of the shacks which gradually took the place of the tents at the settlements (archive ERT, Manolis Megalokonomos collection).

Neighbors in a refugee settlement. Shacks have taken the place of the tents (archive ERT, Manolis Megalokonomos collection).

Drapetsona. Uncle Patzos with his son on his lap, his wife, leftmost, and relatives. The refugee house behind them is probably his.

Better days in Melissia.

Good company and a glass of beer.

«THE REST OF US WERE ALL FATHERLESS, DUE TO THE WAR AND BEING REFUGEES»

BARBARA PARASTATIDOU-APOSTOLIDOU
[1900-1944]

«Mi lete me na tragodo. T' emon e tragodia,
dakra kai ponos 'inetai, do 'k' ech' parigoria.»

(Don't ask me to sing. My song becomes
tears and pain and there is no consolation.)

Barbara and my grandmother Chrysoula were first cousins, daughters of two brothers. Her father, having in addition to his landholdings and livestock both a mill and his own well, was numbered among the wealthier householders of Tantourlouch. His wife was the village midwife, and this professional standing gave even greater worth to their already respected family name.

Barbara had two brothers and one sister, who gradually grew up and started their own households, bringing grandchildren into the world for their parents to enjoy. Thus, in 1913, when a typhoid epidemic struck the village and took the life of their mother, they were all more or less settled except for the youngest, Barbara. The village was left without a midwife, and she without a mother. Most likely it was due to the same cause that her sister was left a widow with four small children.

Not long after, Barbara married a young man from Yetourmaz, a village which was about a four-hour mountain hike from Tantourlouch. Yetourmaz belonged to the prefecture of Lerin[1], and in the early twentieth century it was inhabited by approximately forty ethnic Greek families. No Muslim families lived there.

Her brothers had first met the groom-to-be in Russia, where they had emigrated for better employment opportunities. He seemed to be a good lad, they liked him, and the marriage was arranged. That was it. Barbara had no say in the matter.

In the Pontus, as soon as a wedding was over the bride would go to her husband's home, where she would live in total submission. And so

---

1. A mountain prefecture consisting of 14 villages, the most important of which was also called Lerin.

Barbara went to Yetourmaz and stayed with her mother-in-law. Although Tantourlouch was the nearest Christian village, it was still quite far. The Pontian mountains were difficult to traverse and did not allow for frequent visiting. She would have to resign herself to the fact that she would rarely see her home again, would seldom chat with her girlfriends, nor would she ever see a certain young man who had once made her heart skip a beat. Not long after the wedding her husband returned to work in Russia together with his brothers, leaving his pregnant wife in the care of his mother. Her time came and their son Nikos was born.

That was how things went along, until calamity struck. On January 6, 1918, Yetourmaz, like Tantourlouch and all the other Greek villages of the region, was looted and set on fire. The decision of the new political regime in Russia to withdraw the troops that had been in the eastern Pontus for the last two years provided the opportunity the tsetes were waiting for. They could indulge themselves in every kind of lawlessness, without fear or restraint. Full of hatred, they attacked the villages, doing their part to bring about the Catastrophe. Everything was covered in snow. This pure white scene was blackened by the smoke and reddened by the flames that climbed from the burning houses and storage sheds. The sheer tranquility, the early morning stillness, was shattered by shrieks, lamentations, the bleating of animals and the sound of shots. Tsetes and Turks from the nearby villages charged in, determined to wipe out the indigenous folk. The little Byzantine towns which had been dwelt in by Christian populations for long centuries were now filling up with blood-thirsty usurpers. Where had such hostility lay hidden? What happened to the joint festivals and celebrations? And where had all these maniacal strangers come from? The village would have to be evacuated immediately. They would leave behind everything and get out. They would follow the Russians, who were going back to their homeland.

Had the Christians, perhaps, collaborated with the Russian occupiers, so that the Turks had right on their side? Were they justified in their resentment? No. They had not the least right nor the least justification. In every case the ethnic Greeks had protected them from the Armenians who served in the Russian army, those whose people had been slaughtered a year before the Russian Occupation. Naturally, they had breathed more freely under occupation by a people who shared their Christian faith, but never at the expense of their Muslim neighbors. While it is true that many Greek men traveled to Russia to evade conscription in the army, and far more men went abroad for employment, they would never, for their sake, mistreat people who had actually been in their homes and had eaten at the same table. Could the facts really be quite simple? Could it be that, apart from the propaganda which incited the Turks to action, the achievements of the Greeks, the wealth and possessions they had accumulated through their diligence and by working abroad, were actually the target of a deceitful, treacherous design which had lay hidden in their bosoms until the right moment presented itself?

What would be the result of this evil? No one knew. All that was certain was that they had to get out of there.

When the hordes appeared on the scene, the residents of the village were unarmed, and were, for the most part, terrified women, children and the elderly. From one moment to the next, they found themselves completely at the mercy of ruthless armed gangs. Barbara's mother-in-law was killed instantly, the moment she stepped out into the yard to see what was going on. No one could stay beside her lifeless body. The passage of time worked against them, as each second's delay brought the possibility of another calamity. Her sister-in-law, mother of two small children, was shot in the leg. Her husband was also away. The horrified screams of the children were heartrending. The moment had come for Barbara to make an enormous decision. She grabbed up the three children, the one her own and the other two belonging to her sister-in-law, who followed, dragging her heavily bleeding leg. They reached the road, which was covered in snow so deep that it was higher than their heads. There they met the rest of the villagers, threw a quick glance back as if to say goodbye to their home, and set off.

In a quarter of an hour the entire village had emptied. Not a single Greek was left, except for a few bodies, first and foremost being that of the bravest lad of the village and one of the very few young men who happened to be there and tried to resist. Poor Yetourmaz! Your homes and the church burnt down and your children driven out! Suddenly they were all trudging through the frozen landscape, the freezing air giving them the appearance of marble statues. The older ones did their best to keep up their courage. But what courage could the frightened children muster? The strongest refugees, with their lips tightened and their glance eastward, opened a path through the snow and the rest followed. Where were they headed? For nearby villages? For Kars, where they had many relatives and acquaintances? Would they have to reach Russia, and their fathers, in order to feel secure? Would the tsetes ever stop chasing them? They knew nothing. Nothing was certain.

This tragic flow of people from Yetourmaz was later joined by the residents of two neighboring Greek villages, Lerin and Popadanton[2], so that all together there were over 2,000 people. The altitude was about 2,300 meters. In the dead of winter, this miserable flock secured their lives step by step.

And at night? Those who had the strength pressed on. The feeble trudged along with great difficulty. Those who were completely exhausted turned off to the side of the procession and stayed there, with the snow for their grave. And as if that were not enough, on top of their physical torment was added the plague of the Kurds. Gangs of them lay in wait and demanded ransom to allow them to continue their march. Quite a few years would pass before they would find themselves, in our own times, in the same tragic situation, that is, being exterminated by the Turkish regime. In those days they collaborated with the ones who were slaughtering us.

We Greeks have often suffered at the hands of hostile invaders. But the atrocities which transpired in the Pontus at that time were utterly unprecedented, and have never since been repeated. It was the first time our race was starring in a film of such horrifying dimensions, and the director orchestrating this epic was none other than supreme evil.

When they reached the main thoroughfare connecting Argyroupoli with Erzerum, they had also reached the breaking point. In front of them

---

2. A village in the prefecture of Lerin where 30 ethnic Greek families lived at the beginning of the 20th century.

147

marched the Russian soldiers, while they dragged along behind. That was when the miracle took place. Near the village of Teke a Russian officer, in charge of the transport of munitions, took the initiative and ordered that a great deal of the ammunition be unloaded from the two-wheeled horse-drawn army carts so that the suffering refugees could climb up. He discarded war supplies in order to save the perishing human souls. Just as once the holy rod divided the waters for the passage of the Hebrews, in the same way this decision saved hundreds of lives. Whether this saving resolution, a veritable paradigm of adroit crisis intervention, was officially deemed within the call of duty no one knows. It is certain, however, that it was forever engraved on the hearts of the downtrodden refugees. Thanks to this man, half-frozen infants, weakened mothers, exhausted old people, pregnant women, the ill and the infirm were able to continue their exodus. Among them were Barbara, her sister-in-law, and their children. Only moments before they would have started counting casualties due to so many hours spent in the desperately bitter cold, they were crowded onto those carts of salvation.

Eventually they reached Baipurt, then crossed the man-killer mountain Kop-tagou, and finally ended up in Sarikamis, where they separated from the Russians. Up to this point, their trek had taken place during the same days and hours as that of the villagers from Tantourlouch, and under the same conditions. They continued to travel in an easterly direction, while all around them raged the conflict between the Turks and the Armenians, the latter fighting for their independence. On their march they drank tea and ate dry biscuit, as well as *katsamach*, a stiff mixture of corn meal boiled in salt water, which the Russians had in storage for army use. Barbara and her sister-in-law went to stay with a relative in Yialaoutsam. There, the refugees counted their losses: women who had lost their minds, infants that had frozen to death, old ones who had been buried in the snow, ill ones who had died helplessly. Is there any possible justification for crimes of such a kind or such magnitude? Will Turkey ever be able to present itself as innocent before humanity, no matter how it falsifies the facts?

In March the roads became passable and they headed for the village of Karakilsia. They did not stay there more than two days. The Turks and the Armenians were battling incessantly, so they moved on to Kars. They stayed at the railroad station there for one week, and finally took the train for Tiflida. Again they stayed at the local railroad station for days, until they were able to take a train to the seaside town of Pytsiar.

A ship from Pot took them to Crimea and they made their way to the village of Ortala, where Barbara's husband and his brother had a coffee shop. The women told them of their mother's death and how it had happened, the destruction of Yetourmaz and how they had had to abandon it, and all that they had suffered up until their reunion. There was not a corner–not a barracks, a port, or a train station–where they had not collapsed in near exhaustion along the way.

Nor were they able to rest in Ortala. Though they were now with their husbands, who could protect them, the clashes between the Red and White armies forced them to hide for days at a time in the forests. True, they were not killed, but who can endure for long the frequent knocks at the door, the interminable shooting, and the regularly being questioned, «Whose side are you on?» So they moved to Karasoupazar, where Barbara's husband found a job as a waiter in a café. There their two daughters were born. The family was growing.

That was until the famine of 1921, which devoured millions of victims in Russia. Conditions were barely liveable. The rations of forty grams of bread per person, and that not even daily, were not enough to fill them. Thus, in the winter of 1921 they departed from Theodosia in an Italian freighter which had brought rice and olives to Crimea, and docked in Batumi. They endured months of deprivation and squalid conditions in this floating prison, waiting to set sail for Greece. Meanwhile, the docks at the harbor were filling up with more Pontians from the villages of Kars, among them some of my other relatives. All of them were fleeing to Greece.

When at last they set off, in every corner of the ship, from the hold to the uppermost deck, there were crammed approximately 3,000 souls.

On Easter Day of 1921, they dropped anchor off of St. George, the small island near Salamina which was being used as a quarantine station. Still fresh were the memories of friends and relatives who had died on the way and had been thrown into the sea with a weight around their neck;

yet the sight of dry land once again revived their hopes for a better life. Sadly, such hopes were in vain. Barbara's husband died of typhoid just as they arrived and thus never set foot on Greek soil. Not a week passed before the two little girls followed their father. Many were the Pontians who came to know the motherland only by sight. They gazed briefly on their dream and then expired. That tragic Easter of 1921, together with the paschal lamb of God many of His children were also sacrificed.

For four months they were compelled to stay on the ship, from whose mast flew the yellow flag signaling death, in order to confine the epidemics of typhoid and cholera that were plaguing them. Some of the passengers were transferred to the island of Makronissos. There her brother-in-law's family was wiped out, both parents and two children. Her sister-in-law, with whom they had been through so much together, did not make it this time; none of their family survived. The same ironic fate was shared by the family of her first cousin Sophia, my grandmother Chrysoula's sister. Like so many other Pontian Greeks, they escaped the genocide, only to die in sight of their haven. Every morning, from the deck of the ship, Barbara and her son would watch them load small boats with the dead and the half-dead of the previous day and bury them in lime pits on the island. Many of those who were gravely ill did their utmost to feign health, in order to avoid being tossed into these marine hearses and being buried before their time.

Suffering from typhoid herself, Barbara was moved into isolation quarters on the island of St. George, leaving five-year-old Nikos to fend alone on the ship of the grim reaper. The little boy survived, thanks to the mercy of the sailors and the tender care of a kind woman who looked after him along with her own children, though she did not know his parents. Nikos and this woman's son, a boy of the same age, would carry water to the ill, who were begging for it, helplessly lying on the deck and calling out «Water! Water!»

In exchange for this assistance the sailors gave him food and he did not die of starvation. With what fear did he lay down his little body every night, having lost his father and two sisters in only one week, and with his mother near death, too? What thoughts tormented his child's mind before he fell asleep? Was there room, after all, in the midst of the horror which he was experiencing, for a ray of hope? Did he yearn to someday be able to combat the injustice which surrounded him?

The path he later took in life proved that he would willingly give his life in order for what he regarded as justice to prevail. He lived and died absolutely faithful to his vision, unbendingly dedicated to the struggle to attain it. Of course, an idealism of such magnitude necessarily entails a harsh daily reality for the rest of the family, who lived like collateral victims. Truly, his entire family, but especially the children, were deprived of his fatherly care and protection and were dragged through fierce trials on account of his political actions.

He met his childhood deck-mate again many years later when they were both actively involved in the Drama Uprising, the first mass confrontation with the Axis Powers in Greece. They no longer needed to distribute water to the dying, but they were the same boys, and this time they were willing to sacrifice their own lives. On September 28, 1941, this young man was killed while trying to take over the police station of Nikiforos, which was full of Bulgarians. He was the first casualty of the anti-Occupation resistance.

After a few weeks' stay in the hospital on Saint George, Barbara's health improved. She took her son away from the quarantined ship and headed for Drapetsona, to be near one of her brothers. Her health, however, was still far from good.

When she had to be hospitalized again due to a relapse, little Nikos was forced to work. But what kind of work was there for such a tiny little refugee? Precisely what everyone else refused to do. So he sold water in the brothels around the Piraeus railroad station, saving each penny to have enough money to buy the oranges that would nourish and strengthen his mother.

When all danger to her health had finally passed they moved to a village in the prefecture of Drama, near Barbara's other brother, now father of five girls. There they spent a few peaceful years, albeit in great poverty.

In 1929 Barbara married Giorgos Apostolides, called «Gior's», a man who also hailed from the village of Tantourlouch. He belonged to the

Trechtant' clan, being the son of Yannis «Trechtes» Apostolides, and was an uncle of mine on the other side of the family. He, too, had been widowed. His wife and little daughter died of typhoid in quarantine on the island of Hydra and he had no other family left. Thus, having both gone through similar trials, they decided to start anew: to build a nest for a better tomorrow on the ruins of yesterday. Giorgos adopted Nikos and loved him as his own son.

There had always been something deeper between the couple, ever since Barbara was still living unmarried in Tantourlouch–a love which remained unfulfilled, perhaps because her brothers judged otherwise. They had not married then. Yet the truth was, as she herself later confided, that even on the very day of her *nyfeparma*[3], had Giorgos asked it of her she would have climbed off the white horse leading her to her new life and followed him. In the end, the reversals that had offered them such bitter gall brought those deeply buried and forgotten dreams back to their sorrowful present, with seemingly better prospects this time.

As for Barbara's son, his stepfather became so dear to him that he added the surname Apostolides onto that of his real father. In fact, as time passed, their relationship developed into a special kind of friendship, seeing as it was Gior's who instilled the ideals of social contribution and struggle in that soul. Nikos, for his part, always thirsting for justice as he was, lived his life according to his stepfather's counsel, as if to prove that his love was not in vain, that he was worthy of being his son. He always followed his guidance, defying even the danger of death. Although it is typical in life to look back on the past as rosier than the present, Barbara, for one, must certainly have felt that after all her misfortunes, the future at last held brighter hopes.

The new little family lived in a refugee village called Psilokastro. There Gior's grew tobacco. Their daily staple was *malez*, a flour and

---

3. The ritual of receiving the bride. The groom approaches her house accompanied by friends and relatives, while musicians play and the members of the wedding procession dance or walk to a slow rhythm. Once the bride takes leave of her family and other loved ones, the procession goes on to the church, with the bride normally riding in a buggy.

water concoction that everyone else in the village lived on as well. All the children, most of them orphans, lived a deprived life and had to satisfy their hunger with bread and onions. Nikos was later to write in his memoirs: «We didn't mind, because we were all poor, and from my entire class Melina and Olga Michaelides and George Ampelides were the only kids who had a father. The rest of us were all fatherless, due to the war and our being refugees.»

Barbara's son was very quick at his studies, but he was unable to continue school past the eighth grade. Due to the world financial crisis, the tobacco remained unsold and everyone had to work, simply to get by. A highly conscientious schoolteacher, by the name of Spyros Orologas, a Pontian refugee himself, undertook to help the bright but poor child, and taught him the curriculum for the next two years of school without accepting a penny for tuition. That exceptional man became the bastion of the Pontian refugee community around Drama during those years, devoting himself to his mission with fatherly love and care. He not only taught, but organized food kitchens for the children and implemented a tree-planting program. He advised young and old alike, stood as a model worthy of emulation, and was thoroughly respected by one and all.

Because he spoke Pontian he was able to communicate with the refugees, a thing that non-Pontian teachers who were sometimes appointed to the region found nearly impossible. Was it this ability to communicate, though, that was the main factor in his contribution to the area? Far from it. Rather, it was his great soul.

Who bore the homeland on their shoulders? Who sustained the community during those difficult times? The lives of certain people, like that of the teacher in question, leave no doubt that it is, by and large, through the conscientiousness of the dutiful, anonymous little ants that some degree of moral spirit is salvaged in the world, rather than through those who wear the badge of positions of power.

When Nikos gave up all hope of furthering his education, he turned to cultivating tobacco with Gior's and did his army service in the cavalry. Meanwhile, the region's select-quality tobacco began to provide enough profit for the family to live more comfortably. When he returned from the army he married Theopiste, who would prove to be a heroic woman.

153

She was a lady who suffered in every facet of her life in her effort to be a good mother, wife and daughter-in-law.

Barbara soon became the grandmother of two little girls. The clouds of war, however, darkened the Greek skies with the Italian offensive. Nikos enlisted as a volunteer and was sent to the front, leaving behind in the village his pregnant wife, the two children, and his parents. Even though he had an official exemption from active duty, due to a condition in one of his eyes, he went with the rest of the young men from the village to the Albanian mountains. He made the decision according to his conscience. Under no circumstances would he stand by and not fight for his new homeland. A few years later, two disabled men whom the Germans had exempted from the execution of the men of the Pontian village of Messovouno, Kozani, refused this special treatment and were also executed. They preferred to share the fate of the other men. On that same day another man in Messovouno, who could have saved himself dressed as a woman, upon seeing his fellow townsmen gathered for execution, threw off his feminine attire and was killed with them. It was the same with Nikos. His obligation to respond to the call of patriotism took precedence over all else. He did not seek exemption. In that general climate of enthusiasm, he left the safety of his home and headed for the front.

Regarding Pontian participation at the Albanian front, Lieutenant-Colonel F. Vakalis of the 65th Army Regiment reported: «During the terrible battle of Morava, the Pontian fighters battled aggressively and heroically, seizing 100 captives and 10 cannons, and on November 23 they were the first to enter Korytsa.»[4] Also exalted in this account are their discipline and endurance in the face of adversity. Further, their

---

4. The battle of Morava-Ivan was the first major Greek offensive in the Greco-Italian War of 1940-1941. It took place on the eastern flank of the Greek-Italian front, where the Italian forces had remained on the defensive during the initial Italian invasion toward Epirus. It was a major success for the Greek forces, not only in operational terms, but also as a morale boost, as the breaching of the Morava-Ivan line led to the fall of the city of Korçë (Korytsa) into Greek hands and made news internationally.

self-abnegation, their dignity and their moral fortitude are emphasized. Finally, it is observed that, despite finding themselves on the battle front, they danced to the tune of the Pontian lyre whenever possible. That ever-present companion of the Pontians was heard in the Albanian mountains just as it was heard among those who were exiled in Erzerum and Tokati. Our long-suffering race has always drawn strength and hope from this Orphean device, even though the enemy might lie close by, even though they themselves would very likely not live to see the morrow. It would be no exaggeration to make one more allusion to Thermopylae, where the timeless intrepidity of the Greeks was expressed in their conspicu-ously undaunted stance, over two millennia before the battle of Morava took place: there, three hundred Spartans combed their hair and adorned themselves unperturbed, though they were fully aware of the imminent attack by tens of thousands of Persians.

With the German invasion of Greece, the Pontians behind the lines would demonstrate yet another form of patriotic solidarity, when Greek soldiers returning from the Albanian front, exhausted and famished, would find refuge in their villages. Dimitris Loukatos wrote in his memoirs concern-ing the behavior of the Pontian residents of western Macedonia towards Greek soldiers who were returning from Albania:

«Now these are people. Pontians, the real thing... Here comes a woman down the hill, holding a basket. She comes and stands before us, offering us greens, cheese and a bottle of wine. "Eat up for the road, my lads. Don't worry. God will see the injustice. We'll be free again." I ask her where she is from. "From Samsunta," she tells me. I understand. She must be from one of those remote villages with the kind of people who embody Hellenism one hundred per cent, as well as the biblical sense of hospitality. "What's the name of your village?" I ask. "Agrapidies" is the answer... A little child standing nearby says to me: "Why don't you come up to the village to stay? You'll eat well and sleep." They serve me plenty of hot milk, fresh butter and bread. We start talking. His name is Lazarus Ioakeimides, and his wife is Kyriakitsa... They're Pontians and they used to live in Russia. I realize I have happened upon a home of Abraham-like hospitality. Their children are clean and well-behaved.

One can see clearly that these refugees have brought true civilization to Greece. Here, in this shepherds' village, you see little girls neatly combed, polite, and eager to learn.»

Barbara and her son met again at the end of the Greco-Italian conflict in Albania. The family was reunited, but under conditions of double occupation, since Drama was subjugated by both Germany and Bulgaria. While Nikos was away Theopiste had given birth to a boy, on St. George's Day, in fact, so it was christened Giorgos. Of course, that was also Barbara's second husband's name. At two months old, the baby was left paralyzed by meningitis. His troubled little life began in the absence of his soldier father, and would end that way as well, fourteen years later.

As far as Nikos was concerned, resistance to the Bulgarians was a matter of course. He was mobilized in Christos Kalaitzes' team. They armed themselves with guns which had been hidden in Psilokastro and the entire surrounding region. Those guns belonged to soldiers returning from the Albanian front, who would leave them there so they would not fall into the hands of the invaders. The local inhabitants would find them and hide them in case they were ever needed again.

The day of September 28, 1941 arrived. The events that took place, known as the Drama Uprising and in which Nikos took an active part, included sabotage to the train tracks and the bridge of Fotolivos, an attack on the Bulgarian gendarmerie and on barracks in the city of Drama, and the blowing up of the electric power station. At the same time, they executed village leaders who had been appointed by the Bulgarians. The response of the occupying powers was to massacre hundreds of Greek civilians in Drama and in dozens of villages in eastern Macedonia and Thrace. Among those was, once again, the martyr-village of Doxato. In Ismailova, where the unarmed civilians of Psilokastro and other towns had gathered because they feared reprisals, Nikos was almost killed during a confrontation between the Bulgarian army and about four hundred rebel soldiers. They fought all day, the enemy planes flying low and bombarding indiscriminately. They escaped at night and, with the amnesty offered by the Bulgarians, Nikos returned home. The entire region had victims to mourn, but one fact emerged clearly–the Bulgarization[5] which they were attempting was going to be met with stout resistance.

Historical assessments of the Drama uprising may differ. Was this embroilment a forewarning of all that would beset the Greeks some years later? Was it a provocation by the invaders which the resistance fighters failed to assess correctly? Should the possibility of tough reprisals have been given more serious attention? Or was it a spontaneous resistance action? Much can be said. However, as far as the anonymous young fighters like Nikos were concerned, only one assessment was valid, that of a certain comrade of his: «It doesn't interest me whether it was a provocation or not. We were fighting for a cause and we believed in it.»

Is there such a thing as pointless sacrifice? There is. Can one's objective be illusory? It can. Can there be a wrong assessment of circumstances? There can. However, none of these things can hinder those who believe in their cause from following the course they are steering. The resistance fighters' story was written something like that at the time, without any rationalizing to inhibit their actions.

Nikos' activities, well known to the Bulgarians by now, forced him to move to Kilkis. His stepfather had been openly threatened by the Bulgarian-appointed village commissioner. The invaders were pressuring the youth and able-bodied to move away. That did not mean, of course, that their life would be spared if they were arrested while trying to get away. Many a hope was drowned in the Strymonas River during those years. Nikos' escape, initially towards Kavala, was a conspiracy from start to

---

5. Bulgaria did not constitute merely an occupying force, an ally of the Germans, but had its own long-standing agenda, which was to take back land they considered theirs. Thus, upon the invasion of Greece, they officially annexed all occupied territories as part of so-called *Greater Bulgaria* and launched their Bulgarization campaign. This included the deportation of hundreds of Greek officials–mayors, judges, lawyers, schoolteachers, priests and policemen, the strict enforcement of a total ban on the use of the Greek language and conversion of place names into Bulgarian, as well as repressive economic measures and forced labor for the Greeks, in effect compelling them to emigrate from these territories, while granting incentives for Bulgarians to come and settle there.

finish, but it succeeded in the end. He was unknown in Kavala and from there, in a shabby little boat, he and seven others started in pitch darkness towards Thessaloniki. During that dangerous trip, while fighting the November chill and the turbulent sea, they also had to help a pregnant woman deliver, the only female passenger among them. She had lost her husband in the Drama Uprising. The cries of the newborn baby were lost in the roar of the waves, and the new mother received first aid from a handful of bewildered fugitives.

After their debarkation on a deserted coast near Thessaloniki, Nikos moved on towards the Kilkis villages and quickly got in touch with the local resistance fighters. In the meantime, Barbara and the rest of the family made their way to the nearby village of Kato Potamia, where relatives of Theopiste's lived and generously extended their help, in spite of their own poverty. They had arrived exhausted and miserable, with all their savings gone, for after the Muslims' inhumanity in the Pontus, they faced the rapacity of certain Christians. As they were going through the only northbound pass on Mount Beles, Gior's, who had made quite a profit from the sale of his tobacco, was not able to save his sterling pounds from confiscation at the Bulgarian checkpoint, even though he had taken the precaution of cementing them in cans of olive oil.

Conditions at that time were so desperate that they survived by eating roots and whatever was left over in the fields after the wheat harvest. Skirmishes between the Germans and the resistance fighters were a daily occurrence around them. When Greek accomplices to the Germans, members of PAO[6], were burning Kato Potamia, the panic-stricken residents fled towards Pano Potamia for safety, and vice-versa. Once a landmine exploded under the horse cart that was carrying them. Everyone was thrown off, including little paralyzed Giorgos. Another time, right before their eyes, a PAO member killed a mother in the Kilkis town square. She had put her arms around her dead son's head, which was hanging with the heads of other resistance fighters.

---

6. Panhellenic Liberation Organization, established in 1943 by army officers and state officials towards cooperation with the Allies against the occupying forces, and with a view to preserving national cohesion. In essence, they operated against the leftist organizations EAM-ELAS and among their ranks were quite a few German collaborators.

Barbara and Gior's saw Nikos only a few times. He rarely visited them in the shack they lived in.

Before the end of the Occupation Barbara had already gone mad and, never recovering her lost faculties, she died just after the occupying forces withdrew. She was only forty-four years old. Who knows what role her many trials played in burning out her fuses? Her husband had died shortly before and they buried her alongside him. So the song he used to sing to her when he drank a bit came true: *«When I die, nurse, you die along with me, so they can put us in the same grave, because I love you very much.»*

Their daughter-in-law, Theopiste, and her little orphans, took up a collection in the village to be able to buy a coffin for their grandfather's body, which was kept in the Kilkis hospital for days because they could not afford the burial. In order to pay for Barbara's funeral, they sold their goat.

Nikos, Barbara's one and only son, the volunteer at the Albanian front, the resistance fighter, later a soldier in the Democratic Army, the idealist who wanted to change the world, died inconsolable in Sofia. He never lived on Greek soil again after 1949, and was unable to be near his daughters, who grew up without him, or to attend his young son's funeral in 1954. The sorrows, the disillusionment, the anguish and the joys he had experienced were all silenced by the immense nostalgia that all the relatives who ever visited him remember seeing in his tear-filled eyes.

The Bulgarians, who had invaded Greece, who beat, stole and killed during the Occupation, who condemned his family to hunger and abject poverty, were the people he lived with till the end of his life. His daughters, who lived through the German Occupation, left for the German factories in the 1960s. Nikos, who as a small child had been ousted from the Pontos due to the support which the Bolshevik regime gave to the Kemalian government, fought for the realization of the socialist vision in the world. Who can explain such irony? Is purity of heart a sufficient mitigating factor? Do good intentions always exonerate one? I do not know. I am certain, however, that a pure desire to eradicate injustice constituted the foundation of every sacrifice made not only by Nikos, but by many other uncles of mine. It was a time when circumstances compelled the individual to join one side or the other; there was no middle ground.

Those years when Barbara would get lost in the fields of Kato Potamia, her mind dark and confused, those times she would call for her son to come and appease her fears, those times she could only satisfy her grandchildren's hunger with ears of wheat and water, those times had passed. Only a bitter taste was left for all the pain that was never rendered justice, for all those expectations that proved futile.

Perhaps Turkish cruelty is not to blame for all of Barbara's misfortunes. Perhaps, in fact, the uprooting was not her main concern amidst all the trials that were later added in the course of her life. It was, however, the original cause that forced her and her entire family to face nightmarish conditions. With the knife at their throat, they fled the security of their land, where life had rolled by without change for centuries, and were handed over, naked and unprotected, to the historic gales of the man-killer twentieth century.

Hundreds of kilometers from the Macedonian villages, the cool waters of the Pyxites River flow, right below the monastery of Panagia Soumela[7]. *« 'S sin Panaian tin Soumela, tha pao stephanoumai»*[8] was the wish of lovers in the Pontus. Not many kilometers from there, the mist covers the mountain pastures where Gior's and Barbara once exchanged private glances.

The beginning of the tale of a great love was written in Tantourlouch. The prince was Giorgos, son of the renowned Trechtes, Yannis Apostolides. The princess was Barbara, daughter of his affluent fellow townsman, Damianos Sidiropoulos. As the story continued, however, the fairy tales became entangled. No golden slipper was put on the bare foot and the winner turned out to be the bad wolf, along with the witch, life itself, whose apple was poisoned.

---

7. Our Lady of Soumela, founded in the 4th century, has stood as a symbol of Pontian Hellenism and Christian Orthodoxy for 16 centuries.

8. «To Panagia Soumela I will go to be married.»

View of Yetourmaz today.

The Church of the 40 Martyrs in Yetourmaz. Today it is probably a stable or a shed.

The brave Pontian Greek Israel Balabougiouk, the first to be killed fighting the tsetes who attacked Yetourmaz.

Trekking to the sea (from the book *Certain Samaritans*).

162

Nikos and Barbara. The son, with a book under his arm, shows a protective regard for his tired mother.

Gior's Apostolides, Trechtes' son. The bond between him and his stepson was as genuine as that of father and son.

Tobacco workers in a Greek village.

Spyros Orologas, an exceptional teacher, handing out parcels from the
Greek Red Cross to his pupils, 1948. A genuine altruist.

Nikos, while he was serving in the cavalry.

Greek soldiers at the Albanian front (archive of the Center for Asia Minor Studies, Petros Poulides collection).

On the march at the Albanian front (archive of the War Museum).

A building at Liberty Square in Drama which bears a sign written in Bulgarian (postcard during the Bulgarian Occupation).

Bulgarian retaliation for the Drama Uprising.

Nikos, when he arrived in Bulgaria. He never returned.

Theopiste fought her own battle in Kato Potamia, Kilkis, raising her three children entirely alone.

«GIRLS OF THE HOMELAND»

HARIKLEIA KYRIAKIDOU
[1903-1977]

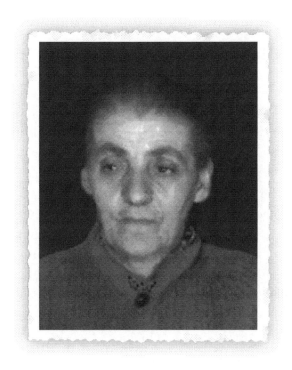

« 'S sin ksenitian p' achpasketai naili kai vai to chal'n at'.
To savano as etoimaz' afka 's so maksilar'n at.»

(Woe to him who is plucked from his home to live
in foreign lands and woe to his plight. Let him prepare
his shroud and keep it under his pillow.)

Harikleia was my grandmother Chrysoula's first cousin on her mother's side. She was born in Tantourlouch, but became an orphan at a very young age, when her mother died in childbirth and left her, her brother and the newborn baby without a mother's tender care. Their father was soon remarried, to a girl quite a bit younger than he was, the oldest of eight sisters. The only condition for the seemingly incompatible marriage was that the groom would, if necessary, escort the bride's family to Greece. According to my grandmother, who was then a small girl, their village wedding celebration lasted for days. Her and Harikleia's Grandfather Trechtes was so pleased that, in his joy, they slaughtered a whole ox and invited the entire village to the feast. To the young couple, life looked as if it would continue smoothly, without further setbacks. Of course, in those days newlyweds could not predict what life held in store for them. They could not imagine that they would soon be driven out of their homeland with the knife at their throat, or that they would go through two quarantines. Nor could they foresee that in a little village of northern Greece, where they would eventually settle, the climate would be so unhealthy that four of their five children would die of malaria, while the fifth would leave for the Beles mountains as a rebel and end up as a political refugee in Poland for 39 years.

At fourteen years old, Aunt Harikleia married Anestes Kyriakides, a fellow villager who was practically a teenager himself. He fell in love with her and she married him. In those days in the Pontus it was normal to marry young, though an additional reason for Aunt Harikleia must have been the new family structure resulting from her father's remarriage.

On that dreadful Sunday of January 6, 1918, when they set off on the road to exile, she believed, like everyone, that they would return. She regarded it as a temporary relocation, a search for interim shelter and safety and not a permanent uprooting, though the frenzy of the flames to which the tsetes had reduced their homes foreshadowed otherwise. Tantourlouch, that remotest Greek village of the Pontus, that unspoiled fastness of our national heritage in the region, was overrun by plunderers. That land through which once echoed the cries of joy and salvation from Xenophon's Myriad would soon be completely blanketed in silence and desolation. In that little Byzantine village the ancient names of Homer, Abraham, Samuel, Deianeira, Isaac and Klemes would no longer be heard. The foothills of Mount Theches would be left bare of the descendants of its ancient inhabitants.

The natural surroundings of that region were the worst possible, with deep snows and arctic cold. In any other situation, they would not even have set foot outside their homes. The freezing cold that seized their bodies became one with the chill that had stolen over their souls. Their dread mounted minute by minute, the many terrors blending–the wild gorges, the sudden, treacherous drop-offs and the ruthless bandits who lay in wait for them. For their psychological devastation was accompanied by material depredation as well. It was common knowledge that the Pontian Greeks had wealth stored up from their work abroad in Russia and, consequently, there was plenty of loot to be grabbed. Regardless of the thieves' patriotic pretext of saving their country from the dangerous infidels, the Greeks' wealth was their primary target. All those who had whetted their appetite on the possessions of the Armenians a few years earlier now greedily anticipated a similar feast. Their degradation was cloaked under the façade of patriotism and faith. To what depths they had fallen! The human beings who were struggling to survive suddenly turned into dangerous enemies who must be wiped out. All at once, the feeble old people and the tragic Pontian mothers with their infants were seen as bloodthirsty foes.
The moment the tsetes came in sight, Anestes and a cousin of his climbed a mountain peak to keep watch. This cousin, having served in the Russian army, tried to avert disaster and rushed off to seek help, but in vain. The Russians retreated quickly. No intervention was possible. Only fifteen Greek soldiers, lads from a village in the Kars region, together with the

strongest men from Tantourlouch, forged ahead of the procession of exiles and opened a path through the snow.

Aunt Harikleia had married young, but before she got a proper taste of life she was forced to swallow the bitterness of being a refugee. After exactly one month of trekking through the snow, via Baipurt and Erzerum, they reached Sarikamis one freezing evening. Their suffering had inspired along the way the creation of a few impromptu rhymes, which, with their relatively light-hearted tone, managed to soothe the pain and sorrow of the refugees somewhat. «Eat and drink with us, so you won't be hungry on Mt. Kop-tagou!» was invented just before they were to start their climb on the formidable mountain. Another was «My fingers froze in the fog of Baipurt; I rested them on the top of your head and they warmed up a little!»[1] Though the rhyme is lost in English, the bantering tone remains.

From the region of Argyroupoli 25,000 people had begun the trek. The refugee committee which the exiles had elected decided they should proceed to Kars, for the hostile gangs were perilously close behind and did actually enter Sarikamis on March 18. The Greek villages of the Kars area had seen astonishing prosperity in the last thirty years, due to the substantial profits made by the Pontian men who worked abroad, mainly in czarist Russia, and who thus contributed not only economic wealth but also cultural richness to the region. Located at the easternmost point of Asia Minor, these small communities created a promising foundation for future development, which, however, would soon be violently cut short.

The residents of Kars opened their homes and hearts, welcoming their relatives and friends. Even refugee weddings took place, like that of another of my grandmother's cousins. But they stayed only three months. The

---

1. *«Fa kai pia me temas, 's so Kop-tagou na min peinas.» «Ta dachtyla m' epagosan 's sin Paipourti tin deisan, eval' na ta 's son korfon sou kai ligon echouleithan.»* (Noteworthy here is the fact that the Pontian word *deisan*, which means moisture, fog, forms a part of the word *paradeisos*, i.e. paradise, a place of moisture and, therefore, lush vegetation.)

relative peace which they had experienced came to an abrupt end, the moment the Turks reached Kars with their savage intentions. They faced yet another upheaval, this time heading towards Crimea. Travelling with the extended Kyriakides family, Anestes and Harikleia started out on their next exile with a group of approximately 7,000 people. They reached Pot in open train cars, without a roof over their heads. There they boarded the ships which would carry them to their final destination. At least, they hoped it would be their last stop.

Not that conditions in the land they reached were favorable, of course. Their ship was greeted by cannon fire from the German and Austrian forces who occupied Crimea at the time, and they were driven off towards Marioupoli[2]. Would the Sea of Azov be more hospitable? They hoped so. Their ocean liner stopped six miles off shore, on account of the very shallow water. There they waited, though no one knew exactly what for. They were simply waiting. A steamship full of Germans and czarists approached and, removing the covers from their cannons, they announced that the refugees were now their prisoners. After five hours of suspense, they were taken ashore in barges. They were detained for twenty days in specially converted army barracks before they were permitted to settle in the approximately twenty-five Greek villages of the area. They stayed there until the end of 1918, cultivating the land and literally vegetating. Still, they slowly began to adjust.

Civil war raged on, however, and the revolutionaries were drawing closer. The fear of being taken hostage compelled the Pontians to take flight once more. Unlike other relatives of mine, who came directly to Greece at that time, my aunt and her family decided on another Russian destination. They arrived in Karasoupazar, where relatives embraced them yet again. Anestes, only 17 years old, worked at a relative's shop, where he sold wine and ouzo. The world around them was endeavoring to catch its breath from the repeated clashes and the alternating occupations. The region was

---

2. A port city of Ukraine, on the northern coast of the Azov Sea. In the city and the many Greek villages of the surrounding countryside lived nearly 150,000 Greeks.

first occupied for three months by the Bolsheviks, but they were soon defeated by the greater forces of the White Army under General Wrangel. The next time, the revolutionary army proved mightier. Anestes, excited by high ideals, enlisted and fought as a volunteer for over two years with the revolutionary Red Army, which had been formed in 1919. He believed passionately in the promise of a more just society and fought zealously for victory. His contribution was accordingly honored, and he was offered a permanent position in the army, which was a great temptation for him. With difficulty he abandoned his dreams and declined the offer. His father had decided they should move to Kuban[3] and Anestes yielded to him. Pontian families functioned according to a strict patriarchal system. He was extremely disappointed, though, for he believed that the earthly paradise would evolve there, in the land they were leaving. No one could have imagined then that he would be haunted for the rest of his life by this forced desertion, and by that incurable longing for an ideal society, which he thought would be built in his absence. Would they live more peacefully in Kuban? So they hoped.

Anestes worked with his father at the bakeries that his cousin had established. It was a big business, the result of many years of hard work, with a staff of forty workers. These bakeries supplied bread to the czarist army, which was in furious battle against the Bolshevik army, and this meant working night and day to meet its needs, as well as the needs of the unarmed civilians, who were sorely tried. Still, the unusual peace that the Kyriakides family were fortunate to enjoy, in a world that was experiencing the throes of change, was itself unstable. Their security was in limbo. Their familiar world had already been upset once by the Turkish genocidal frenzy. Every day new events dramatically increased the sum of the calamities they faced as refugees. Alongside the Kuban River yet other rivers flowed, formed by the blood of the slaughtered. The Greeks made every effort to survive in the midst of the general destruction, which

---

3. Kuban is a geographical region of southern Russia surrounding the Kuban River, on the Black Sea between the Don Steppe, the Volga Delta and the Caucasus.

was to bring about enormous changes to the political face of the region for decades to come. The rival forces, with foreign support, were each trying to unravel a tangle of differences, while the purely innocent ethnic Greeks struggled to endure as they floundered amongst them. The Greek army was a mere shadow amongst all the other forces in Crimea[4].

It was during this period of turmoil that Aunt Harikleia's firstborn son died. He was three years old.

When the Bolsheviks finally prevailed in that region as well, the bakeries were conscripted. The redistribution of wealth and holdings which had been decreed meant that a person's acquisitions could be considered evidence of counterrevolutionary activity and might constitute a reason for persecution. The Kyriakides lost their business and their property, and were in danger of being executed as exploiters of the people. They were saved only when the starving residents of the area testified in their favor; that is, that they had survived only thanks to the Greek bakery owners, who had handed out free flour for months on end.

In May 1922 the extended family left for Greece by way of Batumi. They had spent two years as supervisors in the bakeries which they had once owned, and did not wish to stay any longer. They passed through the Strait of Dardanelles in the Italian ship *Nikolaos*, while their belongings, most of which ended up lost, were on another ship sailing for the same destination, the *Konstantinos*. During the passage of the strait they were protected by a submarine, as Turkish warships were following them with suspicious intentions. They fervently hoped that life would be better in the motherland they were making for.

They reached Piraeus but were not allowed to disembark. For months they were in sight of the motherland, yet were unable to set foot on it. The grim reaper took thousands of lives. Out of the total 11,000 people on the two ships, only 1,500 survived on the *Nikolaos*, and approximately

---

4. In January 1919, by order of Prime Minister Eleftherios Venızelos, two Greek army divisions were sent to Crimea to assist the Entente powers and the Russian General Denikin's anti-Bolshevik army. After approximately three months, the campaign came to a fruitless end and the local Greek population faced persecution.

175

the same number on the *Konstantinos*. In other words, about 8,000 lives were lost onboard these two ships! The main cause of death was the contaminated water. That was how their arrival in Piraeus was marked.

At long last, the order came for their transfer to Makronissos. Upon their arrival there, along with passengers from the ship *Kios*, the number of refugees on the island reached 11,000. The *Kios* was the same ship that on February 7, 1923, would bring the much-tormented monks of St. George Peristereotas to Kavala. The director of the island hospital was an American doctor named Olga Stastny. When friends urged her to leave because her health was in danger, she declared: «I have no other duty which would take precedence over my duties here.» She eventually stayed on Makronissos for over five months. Although her assistant, Dr. Pompouras, died of typhoid fever, she herself came out alive and returned to her home in Nebraska.

On Makronissos there was not an inch of room to spare. The entire island was immersed in misfortune: people jammed together, one on top of another, diseases, deaths. 6,000 refugees had to be transferred elsewhere.

Somehow it was decided that the Turkish prisoners of war should be the ones to enforce order, which they did with excessive zeal by fiercely beating any refugees who did not stay exclusively in their assigned quarters, which had been designated on the basis of their place of origin. A peculiar way of keeping order, and that on Greek land.

Added to this outrageous behavior was the disgrace of theft. The few belongings that the immigrants had managed to save with such great effort and the foodstuffs which the Athens government sent to them were pinched by the Greek commissaries, under the very nose of the island's chief administrator, who not only tolerated it but collaborated with them. These items were then sold on the Attica mainland, across from the island.

Conditions were appalling. They stayed in tents, seven people in each one, and they were allotted just a little over half a liter of water per person per day. Seldom have so few drops of water hidden so much death. The water tanks were mice-infested; hence, cholera and typhoid continued their macabre mission. There were nearly 50 deaths a day, and the dead were thrown into shallow pits of water and lime. Sadly, some of those who were not quite dead yet were also thrown there. Their scattered bones were later found by political exiles, who made the name of this island more familiar to the world. Imagine going through the most grievous hardships in order to reach Greece, only to wind up half-dead in a pit of lime on Makronissos or St. George. Is there any way to characterize such a fate other than as tragedy? Yet another page in the untold Pontian history was added to the silent record.

After a two-month stay, it was decided to send them on to Dedeagach (the former name of the city of Alexandroupoli until 1920) in remote northeastern Greece. They arrived after a seven-day voyage on an exclusive diet of plain beans. The situation there, however, was chaotic, as the Greek army had just returned from Asia Minor, and entrance to the harbor was forbidden. Carts, troops, ammunition and wounded soldiers had created a virtual madhouse of disorganization. Defeated Greece was picking up the pieces from the draining conflict in Asia Minor. Unfulfilled dreams, failed endeavors, mistakes and losses merged into a jumble of bitterness in Dedeagach.

The port authority commanded them not to disembark, but to return to Piraeus. That was the last straw. The refugees decided to take matters into their own hands. They captured the Russian captain and his crew and sent a message of desperation to the shore: «Either sink us or let us off this ship.»

My aunt's father-in-law, the patriarch of the Kyriakides family, was the prime mover in this dynamic effort, in the discussions, the proposals, and the search for alternative options. Eventually it was decided that they would be given provisions in order to make the return to Piraeus. A corner to receive them had not yet been found. So they were sent 5,000 loaves of coarse army bread and stew made with goat's meat. The return trip began, but whoever ate the meat fell ill, and quite a few, mainly the young, succumbed. The first night there were thirty deaths. Having drunk the water of death on the ship *Nikolaos* and on the island of Makronissos, the hour came to eat the food of death as well. The dead were thrown into the furnace along with the coals, as the port authority had commanded that they neither be buried on land nor thrown in the sea. Would this incessant being bandied back and forth end soon? They continued to hope.

When Aunt Harikleia and the other passengers were approaching Piraeus, a new order came which would send them to Parga, a city on the west coast of Greece. It was only natural that there should be an outcry, and there was–shouts, wailing, and despair. Five months had passed, without their knowing even a moment's peace. They had been dragged from one coast to another, yet, with the exception of Makronissos, they had not set foot on Greek land. There were new protests, new proposals and new adjustments. Again Aunt Harkleia's father-in-law was a militant leader, searching for a just solution to the problem.

In the end, permission to disembark was granted only to those who had relatives in Piraeus. 3,500 passengers, those who had no one to support them in Attica, went on to Parga. Very few reached there alive. Aunt Harikleia's family went to Drapetsona in Piraeus.

The destitute shantytown, that ghetto of pride and haven of Pontians, had a place for them. Under tin roofs? Yes! Sharing a room with the goats? Yes! With squalid sanitation facilities? Yes! With a lack of water? Yes! But the Pontian refugees showed kindness and compassion. They gave each other support and comfort. Each and every countryman was «theirs», as if they were members of the same family.

Not fifteen days had gone by when Aunt Harikleia's father-in-law passed away, at the age of 55, from the privation and hardships he had undergone. Those few days were all that rewarded his sanity and prudence throughout their travails–during the exodus from Tantourlouch, in Kuban, in Alexandroupoli and in Piraeus. He was never granted a true homeland. One more Pontian life was wasted. The next day one of his daughters died. She had already become a widow at the age of 21. Two other daughters of his, as well as his daughter-in-law, Aunt Harikleia, were also seriously ill.

That first year they lived in a small one-room adobe house. Anestes worked from sunup to sundown for 12 drachmas a day. They made an attempt to settle in a village, where other relatives lived, but they soon left again. In their weakened physical condition the damp climate was not suitable, although the wages were better: 15 drachmas for a 16-hour day, with room and board, namely, a daily ration of beans and plenty of wine. A charitable doctor who examined them at no charge, a penniless soul whose care they never forgot, urged them to leave as soon as possible when an aunt of theirs died of malaria, at the age of 65. This brave woman had traveled on foot from the Pontus to Russia, begging along the way. Her husband had been exiled and she, with two children and two grandchildren, eventually reached her son, whose wife had also perished in exile. Her sixth child, the son who had walked to Russia with her, died in quarantine on the island of St. George. Her dream back home of having sixteen children, *«na eftaei to psomar»*[5], was never fulfilled.

Aunt Harikleia and Uncle Anestes moved their belongings from the village to the nearest train station in a cart, and from there they traveled by train to Piraeus. Back to Drapetsona again. It was during that period of their life that two more children were born.

Then Anestes found employment as a construction worker for a wage of 80 drachmas a day, so they were able to breathe a little easier. In 1925 he became a member of the Communist Party of Greece. Their secret meetings were held at a dance studio, and Anestes' formal instatement took place there. In 1936 his wife would also join the party. She would be responsible for the circulation of the Communist newspaper *The Radical (Rizospastis)* and the distribution of subsidized foodstuffs to the refugees. During that time her brother was exiled on account of leftist leanings, to a place where their sole food for three months was boiled greens with no oil.

Their health, which was never good, took a turn for the worse. Drapetsona was not the place for them. But there was another matter which worried them, namely, the ever-increasing number of arrests which were being made since the five-day strike at the glass factory in 1929. With the new strike of 1933-34 the situation became unbearable[6]. The danger of being

---

5. A *psomar* was a container for measuring grain, equivalent to 16 modia (1 modi=8.75 liters).
6. During the period of 1933-34, the 120 workers at the glass factory went on strike for months, their main demands being a more just calculation of their wages and the strict observation of an 8-hour work day, which had already been institutionalized in 1929 but was not being properly implemented. There were persecutions, clashes and dismissals.

arrested was the main reason which compelled them to move to Athens, where Anestes' political activities were unknown to anyone. Soon two more babies were born, neither of which lived past the age of two. In 1941, during the German Occupation, they moved again, this time to a village in the prefecture of Kilkis, in northern Greece. A new chapter in their life of hardships was just beginning. Did they believe that they would find an end to their suffering in the countryside? That was their hope, at least.

For Aunt Harikleia, her husband's participation in the National Resistance was the natural evolution of his course in life and she supported his decision as she had always done. The passion to achieve a more just society at all costs consumed him and would not let him rest. He became an officer in ELAS, the Greek People's Liberation Army, while my aunt stayed in the village with their children, who were now three, and two orphans of one of Anestes' sisters, in total five children. Her second son, along with one of the orphans, would herd the villagers' pigs every day and so was able to bring a pittance home. The village people offered them no compassion or assistance whatsoever. They were not eager to suffer the consequences of helping a left-wing family but instead, due to the political turmoil of the times, preferred to keep their distance from trouble and look after their own wants. Besides, while for some people political struggles are a burning passion, for others they are a superfluous and dangerous practice. For this reason, they left the Kyriakides family alone, with both their passion and their afflictions.

The members of PAO (one of many rural security battalions that had been formed–see *Chapter 5*, footnote 6) and every other type of collaborator with the occupying forces, believing themselves to hold a monopoly on patriotism, had become the source of fear and trembling throughout the countryside. The salvation of the country constituted the plausible pretext for every kind of roguery. It was not long before Aunt Harikleia's turn came. They summoned her to the police station for interrogation as to the whereabouts of Anestes.

She refused to reveal his hideout and they beat her so hard that they broke two of her ribs. They shaved her head completely to humiliate her. She began to spit up blood. Outside four of the children were crying, while the fifth, the baby in her arms, sucked the blood from her breasts instead of milk. Some Bulgarian army officers who happened to be at the police station took pity on the family and ordered their release.

Repeatedly, the chests of their belongings were dragged out of the room where they lived and the shabby contents were strewn on the ground. The family was perpetually persecuted. They were cursed, abused, and threatened. One day, while Harikleia was nursing the baby, they cut her nipple with a knife, right before the eyes of her thirteen-year-old son. When they once discovered ammunition hidden away, twelve men of the security battalion lined up to shoot her. She gathered the five children around her and cried out bravely: «Go ahead! Do your job! Here we are. I only beg that you shoot me first, so I will not have to see my children dead.» As before, one of the persecutors spoke up and declared that it was unjust for the woman and her children to pay for the crimes of the father, and they were spared.

Meanwhile promises were made, but few were abided by. After the signing of the Treaty of Varkiza[7] in 1945, Anestes felt thoroughly enraged and irrevocably betrayed. The next year he sought refuge in Boulkes, Yugoslavia, a training camp for communist rebels which was inhabited by approximately 5,000 leftist Greeks. Was it a communist haven? No. In fact, according to Anestes' memoirs, it was Dante's inferno. Anyone suspected of disobedience simply disappeared, and spying on each other was rampant. They went around in groups of five, with those who had secured a place with the authorities keeping an eye on the suspicious ones. Perhaps no one at that time detected a foretaste of the worse misfortunes which were to come and which would manifest themselves in various ways.

The effort to achieve something great blurs the criteria. A person may commit dishonorable acts in the belief that his end, being an honor-

---

7. A pact between the Greek government and the Communist Party of Greece, which specified, among other things, the surrender of arms by all members of EAM-ELAS. It was signed in Varkiza (near Athens) on February 12, 1945, by the Greek Minister of Foreign Affairs and the Secretary of the Communist Party of Greece (KKE) on behalf of EAM-ELAS.

able one, justifies the means. Ultimately, nothing true can be said about humanity if the evil side of our nature is not taken into account, even when it is masked behind some higher purpose.

Their oldest son joined rebel bands in the Paiko mountains. My aunt and the two remaining children could no longer stay in their house, however, because the threats on their life and the violent acts grew worse by the day. So they went to hide with relatives in another village of Kilkis. It would be a breathing spell for them. They started out on foot. On the way, they were stopped by «patriots», who questioned them as before: «Where are you going?» «Where's your father?» The same old questions. They began to beat them. When they had finished, the older boy was nearly unconscious and could not move. My aunt and her six-year-old third son, their souls embittered, continued walking until they reached their destination, where a relative returned with them to carry her wounded son to a safe place. Before they went to hide in another village, Pikrolimne (Bitter Lake), the first son came and met them. They never saw him again after that. In February of 1947 he would be killed in a battle. He was twenty years old.

After their stay in Pikrolimne (Bitter Lake) Aunt Harkleia and the two children went to Mavroneri (Black Water). Even the names of those villages emit despair, as if they were created for the sole purpose of being dwelt in by the hopeless. In this new refuge the older boy was again beaten, and as soon as he recovered he left for the School for Political Commissioners on MountVitsi, which was, in fact, a school for training propagandists. There, after a three-year separation, he met his father, who had come down from Boulkes to join the Democratic Army[8]. That was when Anestes learned of his oldest son's death. His ideological passion leaves no doubt that he wholeheartedly accepted his son's death as a necessary evil in the cause for justice.

Aunt Harikleia went up to the Beles mountains and worked as the head nurse in the infirmary for the rebel army. Because of her self-sacrifice, the wounded soldiers called her «mother». Life brought it about that

---

8. The Democratic Army of Greece (DSE) was the army founded by the Communist Party of Greece during the Greek Civil War, 1946–1949. At its height, it had a force of around 50,000 men and women.

this endearing word, though she would never hear it again from her first son, would be uttered gratefully by his likeminded wounded compatriots. Was this enough for her? Who knows, apart from her own heart? Could she have chosen another path? Clearly, she was on a one-way street.

Her second son brought his younger brother to the mountain on foot, during a torrential rain of several hours. The child wandered from one relative to another before he met his mother again in Gran Korone[9]. After the few days which he spent by her side on Beles, with her consent he was transferred to Yugoslavia. Aunt Harikleia could not have imagined how long it would be before she would hold him in her arms again. The cities of Novisad, Belatsarkva and others, where such children were «accommodated», were more like hell than homes for the underage. There is testimony to the effect that the boys would sneak out at night and gather greens from the fields, eating them raw, in an attempt to satisfy their extreme hunger[10].

After the defeat at Vitsi, Anestes, then a captain in the civil war and known as «the Black Moustache» to his comrades in arms, went to Burreli[11] in Albania. From there, he reached Poland on a Russian ship, by way of Gibraltar and the North Sea. At Piraeus the hold had filled with men from the Democratic Army, who were compelled to stay hidden until they reached the North Sea and eventually Gdansk[12].

For a year Anestes worked as an interpreter at a *kolkhoz*[13] because he spoke Russian. This was until 1951, when he went to Brno, Czechoslova-

---

9. The village of Korona, in Kilkis. It was given the name «Gran Korne» (Big Horn) by the French in WW I.

10. *Long Journey Home. Greek Refugee Children in Yugoslavia 1948-1960*, (in Serbian) Udruženje za društvenu istoriju, Belgrade, 1998.

11. A small town in northern Albania, 91 km from Tirana.

12. A Polish city on the Baltic coast, Poland's principal seaport.

13. The collective farm which replaced family farming in the Soviet Union.

kia[14]. There he met his wife again, after a separation of five years. Aunt Harikleia had crossed the border from Greece to Yugoslavia in 1949, on foot and ill. After a short stay there, she was sent to Bulgaria, and then on to Czechoslovakia. In the meantime her second son was waiting in Kilkis, with an armed band, for the right moment to join battle once more. Though tuberculosis was slowly consuming him, in his not quite twenty-year-old soul the passion for justice and vindication burned still hotter. In the end, along with a group of impaired elderly and other weak companions, he was forced to go to Bulgaria in 1950, where he was treated in a hospital. Upon learning that his mother had been transferred to Brno, he headed for the same place. Their scattered family gathered once more, but without the youngest son. Would this dispersion ever end?

For ten whole years they struggled, until they managed to bring their youngest son to Czechoslovakia. With their bureaucratic evasiveness and deliberate obstacles, which were directly related to the conflict between Tito and Stalin, the authorities delayed his release. After repeated procedures through the United Nations and persistent endeavors, they managed to reunite with their long-lost child. They had left him as a small boy, and now he was a young man. When Aunt Harikleia had crossed into Yugoslavia in 1949 she had not seen him, and had no idea in what part of that country her eight-year-old son might be. A great deal of pain was hidden in the phrase «when the Democratic Army assembled» which was often heard in the accounts of her older son. The little boy had lost his mother, and the mother her son.

During their first years in Brno they had assumed that as soon as things settled down they would return to Greece. The division of the Balkan States, however, was to be more permanent than the leftist refugees had expected.

Especially for the Pontians, the situation was an exact repetition of their previous travails. Just as they had gazed on the Pontus from their

---

14. Brno is the second largest city in the Czech Republic by population and area. Until 1993 it belonged to Czechoslovakia, which had become a sovereign state of Central Europe when it declared its independence from the Austro-Hungarian Empire in 1918. In this town Gregor Mendel, the father of modern genetics, lived, worked and died.

refuge in Russia, expecting to return to their homes before long, now they gazed south and yearned to return to Greece. The thought that they had once again lost their homeland was nightmarish. Would they ever return, as they hoped?

Aunt Harikleia worked in a factory where they sewed military clothing, and from there she was eventually able to draw a retirement pension. Anestes was a painter in a production plant for industrial construction. The boys started families. After the events of the Prague Spring in 1968[15], however, her youngest son went to West Germany, and his wife and child followed shortly thereafter. This was another painful separation for my aunt, who never saw him again. Aunt Harikleia nursed that sorrow for the next eight years, until her death. Only when Anestes died some years later was he able to be present at the departure of one of his parents' from this life, thanks to his brother's connections.

As soon as circumstances permitted, Aunt Harikleia's sons moved back to Greece with their families. The older of the two, in particular, helped me a great deal, as he was always eager to speak with me, although fully aware that we do not share the same convictions on a number of subjects, foremost of which is his obsession with communist ideology. When they slice your mother's breast before your youthful eyes, why should you reconsider your view of things? For the love of what truth should you change your perspective, and adopt a position different from that of your parents'? And, supposing you realized that you ought to, could you actually find it in your heart to do so?

My aunt's exiled brother had the good fortune to return from Poland in 1981. He had lived his entire exile ascetically, without starting a new family. His child, left behind in Greece, had been raised in privation and fear. Sadly, due to his father's political leanings, the boy was unable to get into university although he was very bright.

---

15. Term used for the brief period of time when the government of Czechoslovakia, led by Alexander Dubček, attempted to democratise the nation and lessen the stranglehold Moscow had on the nation's affairs. The Prague Spring ended with a Soviet invasion, the removal of Alexander Dubček as party leader and an end to reform within Czechoslovakia. There were a considerable number of casualties in the clashes which took place between the demonstrators and the Soviet army.

Throughout the dictatorship in Greece which lasted from 1967 to 1974, my Grandmother Chrysoula was the only relative who, despite police threats, continued to correspond with Aunt Harikleia. They had not seen each other for nearly thirty years and they would never meet again. The little girl from Tantourlouch, the companion of her childhood, followed an orbit which separated them forever–from the Pontus to Russia, later to Greece and finally to Czechoslovakia. In essence, they did not live together again after the time when they were neighbors in Drapetsona. Yet they never stopped thinking of each other or loving each other.

Taking a closer look at their lives, it is clear that the uprooting from Tantourlouch overturned every possible logical prospect, while creating many absurd ones. Thus, by the time the two cousins reached the end of their lives, one tucked away in a corner of central Europe, the other in a corner of Attica, they had each faced trials of such magnitude, that neither of them could even have imagined such things were possible when they were young girls. One of them grew old alongside her husband, the other was widowed at 38. One experienced the socialist experiment on the inside, the other from a great distance away. One lost four children, the other lost one. Both of them worked hard, and both of them honored their husbands; both of them knew poverty and persecution. Which one lived a better life? Without a doubt, my grandmother did, for many reasons, the most decisive of them being that she had the privilege of living on Greek soil until her death.

As a young college student, I visited Aunt Harikleia in Czechoslovakia while on a trip organized by the university. At that time I could not understand why the fact that I was Chrysoula's granddaughter held such significance for her. Although she had been immobilized by a stroke and did not have the power of speech, with signs she invited us to stay for dinner. Not for a minute were her eyes dry. She had not seen a relative from Greece in twenty years, and though she was unable to utter a word, the tears overflowed as she silently cried. But what did I know of her other than a photograph I'd once seen, in which the military clothes she was wearing lent her, to my child's mind, mythic proportions? I did not realize then that this gentle, invalid woman whom I was meeting was actually living proof of the wider consequences of the Pontian drama. It did not occur to me that her life was of any direct concern to mine. I dismissed the details because at that time I was historically uninformed.

And yet, her case is quite common among this branch of my relatives, which is full of wives and mothers of leftist men. These women were well-disposed, dedicated, and often brave and combative. They stood by their men's sides and supported their decisions, though they themselves would never take the initiative in the struggle. First their husbands or sons became leftists, and then they did. All these women encountered tempests in their lives which they could never have imagined beforehand and which they generally had not brought about themselves.

When Pontians refer to «girls of the homeland», they mean those traditional Pontian women who were hard-working, patient and deferential, qualities which often bordered on the extreme of absolute sacrifice of their individual will and what today would be considered an inconceivable submission. They were all girls of the homeland. They adopted their husbands' political visions, paying an especially heavy toll. The men made the decisions, the women obeyed. They were transformed, usually uncomplainingly, into dynamic combatants, some courageously looking after their families while the husbands were away, barely managing to satisfy their children's hunger, others going into exile, stigmatized and often taunted, while yet others struggled near their men, in the mountains, through persecution, or in political exile. Theirs was a hard lot, or, as the Greek saying goes: «sweet bread they never ate».

In 1977 Harikleia Kyriakidou departed her trial-filled life in Brno, not having seen Greece since 1949. Apart from her husband and two children, no other relatives lived anywhere near her, though she would certainly have had many friends. She often wrote to my grandmother of the pain and sorrow she felt living in a foreign country. She would send her the couplets she had composed, full of nostalgia:

If only I were a bird, I'd fly
If only I were an eagle, I'd go
And nestle my weary head
In the lands I long for[16].

Approximately a century earlier in Brno, the monk, Mendel, full of scientific concerns, founded the science of genetics by studying the family bonds among peas. In the same city, years later, my aunt lived without the majority of her family bonds–far away from her siblings, dozens of first cousins, nieces and nephews, and others. If a concerned monk took up her case, he would have to compare sorrows rather than colors, crossbreed disillusionments instead of genetic varieties, and fertilize nostalgias, not plants. And, indeed, there is no fear that the law which would eventually be formulated would ever be overturned: when orphanhood is crossed with repeated exiles, refugee flights, deaths and defeats, the pain which is born is forever incurable.

---

16. *«Na em' poulin na epetana, na em' aetos na epaigna, ego kai na etsokeva 's sa mera pou ethelna.»*

Homer Kyriakides with his son Anestes, standing, his daughter-in-law Harikleia in the white head-scarf, their baby son, Homer's wife and daughters in Kuban.

Tsetes (photo by Henri-Paul Boissonnas).

Pontian refugee (archive of NATIONAL GEOGRAPHIC).

Revolutionaries of the Red Army in Crimea, 1918 (from the book *On the Trail of Odysseus*).

Batumi Harbor at the beginning of the 20th century, at a point where the shallowness of the water did not allow large ships to port there.

Another aspect of Batumi Harbor. Here the water is deep enough for large ships.

Pontian refugees on board a ship at Batumi, with members of the authorities on the pier. Headed for Greece, but how many will make it?

Loaded on the ship with whatever they were able to salvage (archive of the Centre for Asia Minor Studies, Manolis Megalokonomos collection).

Transporting the dead from the medical clinics on Makronissos. The man in the middle is dressed in traditional Pontian costume (from the book *Certain Samaritans*).

Makronissos. Pontian man with amputated leg, among other refugees. In the background, graves (from the book *Certain Samaritans*).

Refugees on Makronissos (archive of NATIONAL GEOGRAPHIC).

The ship which was made available to the doctors who volunteered on Makronissos (from the book *Certain Samaritans*).

Olga Stastny.

Harikleia with her cousins and their children.

Soldiers of ELAS on the march (archive of Kostas Balafas).

Harikleia, dressed in military clothing for the purpose of taking the photo, which was sent to Anestes while he was in Poland.

Harikleia, retiree in Brno.

LAZARUS APOSTOLIDES
[1890-1990]

«T' eremon to Kara-Mpournou, triyul'-triyul' taphia.
Anoikste kai teresteta, ola Karsi paidia.»

(The desolate Karabournaki, graves all around.
Open them and look at them, all of them lads from Kars.)

Lazarus Apostolides was first cousin to both my grandmother Chrysoula and Harikleia Kyriakidou. His father was born in Tantourlouch and had been given the name Homer. In the same simplicity with which they ate the ancient *pousinta*[1], they also gave their children ancient names. Historical continuation is not just a matter of theory. It is more a way of life.

After the second Russo-Turkish War of 1877-78, more than 100,000 Pontians moved to the newly-acquired Russian territories in the Caucasus, where the prospects for a better life were abundant. The Treaty of St. Stephen responsible for such favorable conditions, however, was the same one by which Bulgaria, stretching all the way to the Aegean, tightened the noose around the neck of mainland Greece, which was still struggling to free its northern lands from the Ottoman Empire[2].

Uncle Lazarus's father was one of those who emigrated to the new region, to the village of Pagdat, Kars, most of whose inhabitants were also from Tantourlouch. Among them were relatives of his, so he did not feel cut off. First and dearest was his beloved brother.

There he married and had four children. Of them all, Lazarus stood out because of his love of learning, and when he finished primary school he wanted to continue his education. His youthful dreams could not be realized in Pagdat, however. The village was fine, of course, but not for an ambitious scholar, not for him. So his father sent him to Odessa, in

---

1. Cakes made from pre-baked barley flour. This was the thick breadstuff of ancient times.

2. The treaty between Russia and Turkey created an autonomous state called Greater Bulgaria, whose new borders encompassed much of Macedonia. Though this would be rescinded shortly thereafter at the Congress of Berlin, the geographic region of Macedonia has remained a bone of contention ever since.

Crimea, where he could get a better education. Besides, he would not be alone. Two of his uncles, Homer's brothers, had a booming business there: shops, profits, expansion, plans for the future. But was that environment favorable to the charming, intellectually-inclined Lazarus? Unfortunately, it was not. His uncles, being of a more practical turn of mind, kept pressuring him to get involved in trade, which was a prospect that held little appeal for him. He had had a different outlook when he came to live with them, so he left.

The return to Pagdat was undertaken under appalling conditions and left its mark to the end of his life. Due to the extreme cold, as he took off his boots upon his arrival, along with his socks his toenails came off as well. They never grew back. Difficult modes of travel, in difficult times.

He made up his mind to become a policeman in the Russian state, a position that would give him financial security. When he achieved that, he felt he had left country life behind once and for all. Caring for the animals, the feeding and cleaning, the sowing and harvesting, he left them all to his brother. He was now a civil servant and he had excellent prospects for the future: promotion, travel, medals. He married a beautiful girl, who bore him two little daughters.

The political turmoil of the early twentieth century did presage trials to come; but the extremely well-organized social and economic life of the Kars villages veiled the region with a sense of security which, all too soon, would prove to be illusory.

The historical moment, the grand catalyst throughout time, reversed the situation and in 1918, when the Russian troops withdrew from the eastern Pontus, the Greek population found itself in a dire predicament. The Turks appropriated the abundant war supplies belonging to the army which had departed, and charged against the Greeks. They attacked all of the approximately 70 Greek villages of Kars, pursuing the residents maniacally and looting their wealthy homes.

The last one to leave Pagdat was Uncle Lazarus, who perhaps due to his position in the Russian police force was able to delay their departure for over three years.

The year 1922 found Uncle Lazarus with his wife, his children, and his widowed father at the harbor of Batumi, on their way to an impoverished and weakened mainland Greece. But how could that defeated country endure any further burden? Where could it put so many refugees? The ports, islands, quarantine stations, municipal buildings and parks were overcrowded to the point of asphyxiation. So they waited at the Batumi port for months on end, densely packed with another 25,000 Greeks, gazing at the horizon for the ship that would take them to the motherland. A third of them perished there, on the doorstep of their salvation. Their sea, the Pontus, had no room for its own children.

Day after day, waiting patiently for night to fall, they would bury the day's victims by the dozens. Quietly, without a sound, they would perform their heartbreaking task in the dark, seeing to it that the residents of Batumi took no notice of the dangers they themselves ran from the refugees' stay in the harbor. The life of a refugee counted for very little in those days.

At long last they set off. On the ship with Uncle Lazarus 4,500 souls were tightly squeezed, along with quite a few domestic animals, most of which died en route. Jammed against each other amidst bundles of belongings, sleeping mats and makeshift partitions, they fought for a little clean water and a corner to rest in. The wailing of the infants mingled with the moaning of the elderly and the lamentations for the dead. As always, the Pontian lyre accompanied their sorrows, and from it they drew consolation for the tragedy all around them.

And yet, amidst all the pushing and shoving, despite all the misery, hope, that breath of the soul, continued to circulate among them. Who could doubt that their overloaded ship was taking them to the promised land? Who could believe that their future would not be brighter?

Forty days later they arrived at the quarantine station in Karabournaki, or the cape of Kalamaria, just outside Thessaloniki, where they were subjected to mandatory disinfection. In that kingdom of lice and fleas, life went on as if it were Golgotha. Approximately 1,500 passengers had arrived there. The rest had died en route, primarily due to contaminated water. And of those that set foot on land, only about half survived. Of the original 4,500 only 800 were spared! In the space of one year, 25,000 refugees had lost their lives[3]. Double barbed-wire fences and guards kept the outcasts away from Thessaloniki. You needed special permission to go there.

Ifigeneia Chrysochoou[4] writes in her book *Uprooted Generation*: «From the quarantine station at Kalamaria they were transferred to the wards. There were 60 wards, 1,000 meters from the sea, all built of wood, standing on poles half a meter above ground, the roofs covered with tar paper. Each ward measured 15x4 meters, most of them in the shape of a Greek Π, with the common toilet in the center. (...) Those in whose speech the language of Homer is still preserved, those faithful guardians of country, family and religion, those who are overcome with emotion and trembling, their hearts racing, upon hearing the word "Greece", will they live in this utter desert, this abandonment, this isolation?

»[...] The door doesn't stop opening and closing. That's good. You don't suffocate from the stench of some 80 people.

»[...] The nights are awful. The odor of bad breath is mixed with smelly feet, the gas of the lamps, the stench of pee. How can the children and the elderly go out in the freezing darkness? Everyone urinates in the can. Sometimes one's nose doesn't notice, because another stink dominates everything else. There is no lack of dead in the ward, let alone the hospital. In bunches they go in, in bunches they're buried... Typhoid, measles, malaria, abdominal ailments, bronchitis. Every kind of illness. Most of the dead were taken by typhoid. Here, death set out to finish off whatever had escaped the Turk!»

During that time of hardship and suffering at the Batumi port, Uncle Lazarus's father, Homer, would often say «Just let me get to Greece and I don't care if I die there.»[5] It seems his prayer was answered, for that is

---

3. According to the testimony of P. Fokaides, secretary of the Committee for Settlement of the Refugees of Kalamaria for one year.

4. This much-awarded writer was born in Asia Minor but left there as a refugee at the age of 13. Her best-known books are the trilogy: *Burnt Land, March of Torment*, and *Uprooted Generation*, as well as *Here Lies Smyrna*, which completes their story.

5. *« 'S sin Ellada as erxoumai ki as teleitai i psy m'.»*

exactly how it happened. Indeed, his wish was granted beyond his expectations: not only did his own life end there in Karabournaki, but also that of his daughter-in-law, Lazarus's wife, and the lives of their two little girls. He himself died of a heart attack the day after they arrived, having lived in the motherland only one day.

So ended the odyssey of Homer.

At thirty-two, Uncle Lazarus found himself all alone, counting his misfortunes in the swampland outside a terrified and harshly indifferent Thessaloniki. When he was allowed to leave the place of suffering, he went to a village to be near two of his father's brothers. From there they were sent to colonize Eastern Thrace, in a village called Saranta Ekklisies (40 Churches). Not even there were they able to establish a home. Once again, they were dragged into emigration against their will. Others made the decision without their knowledge or consent. The area was given to the Turks under the Treaty of Lausanne and they were forced to leave.

Ernest Hemingway, then a young correspondent for the *Toronto Daily Star*, writes thusly about the flight of the residents of Eastern Thrace: «In a never-ending, staggering march the Christian population of Eastern Thrace is jamming the roads towards Macedonia... Twenty miles of carts drawn by cows, bullocks and muddy-flanked water buffalo, with exhausted, staggering men, women and children, blankets over their heads, walking blindly along in the rain beside their worldly goods... It is a silent procession. Nobody even grunts. It is all they can do to keep moving...»[6]

Thousands of the inhabitants of Eastern Thrace took the road to exile. Conditions were exacerbated by the fact that all the means of transportation had been conscripted by the Turkish army. Worse yet, by Kemal's decree, the deadline for departure was moved up from fifteen days to barely three. Our former allies, the French, took it upon themselves to implement the change by applying unbearable pressure.

Eventually, Uncle Lazarus settled in the prefecture of Drama, in a small village which later changed its Turkish name to Psilokastro. There his

---

6. «A Silent, Ghastly Procession Wends Way from Thrace», *Toronto Daily Star*, Oct. 20, 1922, p. 17.

father's two brothers–the ones who had tried to push him into trade in Odessa–had already arrived. For a year they lived with the Muslim residents of that village. The uprooted Pontians were waiting to put out new roots by uprooting the locals, who would in turn take root in the very land they themselves had been uprooted from. What an amusing anecdote! Yet it was all too true.

But while the Pontians had been literally chased out of their land, exactly the opposite took place with the Turks of the so-called population exchange. Without, of course, downplaying the latter's justified frustration regarding the compulsory emigration, they were given the opportunity to take all their moveable property with them. They transported entire herds of cattle on trains. The only thing they left behind were the walls of their homes. Most importantly, they left peacefully and were not subjected to threats and dangers. We left with the knife at our throats.

A typical example of the profound respect the first-generation Pontians had for their religious tradition was the rescue and preservation of the treasures and the bell of the Church of the Transfiguration of Our Savior in Pagdat, which Uncle Lazarus and another man from his village carried to the new place of residence, despite their unprecedentedly convoluted wanderings.

Psilokastro is representative of all refugee villages in northern Greece. The newcomers lived in the homes of the Muslims who had left and started to cultivate the land. They built a church and a school, and would go to a neighboring town for whatever needs the village could not supply. In the village they grew tobacco of excellent quality, so that, in spite of the merchants' greed and the middlemen's conniving, they still made a fairly good living. Though their finances were limited, the Pontians had large families, and there was no lack of feasting and dancing to the accompanying lyre.

But did they live a carefree life? Certainly not. The refugees were nothing like the inhabitants of other parts of Greece, because they had undergone significantly different experiences. Absolutely everyone in the refugee villages were the victims of a slaughter the magnitude of which the world had never witnessed before, a fact that scarred them for life. Only by mentioning a few examples does the abyss which separated them from the local Greeks become somewhat fathomable.

Their first two priests who served at the church of the Transfiguration of Our Savior, named after the church back in Pagdat, were Christos Papadopoulos and Elladios Karapanagiotides. They had both suffered near-martyrdom in Samsunta and arrived in Greece desolate and alone.

Father Christos had sought refuge in the Pontian mountains with the rebel forces because the Turks were after him. When the massacre in Kato Tsinik, Samsunta, was ordered, his wife, his mother, and their four children also went to hide in the mountains. But their newborn child was crying, which might betray them to the enemy. It was decided by the rebels that the babies should either be killed or taken away. At that point, Father Christos' mother picked up the baby and headed into the unknown. She was later found in a ravine, dead, with the baby strapped to her back. His wife and the other three children fell into the hands of the Turks and were exiled. No one ever learned what happened to them. Father Christos was left completely alone, with only his faith to console him.

For some years he served the church in Psilokastro and the surrounding villages. His vestments were paid for with money given him by his first cousin, a worker in the tobacco fields, in order to replace the rags he had been wearing when he arrived from the Pontus. He often gave the children he baptized the names of his own children. During the dictatorship of Metaxas, he was arrested and led to the police station. Despite the official ban on the Pontian language, he had uttered the phrase *«As trogomen enan xygalan»* which means, «Let's eat some yoghurt». The champion of law and order, in an effort to discourage the use of a language which to the mainland Greeks sounded illiterate and broken, said to him: «You speak corrupt Greek»[7].

---

7. A ludicrous, unfounded accusation, as can be seen from only a few citations of ancient usage: Ctesias, the 5th century BC Greek physician and historian, recording the habits of the tribe of Kynokefaloi states «πίνουσι δὲ γάλα καὶ ὀξύγαλα τῶν προβάτων» («they drank milk and yoghurt (*oxygala*) from sheep»). Strabo (63 BC-24 AD) in his *Geography* mentions that Skythes, Asian nomadic tribes, fed on milk and oxygala from horses. Galen (2nd century AD) in his book *Περί τῶν ἁπλῶν φαρμάκων κράσεως καί δυνάμεως* attaches healing properties to oxygala. Finally, Ptohoprodromos (12th century) refers to the profession of ὀξυγαλατᾶ.

Eventually Father Christos, urged by Bishop Chrysanthos, Metropolitan of Trapezunta and later Metropolitan of Athens and All Greece, left for the Monastery of Panagia Faneromeni (Our Lady Revealed) on the island of Salamina, where he lived out the last years of his tormented life.

Father Elladios, the priest who succeeded him in Psilokastro and who was also from Kato Tsinik, had a permanently clouded countenance and sometimes gave the impression that he was not quite in his right mind. Tsetes had forced him to dig his own grave. They commanded him to lie facedown on the ground and raped his wife on his back before killing her and his four children right in front of him. Then they hanged him from a mulberry tree, and thinking he was dead, left him hanging there. An old Pontian woman rescued him, and that is how he ended up in Greece. He would wander around Psilokastro for hours at a time, with a dog at his heels, going from home to home and handing out charity, until he would eventually return to his solitude.

The Turkish fury against the Christian clergy left many victims in its wake, but also staggering proof of the magnitude and kind of crimes that can result when Satan is pulling the strings. Seven priests were crucified in Pafra, another one in the village of Ada in Samsunta, Father Minas, in the village of Tepetsik, after they had cut off his beard and skinned him, as well as many others. How much more preferable is defeat, when victory brings with it such horrors!

When Giorgos and Melpomeni Spanidou arrived in Psilokastro, all twelve of their children had either been lost or killed or snatched from them. Even Job had lost two less. They summoned the courage to have one more, their son Theophilos, who now lives in Thessaloniki. Have there been many parents on this earth more orphaned than those two?

Another example of the life of one of the Psilokastro refugees is that of Chrysoula Symeonidou. Twice she was exiled from her village in the Pontus and yet survived. Both times she returned to find her house burnt down. Her husband was a deserter and his grandmother and parents were sent into exile, after which no one ever saw them again. Chrysoula took her baby and sought refuge near the Pontian rebels, taking care to keep her distance so that the baby's crying would endanger neither their own lives nor those of the rest of the unarmed people following the rebels.

On June 21, 1921, she was near the renowned rebel chieftans in the mountain range of Agiou-Tepe[8], that blood-drenched mountain of martyred Samsunta. The Christian villages of the area had been burnt down and thousands of women and children, like her, had hidden in the Saltouch Forest. The Turks, with their mighty armed forces and artillery, reinforced by 400 tsetes who were led by that self-same Topal Osman, attacked the rebels, whose forces were hopelessly smaller: a few rifles, a few shells. When the rebel forces of the heroic leader Pantelis Anastasiades[9] united on the edge of the forest in order to protect the terrified unarmed civilians, the Turks began their strike with machine guns, weapons capable of wielding death from a distance.

The rebel captain commanded the women and children to scatter in the forest immediately, while they fought on and gave them cover, with no thought for themselves. In the pandemonium of enemy fire the refugees ran here and there, panic-stricken. There were already 72 dead among them. For whole days Kemal's army pursued them in the forest of Saltouch, even using specially trained dogs to track them down. Hundreds were trapped and butchered on the spot, while others were burned in villages nearby.

When young Chrysoula managed to find a safe place to rest, she took her baby in her arms. She had strapped it to her back in order to be able to run. To her horror, she now saw that it had been struck by a bullet and was dead. In the uproar and panic, the innocent soul had silently departed, perhaps even serenely, incapable of grasping the extreme agony of its mother. Weeping and sobbing, she buried the child in the woods, digging its grave in the dirt with her hands. She never saw her husband again.

It is worth noting here that on that same day of June 1921, while the Christians were being slaughtered on Agiou-Tepe, a young man from Oinoe by

---

8. Hill of the Bear.

9. Pantelis Anastasiades (1896-1969) was born in Samsunta. In the mountains at the early age of 18, he struggled, fought, and rescued countless women and children. In 1923 he arrived in Greece, by way of Russia and Bulgaria.

the name of Chrysostomos Karaiskos, a great Pontian patriot and a captain in the Greek army, tried to persuade the chief commander Papoulas[10] to make use of the Pontian rebel forces. With him were fighters eager to strike at Kemal from the south, in coordination with the Greek army. He was not listened to. Reluctance on the part of Athens? Lack of boldness to take the initiative? As it later proved, the times demanded more drastic decisions if they were to avert ethnic genocide. The heroic Pontian epic was composed to the dramatic tune of abandonment.

In Psilokastro, Uncle Lazarus dwelt in a Turkish house with his new wife, herself a Pontian, whose spouse was also dead. With mutual shares in sorrow, though in different percentages, they started their life together. They had four sons. One of them died young, his laughter never to be heard again among the noisy clusters of children in the village. Once again, they mustered their strength and devoted their love to the other three.

After the Greco-Italian War, Greece was occupied in 1941 by both the Germans and the Bulgarians. The latter, who were German allies, surpassed the Nazis in persecutions and violence. Their wrath against the Greeks was far greater than that of the Germans, because it had been incited by the poison of poor relations between neighbors and by land claims over long-suffering Macedonia. The Bulgarians compelled Uncle Lazarus's twenty-six-year-old first son to do forced labor on the banks of the Danube for six months as a *dourdouvaki*. He was there when the Occupation ended and liberty was declared. His second son was a street vendor at the time, selling cigarettes out of a crate in order to contribute to the support of the family. Until civil war broke out. The age old Greek plague once again made its appearance on the stage of history, mercilessly extorting the highest of taxes: a brother's blood. Then their life, which had been rebuilt so many times, was literally shattered by another devastating event.

Uncle 's Lazarus second son was killed in the vicinity of Drama, just a few kilometers from Psilokastro. He was barely seventeen. The specula-

---

10. Anastasios Papoulas was commander in chief of the Greek forces during the Asia Minor campaign. He was later executed for taking part in an attempted coup (March 1, 1935) on the part of supporters of Venizelos.

tion as to how he died caused yet more bitterness to his parents. Did he die at the hand of the enemy? Was he killed by his comrades? Was he trying to escape from the rebels? Had they sent him to dig up potatoes in a dangerous spot? Did he climb the mountain on his own initiative? Was he conscripted along with other village youth after an ambush? It might be interesting to pursue all these speculations, but the fact remains that the father, my Uncle Lazarus, saw a fourth child die before he did. That is the essential fact; everything else is insignificant by comparison.

Then came the 1960s. With the roads to immigration wide open, poverty-stricken Greece became the source of an abundant, cheap work force. The youth left in successive waves, in search of a better life. Special German envoys arrived in the Drama area, compiling lists of candidates and making their selection of potential immigrants. The countryside was deserted, production was undermined and the youth were turned into cheap tools for the industrial development of the booming German economy.

It is a curious fact, indeed, that the occupying forces turned into saviors, just a few short years after their boots had trodden authoritatively on the soil of our unfortunate homeland. But it did happen, and it proves the transience innate to life and human affairs.

From Psilokastro, which was likewise drained of its youth, both of Uncle Lazarus's remaining sons emigrated. They followed the typical path of the second-generation Pontian refugees who grew up in the villages of Macedonia. After the one-way street of the tobacco fields and the general lack of opportunity, there arose the prospect of emigration, full of promise. After the Turks' violent, compulsory child abduction policy came the Germans' peaceful luring of young refugees on a voluntary basis. The times decided their routes and the conditions determined their choices. Life was never granted freely to the refugees.

Uncle Lazarus, listening to Pontian songs, would let out a sigh now and then, and that was all. He rarely spoke. On the few occasions I met him, I remember his being totally passive and completely introverted. His extremely tall form moved slowly and calmly, and in his strikingly blue, pensive eyes there was imprinted a deep sadness.

He had wanted to get an education but was not able to. He tried to become a high-ranking officer in the Russian police but was thwarted by events. He had wished to live in Pagdat with his family; they were exiled. He tried to save them all but lost every one of them. He was left completely alone. It had been his heart's desire to see his sons happy around him. Two of them took a path that offered a possible return. The other two took the path of no return. He longed to close his eyes once and for all in Psilokastro, yet he was not even granted that wish.

He died at exactly 100 years old in a German workers' town near Stuttgart, where he lived with his children and their families. One day he lay down and passed away, quietly and simply, just like that. Was he the perfect human being? Had the tragedies of his life perhaps sanctified him? Certainly not, as is the case with all of us. Our trials serve to balance out existing faults, but they do not create ideal characters. They lighten the blame, but they are not cathartic fire. From this perspective, one cannot judge harshly someone who submitted stoically to three expulsions, who carried the burden of his losses in silence, and who treaded wearily and passively to his end. A somewhat excessive tendency to complain may be forgiven, even if it lasts a lifetime. At any rate, it is often the case that we humans focus on the more trivial side of life, to avoid being devastated by that which is genuinely significant.

Pagdat today.

The impenetrable masses at the harbors (archive of ERT, Petros Poulides collection).

Jammed together on deck.

Departure from Batumi. For hundreds of refugees, the ship of their salvation became a death trap.

Arrival of Pontian refugees at Kalamaria, Thessaloniki.

The wards at Kalamaria (from the book *Kalamaria Between the Wars 1920-1940*).

Ward at Kalamaria (archive of NATIONAL GEOGRAPHIC).

A refugee family outside the ward they inhabit (archive of Ioanna Pasalidou).

Tents at Kalamaria. In the background the wards can be seen (archive of Anna Theophylactou).

Kalamaria (archive of Anna Theophylactou).

The railway station of Saranta Ekklisies during the evacuation of Eastern Thrace (from the book *From the History of Thrace 1875-1925*).

Pontian refugees in Thessaloniki, dressed in traditional costume and looking troubled. Like fish out of water (from Santeos.blogspot.gr).

Pontian youth of Psilokastro in a commemorative photo. Like the majority of those in the area, they spent the prime of their life working in German factories.

Psilokastro, Drama, a typical Pontian village. The youth are dancing to the strains of the Pontian lyre.

Father Christos Papadopoulos.

Father Elladios Karapanagiotides. Both priests came to Greece completely alone, their families butchered by Topal's hordes.

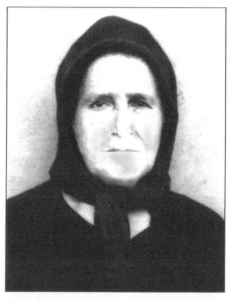

The tragic Melpo Spanidou. She lost 12 children in the persecutions.

Chrysoula Symeonidou. The baby strapped to her back was killed by a bullet on Agiou-Tepe, Samsunta.

«WHEN THE LIVING
ENVY THE DEAD»

MARIA SIDIROPOULOU
[1867-1942]

«Polla na leo 'ki poro ki oliga 'ki kaneintan,
Ta terta m' ola na lego, meron' kai 'ki teleintan.»

(I cannot say a lot, and a little won't suffice. To tell all my trials
would take till morning and I won't have finished.)

Maria Sidiropoulou was my grandmother Chrysoula's mother. She was born in Tantourlouch, Chaldia, the most isolated little village with an unmixed Greek population on the Pontian mountains. Of the approximately three hundred families who lived there in 1829, two hundred emigrated to the Kars region, which was under Russian rule. Most of them went to Artachan, others to Pagdat and Pelikpas, and a few to Alisophe. Some, mostly men, went to the coastal areas of the ancient Greek Tavris, otherwise known as Crimea. Their ranks were later swollen in the early twentieth century by draft-dodgers who were seeking to avoid the forced labor camps of the Turks. Around 1908, another forty families left Tantourlouch.

When my great-grandmother was born, in the mid-nineteenth century, there were about three hundred people left in the village. Two hundred and twenty were openly practicing Christians, sixty were secret Christians, and about twenty practiced the Muslim religion. In a cave some fifteen minutes from the center of the village lay the ruins of a church where Christians had worshipped in secret[1], while in 1871, a church dedicated to St. Stephen was secretly built overnight, in one of the Kyriakides family's fields. Four years later the school was built, in the yard of St. George's, the main church of the village. My great-grandmother's brothers went to school there, for girls did not have the right to an education yet.

Women may not have gone to school in the nineteenth century, but they certainly did not lag behind the men when it came to hard labor.

---

1. Chrysanthos, Bishop of Trapezunta, *The Church of Trapezunta*, Estia, Athens 1933.

Indeed, when the Russians arrived in 1916, women from Tantourlouch loaded sacks of wheat on their backs and carried them to the seven villages of Santa, eight hours away. Did they have to work in order to be able to eat, as they later testified in the Turkish court? Were they taking supplies to the Russian soldiers in order to help them? No one knows. What is certain is that those women had the strength to load themselves like pack animals and walk for hours up and down steep slopes. At the same time, they were used to having to abandon their homes from time to time. It was not uncommon, during conflicts between the Russians and the Turks, for them to be moved to the neighboring unmixed Turkish village of Demiroren for several months. Often enough, when they returned they found that all their belongings had been stolen. Yet the Pontian women of Tantourlouch endured. Besides, all of them knew how to handle a gun, to scare off the Turks when they tried to steal from them.

My great-grandmother's father, Yannis Apostolides, was known by the name of Trechtes (meaning «running» or «flowing») because he was dynamic, always active and hard-working, but also because money just seemed to flow from him. The name by which the whole clan was known, Trechtant', originated with him. He and his wife had twelve children, eleven of whom survived, among them Lazarus Apostolides' and Harikleia Kyriakidou's fathers, and Gior's, Barbara Parastatidou's second husband. Their stables were full of animals and so were the chicken coops; cattle, oxen, sheep and hens supplied them with meat and dairy products, allowing them to spread many an abundant feast at holiday celebrations, weddings and *soumadia*[2].

Trechtes' main occupation, however, was the breeding and training of thoroughbred horses on the mountains of that region, which were ideal for the purpose. On average, he bred sixty horses a year and sold them in Argyroupoli or Trapezunta. He sold exclusively to discriminating buyers, the wealthy riders of the area.

In 1918, the year Tantourlouch fell to the Turks, Trechtes and his wife had already died. Thus, they never learned of the storms which life

---

2. Engagement celebrations.

held in store for their children. They belonged to the last generation of Pontians who had the privilege of departing from this world in the land where they and long generations of their forefathers had been born. Their children composed the first generation of refugees. They died in distant lands, having first suffered every ordeal possible. It was a time when «the living envied the dead.»[3]

My great-grandmother Maria married Isaac Sidiropoulos, a fellow villager. They had eight children, one of which died when it was quite small. Twice, she gave birth to twins. The second time she brought into the world Chrysoula, my mother's mother, and her sister. They had a good life, though they worked hard. Their two sons, Yangos and Vassilis, had barely turned eighteen when they moved to Russia. Some of their uncles, Maria's brothers, were already settled in Sudak, so the boys opened shops there too, selling yard goods, and business went very well. The eldest daughter also moved to Crimea, where her husband had gone to avoid being drafted into the Turkish army.

The occupation of the eastern Pontus by the Russians caused the optimism of the Greeks to soar, and the boys opened yet another business. The industriousness of the Greeks had found fertile soil. The elder son, Yangos, decided to let Vassilis run the shops in Sudak while he would open another one in Baipurt, where apart from the wealthy Armenian community there was also a thriving Greek community, small in number but dynamic and prosperous. Trade was conducted in gold lire and Yangos' daily earnings were considerable.

The rest of Maria Sidiropoulou's family lived in Tantourlouch, and her husband would travel to Russia from time to time. Their success abroad afforded them a comfortable daily life, and they built a big, new house around 1915. It was constructed only after careful planning. They even had an interior well, by building one of the rooms over it and making a small aperture in the floor. This way, they were able to get water even when everything outside was frozen.

---

3. Goethe.

At some point Yangos decided to marry. His wedding took place near the end of 1917, on the same day his sister Sophia married their fellow villager and local schoolteacher. He and an escort of forty more riders brought his wife on horseback from the neighboring village of Lerin, despite the deep snow. Of course, in the Pontus, «neighboring» often meant about a day's horse ride.

Yangos' wedding took place in the morning, at the bride's family home, and Sophia's followed that evening in Tantourlouch. Everything was done according to tradition: the nyfeparma, the *foustron*[4], the feasting. The *kemetzes*[5] played all night, and the abundant food and flowing *tsipouro*[6] completed the great joy of the household. There was not the slightest foreshadowing of the disastrous hurricane which would sweep them away less than two months later. No one imagined that behind these hopeful marriages lurked their ruin, waiting its turn.

The day after the wedding, Yangos and his wife left for Baipurt, where they had rented part of the luxurious home of a certain bey. The rest of the house was lived in by Russian officers. Sophia and her husband went to live with his parents, near her own family's home.

Then came that dreadful January of 1918, when time froze for them. The mountains had filled with Turkish rebels and fortune-hunters of all sorts from the wider region, who stormed the neat little Greek villages. Before the residents were forced to abandon the village, they were taken captive and held inside the school. From there they could see their houses being burnt and pillaged, yet they were unable to do anything to save them. They stood by helplessly, watching the mania of destruction and predation. As they had good relations with the Turks of the surrounding area, they could not believe their eyes. Where had all these people come from? Where had all this hatred lain hidden?

---

4. An omelette made with fresh butter, the Italian sfougato.
5. The Pontian term for the lyre.
6. An alcoholic beverage similar to ouzo.

In a short while the *Turkant* [7] had taken everything, having burnt and plundered unceasingly. And yet, the tragedy lay not in what had just happened but in what the next hours would bring, which would utterly eclipse all material loss.

It was early afternoon when they were thrown out into the road, that is, into nowhere, as the snow blanketed everything and there was no passage. For the most part, they were women, children or the aged. The women of Tantourlouch, like all the women of the Pontian mountains, may have been accustomed to living without their husbands and have acquired courage and a cool head, but on the day they were forced to abandon Tantourlouch, the temperatures were below zero and the snow was deeper than they were tall. The conditions were such that no matter how much courage the women like my great-grandmother had in them, it would not be enough. With so many children and old folks on the road to exile, and with such savagery around them, they quickly realized that their life was entering its most dramatic phase.

The family reached Sudak after an excruciating three-month ordeal. Their trials were offset by the fact that they had all arrived alive, in spite of the unprecedentedly severe weather conditions and the pursuit by bloodthirsty gangs. They accommodated themselves in the rented house Yangos was living in, and perhaps they thought they would not have to leave again. A private field of about two and a half acres was being rented to a Russian farmer, and their shops were doing well, despite the political unrest. They might just manage to stay there after all.

Did they feel safe, though? Could they relax at last? They could not. The place was given over to a relentless struggle for domination between the Red and White armies, as well as many others. They were not exactly sure who was fighting who. The Greeks living there were not a target, it is true, but they found themselves in the middle of the conflict. Though they themselves were not victims, the human sacrifice taking place before their eyes in this civil war was terrifying. Nor could they imagine then that several years later they would live through a similar calamity in the mother-

---

7. The Turks as a people.

land, Greece. The Germano-Austrians had been in Crimea since March of 1918[8]. On January 7, 1919, ten days after British troops landed there, the Greek army also arrived–25,000 men on the side of the Entente powers.

When the Allies were defeated, the Pontian Greek refugees were in a dire situation. They belonged to a power that was hostile to the new regime, and their safety was doubtful. They would have to go through another uprooting. They had to get out of there. Their plans for building a house in Sudak fell through. A return to the other side of the Black Sea, to their own lands again, was impossible. There, the scheme to slaughter the indigenous peoples continued unceasingly, and they would be lost for certain. The only place of refuge left was mainland Greece.

My relatives left Crimea after a year's stay, with the first shipload of refugees that was organized. Yangos went to Theodosia and arranged for their departure with a committee of Pontians. «Drop everything and come at once!» he notified the family. Maria Sidiropoulou would look on many new places, a thing she had never imagined while living in Tantourlouch. The horizons of her world were radically widened. Beyond the mountains that surrounded her village, Tsatima, Ormin, Chatsar and Tsam-Tsouchor, there were cities, trains, stations and ports. There was the strait of Bosporus, the city of Constantinople, the Aegean. And there was Greece. She came to know them all, without having foreseen such a thing, without ever desiring it. The land where she was born, though, she never saw again.

The ship *Patris*[9] took them to the island of Aegina[10] in a few days' voyage. Others were taken to the island of Hydra. Ten days later the same ship, loaded with soldiers, would head for the landing at Smyrna.

---

8. In accordance with the Brest-Litovsk Treaty of March 1918, not only were the eastern Pontus, Kars and Armenia given to the Turks, but Crimea was given to the Germano-Austrians.

9. The ocean liner *Patris* belonged to the National Steamships of Greece, owned by the Empeirikos Brothers, and had been conscripted for use by the Greek state. It had a capacity of 4,890 registered tons.

10. One of the Saronic Islands of Greece in the Saronic Gulf, 27 km from Athens. Tradition derives the name from Aegina, mother of the hero Aeacus, who was born on the island and became its king.

They arrived on April 7, 1919. It was Easter and they celebrated it on the ship. On the island the authorities and the residents greeted them with eggs dyed red, as is still the custom, and with *tsoureki*, a delicious, sweet bread which is always baked at Easter. They had left Theodosia at the beginning of Holy Week, the week of Christ's passion. Yet the Resurrection, which they were so looking forward to experiencing in the motherland, was marked by another loss. All their belongings were stolen, though they were told that they had fallen into the sea and that the local Aeginite divers were unable to recover them. In vain did my great-grandfather Isaac go and inquire after them, day after day. They had been deprived of even the most essential items and were left with only the clothes on their backs.

The local government provided them with makeshift housing in the fields and a common meal. They started working immediately. They picked olives at the monastery of Chrysoleontissa and pistachios at the village of Messagros, while illnesses ravaged their weakened forms. With their eyes in pain from trachoma[11], they struggled to survive, under the scorching heat of the sun and in the cold. They tilled, they watered, they pruned and they gathered the harvest. In spite of their calloused hands and their tired, sun-burnt faces, however, they persisted bravely in the face of these trials, a fact that soon became known all over the island. The initial suspicion with which they had been received was followed by unequivocal respect.

My great-grandmother's was one case among thousands. She was a typical refugee, in that everyone was in difficulties. Of Pontian housewives who suddenly found themselves without a home there were many. But who would dare to say that the impact of the injustice diminishes with an increase in the frequency? True, a general climate of misfortune tends to be created, but one's personal sorrow remains intact in the soul. How much more so in the case of my great-grandmother, who was destined

---

11. An infection caused by the bacterium *Chlamydia trachomatis*, and a major cause of blindness in underdeveloped countries even today.

to suffer more pain still. One of her sisters and her husband had already been slain by the Turks in Tantourlouch at the outbreak of World War I, before their four children's very eyes. Their only daughter, who as the oldest had taken the place of their mother for the three younger siblings, died of typhoid fever on the voyage from Russia to Greece, along with her husband and their two children. It was a terrible loss.

Her brother Homer died of heart failure in Karabournaki, together with his son Lazarus' wife and two children, who succumbed to illnesses. Another brother, Gior's, lost his wife and daughter on Hydra, where they had disembarked on their arrival in Greece. This recital of unremitting tragedy may sound like raving, but it is an entirely accurate description of how the noose of death grew ever tighter around the neck of Maria's family.

In 1921 they crossed from Aegina to Piraeus, on the mainland, where they settled in the shantytowns of Drapetsona. For a home they were given two tiny rooms with no roof. They had to set up a tent in one of the rooms until they were able to make a roof out of tar paper. Eight people lived in there: the parents, three daughters, two sons and one daughter-in-law. On top of that, they had to squeeze their goat inside as well, so that it would not be stolen by various petty thieves who hung around the wide-open homes. Why did they not close their doors? Because the heat inside was suffocating, of course!

It was in the midst of this misery as refugees in Drapetsona that Maria had to bear her heaviest cross: the death of her own daughter, Sophia, in 1921. She had been sent to the island of Makronissos to stay in quarantine, from a country that was overwhelmed by calamity.

Esther Lovejoy, the volunteer doctor through whose efforts three temporary hospitals were set up on the island and where many of the lives of the downtrodden were thus saved, writes: «A tragic procession of women, children, the elderly, and very few whole men trudged through the sand, loaded down with their bundles. Many of the elderly were so weak and exhausted that they needed help to reach the camp for the "unclean", where it was mandatory for all new arrivals to stay until they and their sparse belongings had been disinfected of lice. The conditions of the

The funeral of tragic Sophia (archive of Theodora Ioannidou).

refugees are indescribable. Human beings, usually women and children, without a country, cast out by the world. Unable to speak Greek. They move them from place to place. They do not have blankets... clothing. They are cold, hungry and ill.»[12]

The photograph of Sophia's funeral was for me a genuine invitation from my deceased relatives who once lived in Drapetsona. Luckily, the Pontian custom of photographing the dead, established as a means of informing relatives who lived abroad of the event, was adhered to in the case of my twenty-six-year-old aunt. Otherwise, it would have been difficult to form the slightest idea of the storm that struck the refugee hovels, or the wretchedness to which my unfortunate relatives had been committed.

First and foremost in the tragedy was my great-grandmother, Maria, the black-clad figure in the center of the photo, with her eyes fixed on her dead daughter. My great-grandfather, Isaac, in ragged clothing, is second from the left, staring off as if stunned.

Standing near their mother are my grandmother Chrysoula and two of her sisters, their faces darkened. Yangos' wife, who loved her worthy, capable sister-in-law dearly, is also standing beside Maria, her face gloomy.

Other figures from the refugee ghetto fill the background of the tragedy, relatives and friends unknown to me. A few humble flowers in the wooden coffin cover the skeletal shell of a tyrannized soul, and an icon of Christ is in her hands. The presence of the priest, also raggedly dressed, alludes to the ultimate meaning of such pain: perhaps reward in another world in recompense for calamity suffered, or the assurance of a heavenly destination in response to justified protestation. However, the bitterness frozen on all their faces indicates that, for the time being,

12. Lovejoy, Esther Pohl, M.D., *Certain Samaritans*, Chapter XXV, The Macmillan Co., New York 1933. According to her, World War I, of which she had experience, was a feast compared to the horrific crimes of the Turkish people against the Christians. She blamed the "civilized world" for remaining indifferent and often cooperating with the criminals. Once there was an incident she saw with her own eyes where American sailors handed over to Turkish soldiers two refugees who were trying to swim to their ship. On Makronissos she coordinated the team of American doctors who operated three hospitals: one for smallpox, one for typhus and another one for non-contagious diseases.

at least, they have distanced themselves from any such hopes and have irrevocably transcended the luxury of complaining. Why do they seem impervious to the deadly dose of bitterness they have just swallowed? Is it because for a long time they had been imbibing smaller doses of refugee poison? Had these Mithridates[13] of Drapetsona become accustomed to the poison by now?

Before she departed from this life, Sophia, a worthy and courageous woman by all accounts, had lost her husband and two children en route to Greece. She who had been her mother's right hand back in their home in Tantourlouch, who had dressed and combed her little sisters and taken them to school through the snow and the rain, who looked after the animals and the fields since the men of the house were abroad, she did not endure. Yet it was she who single-handedly managed to scare off the Turks that had tried to break into their home by way of the roof to steal the silk goods they had from Russia.

Her self-possession and courage were known to all, as was her proud soul. She only went to the annual matchmaking after years of pressure on the part of her family. She felt it was beneath her dignity to declare her candidacy by joining the circle of girls who would dance at the summer fair and exchange interested glances with the men who made up the circle of prospective grooms. The mountain pastures rang with song, and the young men, dressed in different colors according to the village they were from, would search for a mate. In Sophia's eyes, this ritual was demeaning. She had finally been pressured into climbing up the mountain that summer of 1917 when she was affianced.

Where did such an imperious soul go? What salty brine swallowed up forever all that she had loved? The decision, or perhaps it was a weakness, to leave Russia with her relatives in 1919 proved to be disastrous. Had they thrown her dead children and husband in the sea, or in the smokestack of the ship? I never learned, but it is of no significance. Before she

---

13. Mithridates VI, King of the Pontus, regularly ingested small doses of various poisons so that he would be unaffected by any if an enemy tried to poison him.

escaped this world, dying in the hospital in Athens where she had been transferred from Makronissos, my grandmother Chrysoula's much-loved sister had suffered the ultimate misfortune. That is the important thing. If the term «plunder» can be used to refer to lives, then a more perfect example than the life of Sophia could not be found, regardless of the fact that such experiences were hopelessly frequent in the history of Pontian Hellenism. The mournful lament of the kemetzedes resounded through the narrow streets of the refugee shantytowns, among the tents and the shacks, grieving for all the human beings who were lost in the same way. Thousands are the plundered Pontians.

Within the next few years, the single girls of the family married hardworking men, all of whom, naturally, were Pontians. The local Greeks had not yet accepted these peculiar people far enough to approve of intermarriage with them, despite their being of the same race. Mainly, though, the Pontians themselves considered it an essential prerequisite for marriage that the partner be «one of them». Only then did they feel secure.

Yangos opened a coffee shop in Drapetsona, whose patrons made it the hub of the leftist element in the area. There the refugees would gather after work to see each other, to chat or play backgammon, but also to find respite. Besides, in their homes there was hardly room to move.

As the years passed, my great-grandmother saw more and more grandchildren. Each new birth softened the pain of a previous loss. But conditions of hygiene in the district were extremely poor. The children were in danger of becoming blind due to eye infections. Many of the children went to a special school for those who were afflicted with trachoma. Among them were two of Maria's grandchildren.

The cement and gypsum factories may have given the refugees work, albeit low-paying, but they also took their toll with regard to their health. The magnificent clouds over the Pontian mountains were replaced by the dust clouds from these factories. Respiratory ailments were on the rise. The three orphaned boys who were the sons of Maria's unjustly killed sister, all young men by now, had tuberculosis, as did her twenty-year-old grandson, the oldest of Yangos' four boys. Another grandson also had tuberculosis. Both of these grandchildren died.

Life had a different yet equally dramatic scenario in store for another grandson of Maria's, the son of Chrysoula's twin sister. During the Occupation, the Bulgarians sent him from his home in Psilokastro into forced labor in Koumanovo, Serbia, which they also held in occupation. He never returned. There are rumors that he joined the rebels supporting Tito and that he was killed by Croatians. I remember the suspense when I was a child as we would listen to the Greek Red Cross announcements concerning people searching for their loved ones. We sat gathered around the radio, young and old, all completely silent, in anticipation of the good news which never came. And when one day we heard that a man by the same name as my uncle was looking for his mother, whose name matched my great-aunt's? What a thrill of excitement, what wild joy, how our hearts fluttered! Until we heard the father's name, which did not correspond, and we sank back into hopelessness. It was the second time that my grandmother's twin sister had lost a child. Near the beginning of her marriage she had fallen asleep while nursing her child, and when she woke up in the morning she found it dead. She had never gotten over her feelings of guilt. Then came the disappearance of her son. What more was needed to plunge her into protracted grief?

Of all Maria Sidiropoulou's children, only her extremely withdrawn second son, Vassilis, was late in marrying. This brother of my grandmother's, by all accounts, was a model of integrity and magnanimity. He had a terrible time adjusting to a community that was so suspicious of the newcomers. His gentility found that the best way to deal with these strangers was by keeping his distance. So that his little nieces and nephews would not be hurt by the gibes of the local children, he advised them not to speak Pontian in front of them. He had even come up with the idea for two of his nephews to take on names totally foreign to the Pontus: one was «Errikos», extremely incongruous for Drapetsona, and the other «Johnny», of equally foreign extraction, in place of his given name, Isaac. Was it that Vassilis was attracted to things foreign? Absolutely not. Rather, he was deeply disappointed by what he himself had been through, and wanted to protect these little children. I remember him warning me, in his soft, throaty voice, to be careful, because «the country has been surrendered to powers higher than the dictator, Papadopoulos». This was at the very moment when events at the Athens Polytechnic were unfolding, exactly opposite his photography shop[14]. My beloved Uncle Vassilis is the prime example of those who not only never laughed, but who had withdrawn into themselves for the remainder of their lives. He seemed a total stranger to the society he was obliged to live in and which bore no relation whatever to this veritable font of nobility.

The truth is that the psychological damage done to the victims of the Pontian drama has never been studied medically. The scientific community never concerned itself with this, and the precise threshold for a nervous breakdown in such calamities was never documented. Uncle Vassilis, who because of his experience as a refugee had developed certain coping mechanisms, was a victim of permanent depression on account of his unusual degree of sensitivity. Many others were correspondingly affected. There is the case of a distant aunt who never ate meat again, because she and her sister, who afterwards lost her mind entirely, had been unable to hide their three brothers in time and the Turks had executed them before their eyes. What diagnosis would psychiatrists establish if they took an interest? Or could it be the case that even the cold, scientific eye cannot endure in the face of so much pain, so that they will never take an interest? Can a Pontian woman who would leave her child in the snow be considered sane? Or those others, who killed their own children so that their cries would not give away hundreds of other unarmed civilians? Will the ultimate torture–the struggle between the instinct for survival and doing one's duty–ever be scientifically investigated? Is anyone interested in walking on the edge of insanity in order to study such cases? Under what psychological pressure did a distant relative of mine from Kerasunta live the rest of her life, when she watched

---

14. The Athens Polytechnic uprising in 1973 was a massive demonstration of popular rejection of the Greek military junta of 1967-1974. The uprising began on November 14, 1973, escalated to an open anti-junta revolt and ended in bloodshed in the early morning of November 17 after a series of events, starting with a tank crashing through the gates of the Polytechnic university grounds. 24 people were killed.

her four sons and four brothers-in-law being slain before her very eyes? How much comfort was it to her that she gave birth to four more boys in Greece and gave them all the names of their dead brothers? The word *persecution* does not suffice to plumb the depth of this tragedy. The word *exile* does not convey the essence. The word *execution* is inadequate. Only the term *genocide* expresses the tactics which provoked so much and such a variety of total psychopathological abuse.

Yangos' indubitable ability to always have savings put aside considerably improved their living conditions. My great-grandmother Maria began to live better, as did the rest of the family. They moved to the Drapetsona town square, where the state had allotted them a plot of land, and built a trim stone house. Across from them was the dancing school of a Pontian visionary who considered it necessary for the Pontian community to assimilate western innovations.

Also nearby were the Turkish baths «The Balkans», owned by an Armenian who had created a lucrative business. This cunning entrepreneur took over the best well in Drapetsona and provided not only the pleasure of the baths, a treat which the refugees confessed to have been painfully lacking from their lives, but also hair removal services! This well, which had fallen from the Turks into the hands of the Greeks thanks to the bravery of Karaiskakis, was destined to become a business venture. From the look of things, pleasure finds cracks, even in the poorest of hovels, yet without bringing about any substantial change in the overall living conditions. For the misery of Drapetsona remained almost unchanged for quite a few years to come, despite glimpses of the good life, like the Turkish bath or the fox trot.

My great-grandmother became a widow in 1927. Isaac Sidiropoulos died of a heart attack, according to the death certificate I was able to locate. She herself died during the German Occupation, in central Athens, in a house which Yangos had rented after the 1940 bombing of Piraeus by the Italians. They had not had the chance to enjoy the newly-built house in Drapetsona for long. Yet another dream unfulfilled, and another house abandoned. In the 1960s Yangos and his family settled permanently in Rosochori (literally, Russian Village and now called

Drossia) near Athens. There, they built a house of exceptional architectural beauty which all of us relatives took pleasure in.

As for the rest of Maria Sidiropoulou's family, the siblings who had survived scattered with their children all over northern Greece, to Komotini, Drama, or Thessaloniki. There they built poor little homes, barely enough to find shelter from the rain, and they worked hard just to survive. Several of her nephews were forced to expatriate after the Civil War. This branch of my family tree is full of leftists. One by one the earth received them, laden with suffering. It would have been a blessed work, had it not received them laden with disappointment as well.

Only one of her brothers, I suppose the most independent of them all, went to Lebanon via Constantinople in 1919. He was the owner of a large kolkhoz in Russia, and when he realized that his position was not viable in the new regime, he offered to leave it to one of his siblings before he left the country.

No one accepted the offer. No one stayed behind. The kolkhoz suffered the same fate as the property and the shops in Sudak and Baipurt. This great uncle of mine died in Beirut, and only his nephew of the same name brought him vaguely to his relatives' minds. Several of his offspring went all the way to Australia, and for decades we were unaware of their existence. I must admit that my recent contact with members of these family branches, though quite difficult to achieve, was especially interesting. It brought me in touch with some very kind relatives, as well as determining the extent of our dispersal around the world. We Pontians are everywhere. Like autumn leaves that the wind has blown, we have reached the four corners of the earth.

Today Tantourlouch is practically deserted, and there is every indication that it was anything but a blessing which ousted the Greeks from their land. Thirteen residents live there in the summer, as many as the members of Trechtes' immediate family. The surrounding mountains, no longer covered by those dense old forests, continue to blossom with those humble, simple, golden flowers, the amaranth, «the tears of Holy Mary». Many, many tears.

The waters of the river where they slaughtered the Armenians continue to flow into the depths of a nearby valley, its roar now uninterrupted by the heartrending wailing that reached the ears of my great-grandmother. A part of the newly-built house they were forced to abandon in 1918 still stands today. The rest has been torn down. Of course it belongs to others now. Upon its walls, snow from Mt. Chatsar continues to fall for six months out of the year, and in their cracks the North winds still sing of dreams that never came true. Its stones, unshaken audience of laments and silent witnesses to vanity, are still there and will always be there... eternally sunken in the tranquility of the inanimate, and in the end, the only lucky ones.

The school at Tantourlouch, left, and next to it the Church of St. George, now a mosque. This is where the tsetes rounded up the women and children while they were burning the village.

The house that not a single member of the Sidiropoulos family enjoyed for long, as it is today. Its owner lives in Constantinople and rarely visits it.

The minaret that was built after 2009 beside St. George, now a mosque.

The Bolshevik delegation at Brest-Litovsk, where the treaty of the same name surrendered the indigenous people of the Pontus to the slaughter. Standing third from the left is Trotsky.

Theodosia. From this port the uprooted Pontians abandoned unstable Crimea for safer destinations.

Sudak. A place of prosperity for my emigrant ancestors.

Kerch. The ancient Milesian colony of Pantikapaion, founded 2600 year ago.

Patris. The first ship that brought the Pontian refugees from war-torn Crimea to Greece. Among them were my relatives.

The ship *Patris*, loaded with soldiers off Smyrna.

Uncle Vassilis, Maria's especially gentle
second son. His face reflects his personality.

Esther Lovejoy.

Drapetsona. The shantytown youth in a serious pose, holding glasses of wine. Most of
them are nephews of my great-grandmother's, and make up the administrative council of
the Pontian Association.

«INDOMITABLE COMRADES OF THE PONTUS, INSTRUMENTS OF FRATRICIDE IN GREECE»

CHRISTOFOROS TSACHIRIDES [1894-1957]

«Mana, na syro k' eporo aouto tin sklavian.
Tha pairo to marten 's s'omi m' ki evyaino 's 'sa rachia.»

(Mother, I cannot stand this subjugation.
I'll take my rifle on my shoulder and go to the mountains.)

Christoforos and my grandfather Thodoros were the sons of two brothers. The poor little village where they were born, Skopia[1], lay a short distance from the monastery of Panagia Soumela and, along with a few other villages, belonged to its exarchate. There the Christians of the region found not only spiritual guidance, but also education and protection. In fact, during the great persecutions, both Greeks and Armenians, rebels as well as the unarmed populace, found refuge and salvation within its well-fortified walls, just as they did elsewhere, in St. George Peristereotas[2], St. John Vazelonas, and other smaller monasteries of the area.

As they grew up, the two cousins felt constrained in their village. Poverty on the one side and the risk of being conscripted by the Turkish army on the other compelled them to leave. When Christoforos was 18 years old he went to Constantinople. After a short while Thodoros would take the same road.

Emigration was not an easy matter in their part of the world. There were few means of transport and a great part of the journey had to be covered on foot. The husband, brother, or son who had left would not return home for about two years. Besides Constantinople, many of the young chose to emigrate to czarist Russia, where the opportunities for

---

1. Skopia belonged to the district of Matsouka (now Macka), which was situated on the Teheran-Trabzon trade route and was an important stopping place on the Silk Road to Europe. Up until 1923 the district consisted of 70 villages, 47 of which were inhabited by all-Greek populations. The biggest Greek Orthodox monasteries were located in the Matsouka region.

2. The ruins of the monastery of St. George Peristereotas are located in the district of Macka. Originally founded in 752 AD, it was finally closed on January 17, 1923, when the monks were expelled to Greece, along with the general population.

work were ample, the profits substantial, and the conduct of the local people friendly. They emigrated in small groups of at least two. When the day came for parting, however, their courage diminished. Support was needed not only by those who were departing but also by those who would be awaiting their return. The atmosphere was laden with the painful awareness that there would be no one nearby to care for them when tough times came–and they were sure to come. «In foreign lands I have been taken ill and in a bed I lie. A thousand doctors are looking after me, but none are like my mother,»[3] was one of the verses the people would sing.

It had become standard practice for large groups to see off those who were departing. Friends and relatives were all there, lending the event dimensions that today are hard to comprehend. For those times, however, the whole procedure was completely justified. Those who were leaving were undoubtedly troubled by the likelihood that on their return they might not find some of those they left behind. On the other hand, those who remained, basically simple peasants, were also disturbed by the potential hazards of emigration. Could they possibly fathom how big the countries beyond the mountains were? Could they imagine the huge streets, the many-storied houses, and the crowded markets of the cities? Surely not. Whole generations had lived and died, isolated in the majestic mountain cloister of the Pontus, without any idea of the vastness of the world.

All together they would walk from the village until they reached the main road, where the caravans passed through. The procession of villagers sang songs of emigration, to the sorrowful accompaniment of the Pontian lyre, often with the *angeio*[4] as well. Rarely does one find in folk music an instrument which expresses heartfelt sorrow so perfectly as the lyre, as the horsetail hair bow slides over that simple contrivance made from the wood

---

3. *« 'S sin ksenitian errostesa kai 's sa krevata keimai. Chilioi yiatroi teroune me, amon ti mana m' 'k' einai.»*

4. The Pontian instruments are: the Pontian lyre; the *taoul* (drum); the *zournas* (a reed instrument descended from the ancient oboe); the *angeio* (the ancient bagpipe); and the *cheilavr'* (the fife, known in antiquity as the *cheiliavlos*).

of a plum tree. Joyous Pontian songs do abound, but the ultimate destination of the lyre's plaintive sound seems to be the pain of the human psyche. Crying and blessing each other, they would separate. The women–mothers, wives, daughters–and the elderly parents and grandparents would return to their homes, while the emigrants would head for the unknown. True, many of them were not leaving for the first time. Yet their future, too, was unknown, compared to the thoroughly predictable life in Skopia.

Uncle Christoforos worked in Constantinople, at the tinsmith shop owned by his father and his uncle, my great-grandfather. But people from Matsouka were not known for their mild natures; the *meizeteroi*[5] were tough and demanding of him, and it was not long before he left for Russia with a friend of his. He worked for some years there for a *baksevanes*[6], who almost became his father-in-law. But he did not settle down.

It was four years later when he retraced his steps back to the the village. He'd gone away a young lad and returned a man. His dynamic grandmother had already decided that there was no better-suited bride for him than a young neighbor of theirs, the lovely Anna, who thus became his wife. Soon she made him a father, bearing him a son. With her, he experienced complete happiness for some months. He literally worshiped her.

Then he lost her to an epidemic of *gourzoula*[7], which once again struck the Pontian mountain villages. The people would shiver in fear when a yellow bird, the harbinger of calamity, appeared in their parts. They knew death would follow. Along with Anna, on the very day and by the same cause, he lost his only brother. Uncle Christoforos had wrestled with death as well, but though he came out the winner in his own battle, he was like a wounded beast. Still weak, he ran up to a mountain peak to grieve and moan. His wailing tore the air and the echo could be heard as far as the village: «Annaaaaaaaa!» He was left with the child of the love he would never get over.

---

5. The older ones. *Meizeteros* is the Pontian form of *meizon*, which is the comparative degree of the ancient Greek adjective *megas* («big», in this case with reference to age).

6. Turkish for a vegetable farmer.

7. The plague.

He later married Anasta, who was considered an old maid at the time, though only 24 years old. The fact that she knew how to read and write may have been daunting to prospective grooms. Or she may have had a condescending air, though not without reason. She was the daughter of Giorgos Mylonides, a teacher who served five villages in their region, and the granddaughter of a wrongfully killed elder of the Panagia Soumela monastery, who died an unsung death after being struck by a stone during an attack by bandits. Even more impressive, however, on her mother's side she was the niece of the well-known hieromonk Jeremiah (born Giorgos Tsarides). Living in destitution with her five fatherless children, his widowed mother had entrusted him, then 10 years old and the youngest, to the care of the Soumela monastery monks. The boy was brought up and educated by them, and he never left the monastery. Instead he became a hieromonk, a lifelong worker in poverty and obedience. After forty years of life at the monastery, he had become the very personification of its history in the last decades before the Catastrophe.

More than once he had been threatened to death during lootings of the monastery by Turkish outlaws. Three times they hung him over the steep rocks in order to terrify him into surrendering money and valuables, but he remained steadfast and did not reveal a thing. When the Turks commenced their slaughter of the indigenous peoples, initially the Armenians, Jeremiah and the other monks hid and protected the victims. He knew well of persecutions, and of treachery regarding lives and property. During WWI, not even a blanket was left in the monastery. They emptied it of everything, even the livestock and foodstuffs, in order to meet the needs of the Turkish hospitals. In April 1916, all the monks of the monastery took refuge in nearby Russian-ruled Livera[8]. Eventually, after appalling travails, Jeremiah found his way to Greece by way of Trapezunta. By then he was in rags. His monastery had been plundered. The crystal jewels from the church's chandeliers were used to make necklaces

---

8. A village in the district of Matsouka with 1,500 Christians and 500 Muslims until the beginning of the 20th century.

which were hung around the necks of cows, while Christ's sepulcher was used to make saddles, an indication of the intellectual and cultural level of the gangs involved. These were things that Jeremiah was sure to have cleaned and cared for with his own hands, yet he could not save them.

He and two fellow ascetics, however, had seen to it that the miraculous icon of Our Lady and a few other religious treasures were carefully hidden in St. Barbara's annex, which was relatively near the monastery. If he had not been suffering so badly from acute kidney disease, and so near his end, he would have been part of the delegation which in 1931 officially reclaimed these treasures and brought them to Greece. He was the only one still alive who knew their hiding place, and they were found according to the directions he gave. If the whole procedure had been delayed by a year, Pontian Hellenism might have lost its most cherished icon, because Jeremiah died some months later.

In 1932 he was serving as a priest at a church only a short distance from Thessaloniki, when a 7.0 Richter earthquake hit Ierissos, Halkidiki, resulting in 161 deaths. During a strong aftershock which occurred while he was reading the gospel to the congregation, everyone dashed out in panic. The walls were badly jarred and looked as though they would collapse into pieces, like those that covered all of Ierissos. Father Jeremiah continued reading, unperturbed. When the liturgy was over, they were all astonished to find that the church had moved so much that the sanctuary was now facing south instead of its original eastward direction.

Jeremiah drew his last breath at the age of 55, in one of the tents put up for the earthquake victims. I hardly consider myself worthy to remark, unless it be to note that the spiritual wealth of the Pontian monastic community was yet another victim of the cultural genocide we suffered. I do not know if Anasta was worthy of such an uncle, no matter how often she would proudly declare whose niece she was, especially when she felt she was the object of unfair treatment. Living as she did in the shadow of the deceased Anna, she probably said it often.

At the time that Uncle Christoforos was conscripted by the army, his second child had already been born, a girl he named after his first wife, whom he could not forget. With two children now, one from each marriage, and no one to protect his wife and parents in the village, he was sent to the *Amele Tampourou*. He was going to learn firsthand of that martyrdom which was specially designed for the ethnic Greeks. It was not long before he discovered for himself that the battalions had been created to exterminate them. They broke rocks from morning till night, starving and exhausted. Not only were the snows, rains and winds *not* a reason to change their schedule, but rather, they presented all the more reason to be constantly out in the open. According to an official telegram that has been preserved, the administrator at Argana ordered that the Greeks be forced to work under the worst weather conditions; otherwise «it is impossible to achieve our purpose»[9]. He was compelled to escape.

After a breathing spell he showed up again, when amnesty was being granted to draft-dodgers. Was it because he thought he would be given money, shoes and clothes again? Was it because he couldn't stand hiding out in the woods anymore? Or was it because the authorities were abusing his family? It could have been one of these reasons or it could have been all of them. He escaped again, but was eventually arrested and then sent to Erzerum.

The people sang about the adventure of exile in that particular place in this way:
«On the ridges and on the mountains and in the cities,
many Greeks were lost far away in exile.
Oh, what has become of our Santian neighbors?
They have filled graves in Erzerum's plains.»[10]

---

9. Written order from the chief engineer of municipal construction, Omer, to the commander of labor battalions at Argana Maden, foreman supervisor Loufti bey: «We were informed that the traitors of our country, Greek soldiers, do not work whenever it rains. Because, on the one hand, the pay office is being charged on a daily basis for 860gr of wheat and, on the other hand, we are unable to achieve our purpose, we instruct that from now on the soldiers are to be sent to work in rain and snow, without any exception» (Antonios Gavrielides, *Pages from the Black National Disaster of Pontus*, p. 224).

10. *'S sa rachia kai 's sa vouna ki apes' 's sa politeias / polloi Romaioi echathane makra 's sa eksorias. / Nt' eyentane kai oi Santet' t' emon oi yeitonades? / Atein' taphia egomosan t' Erzeroumi ta ovades.*

Uncle Christoforos drew strength from a type of phylactery given to him by Jeremiah and which he wore near his chest.

It was a small, triangular piece of cloth, inside which was sewn a carefully folded, relatively large paper on which were blessings and prayers, beautifully handwritten by Jeremiah himself. The torture was incessant, however, and despite his efforts to be strong, he could not endure it. He escaped again. He hid in the towering mountains of the surrounding area and started on his way back, walking only at night. He assuaged his hunger by eating wild greens and slept wherever he found a spot. If he were caught, he would certainly be hanged.

Once he came face to face with an armed Turk in the forest. He pretended to be a fellow Turk but could not pull it off, as he had the appearance of a draft-dodger. The Turk told him to prepare to die. The only thing he considered necessary was to satisfy his captive's hunger before he killed him. He gave him food and my uncle started to eat, with a pistol to his head. Why would the Turk have cared to fill his stomach? Was it a religious commandment, or perhaps an effort to give the ruthless murder a human visage? Nobody really knows. My uncle began with difficulty to swallow the morsels of horror, each one bringing him closer to death. Their end would be his end, too.

The first time the Turk pulled the trigger, the gun did not go off. The same thing happened a second and a third time. Then the unheard of happened: this freakish persecutor fell to his knees and, raising his hands to heaven, begged forgiveness from God. And in order to avert an avalanche of bad luck incurred by the strange event, he gave my uncle provisions and steered him clear of dangerous areas, pointing the way to safety in the Greek villages in the distance. Instead of losing his life to the Turk's fierce fanaticism, my uncle was spared by his superstition. He always said, though, that he owed his salvation to the holy phylactery from Jeremiah.

When he eventually arrived in Matsouka, he immediately enlisted in the rebel forces headed by Aristeides Petrides, renowned for his bravery among Greeks and Turks alike. There was an ancient dance called «The Duel», introduced to them centuries before by The Myriad, the ten-thousand-strong Persian army whom the Greeks had hosted near Kerasunta. In this dance, the male dancers threw their two-edged knives high into the air and caught the blade with their bare hands. Petrides always insisted on catching it in his teeth.

The presence of Petrides' men surrounding the villages of the area meant protection for the unarmed, namely, the women, children, and the remaining elderly. Not a single young man was left at home. My uncle was an excellent marksman, and his enlistment added to the effectiveness of the rebel band. Once, when Aristeides was about to free his brother, who was being led to prison, he asked Christoforos Tsachirides to be by his side along with three other men. After the first few shots, the Turks ran for their lives and the prisoner was freed.

Soon afterwards Uncle Christoforos joined the Santa[11] rebels of Captain Eucleides Kourtides[12], a band of 141 men renowned for its heroic feats, and the last to give up the fight in 1924. For seven whole years, Eucleides was a living terror to the Turks. Government schemes for his assassination came one after the other and both the army and its lawless followers were on full alert against him. His foresight and adept organizational skills saved the unarmed civilians, as well as his own group of men, from starvation and death on numerous occasions. Like the majority of the Pontian rebel captains, he saw to it that the unarmed masses had their share of food first, then his own men, and he himself would eat last of all. Very often their meal consisted only of *pileki*, a mixture of flour and water baked on a heated stone. They sometimes even had to eat bear, cut off as they were from everyone and everything.

When it was decided that the Turk Isein, the ruthless murderer of the Pontian Greeks, had to be punished for his atrocities against the Chris-

---

11. A total of 7 Greek villages in the district of Argyroupoli, first settled in the 16th century. With the 1918 departure of Russian troops, they were attacked by tsetes and in order to defend themselves, armed groups were formed. It was their self- sacrifice that kept the region from being conquered until 1921, when deportations of civilians and rebels began. The Santian rebels were the last to abandon their land for Greece in 1924.

12. Eucleides Kourtides was born in Santa of the Pontus in 1885 and died in Nea Santa, Kilkis (Greece) in 1937. He became one of the most famous freedom fighters in the region of Santa and the entire Pontus, influencing a generation of men who have now become a legend.

tian women of Matsouka, the cold-blooded murders, and the unbearable taxation he imposed on the villages, Eucleides laid his plan: Uncle Christoforos and Konstantinos Kourtides, the captain's brother, would lie in wait for him near a small country inn. Aristeides agreed to lend a hand in the attack. They killed Isein at daybreak, as he was returning from the village of Hortokop where he had gone to collect taxes. One more merciless criminal would no longer prey on the region. The song recounting the rebels' feat could be heard till fairly recently at Pontian gatherings in the village of Komnena in Ptolemaida, Greece:

«The handsome Kourtides with his gun killed Isein by the little inn.»[13]

Nor did the folk muse leave unsung the bravery of Eucleides:
«Sapan Mousa, Seit agas and Kalfas from Yemoura
were terrified when they heard the name Eucleides the Santian.»[14]

Those tsetes mentioned in the verse, who had sworn to wipe out the ethnic Greeks, were constantly confronted by the bold Eucleides, determined to hold Pontian Hellenism erect at any sacrifice. He struggled until the end. After his death, in New Santa in Kilkis, a comrade of his wrote another song: «Seven years with the rebel forces in the mountains of Santa, seven years he tyrannized Turkish souls, eh, poor captain,»[15] is just a part of the whole.

The rebels fought under unequal conditions. Against the Turks' cannons, machine guns, sub-machine guns and plentiful supply of hand grenades and bullets, they had very few guns and ammunition, which they used frugally. Despite the terrible lack of weaponry, though, they managed to protect many villages and their residents all the way up to 1924. Most of

---

13. *O giosmas o Kiourtogles me to tyfekopon eskotose ton Isein afka so tikienopon.*
14. *Sapan Mousa, Seit agas, Kalfas o Yiomouretes / etromazan pou akougan Eucleides o Santetes.*
15. *...Ephta chrona 's 's'antartika 's si Santas ta rachia, ephta chrona turannize ta tourkika ta psua, e, mavren kapetane...*

them were excellent marksmen. A certain exaggeration in the memoirs of one of the rebels is indicative of their ability. According to a fighter from Samsunta, Demosthenes Kelekides: «They were able to shoot a bullet through a finger ring from a thousand meters away! They hit their mark because, during peaceful times, they used to make that kind of bet.»

In the diary of Eucleides' comrade and brother, Konstantinos Kourtides, Uncle Christoforos is referred to as «Tsiahur». Also mentioned in his diary is the decapitation of two rebels behind his house in Skopia, along with the fact that this little village kept supplying the rebels with food and ammunition. While the Skopians lived on a starvation diet consisting strictly of greens and potatoes for months on end, since their livestock and meager produce had been seized by the Turks, they also found a way to support the freedom fighters, as well as the crowd of unarmed civilians who often followed them.

The history of the rebel army of Santa is full of heroic feats, but also of extreme desperation. The Turkish army and its fanatic, unenlisted followers launched continual attacks against the seven Santian villages. They used the wives and children of the rebels as beasts of burden, to carry the very weapons that would be used against their husbands and fathers. The uttermost limit of desperation which they faced was during the events at Mertzan Lithar. There the rebels were forced to kill seven babies whose wailing would betray their presence! Hundreds of residents of the Santian villages had taken refuge in their hideout. The Turkish army was very close by and the tiniest noise would bring catastrophe upon them. Frozen with fear, they did not make a sound. Their babies, though? What about their babies? They did not even have water to quench their thirst. The panic-stricken mothers tried to quieten them by putting their own spit in the mouths of the thirsty babies, but it was futile. The order came to kill them. A Turkish divisional commander later declared with disgust that people who reach such an extreme cannot be beaten, and he withdrew his forces. He was spouting wisdom from his safe corner, of course. It would have been more honest if he had admitted that those angelic souls were victims of the merciless slaughter which his own people had launched against our race. This is what justice demands from the perpetrators of such terror.

This case of infanticide must be judged in the light of the great like-lihood that hundreds of other unarmed civilians would otherwise have been slaughtered. Only in this way does the abhorrent side of its charac-ter recede and the essential one emerge, which is, exclusively, the tragic.

A similar trial was experienced by the hapless mother of Makrygiannis[16] about one hundred years earlier, which, fortunately for Greece, had a dif-ferent outcome. Again there was danger from the Turks, and the wailing of the newborn Makrygiannis could have brought death to the rest. His mother took him and left, but in the end the baby did not cry and they were saved. With many such tortuous trials have we paid for our baneful proximity to this hostile power.

Demosthenes Kelekides writes in his memoirs about the tragic aspects of rebel life: «Do you know what it is, after a battle, to be sitting on a fallen tree trunk, one man crying over his wife, another crying over the fallen corpses? Their vision blurred because they've "drunk blood"? The wire on the captains' hats shining in the sun? And all that they put aside, because some blind old man takes up the lyre and they begin to cry, remembering what they've been through.

»The infants, the lakes, the drowned babies, who floated on the water like mushrooms, and the mother, with her broken heart, unable to utter a sound, unable to cry. To be surrounded by the enemy, and the women to be cooking, with their children hanging on to their sides.

»At night, the moon beating down. The captains held in their hands the lands that had been granted them by birth, and they had become as light as a feather; for they had been praying and were no longer them-selves; they had committed themselves into God's hands. True, in Mess-

---

16. (1797-1864) A distinguished military officer active during the Greek War of Indepen-dence and later an indefatigable politician, who fought for the constitutional rights of the people. He was one of the three leaders of the September 3, 1843 Revolution against the king, which led to the granting of the first constitution. He is best known for his *Memoirs*.

olonghi[17] there had taken place a sudden advance, in the hope that if they broke through the line, they would reach the plains and would be united with their free brothers and would live, but us? What line was there for us to break through? We were blocked by all the nations. There was no road. There was no salvation to come from anywhere. In the European war, in which Russia protected us, we seized ships and boats and went and told them our pain and they sent reinforcements.

»Now, as we gazed searchingly at the sea, remembering the past, it seemed as if even the sea was capable of irony. Now it was wilder, more eager, calling to us: 'Jump in and I'll drown you!' Others, who looked at the mountains and the gorges, saw them as fierce, as if they no longer wanted to receive us, because we were a cursed people! To such an extent had we been isolated on all sides by humanity, and even by the elements of nature! The lyre of the lyrist thrummed against our aching souls, and his hoarse voice pierced us, as if even his vitals themselves had cracked, as if everything was finished.»[18]

Words cannot suffice when trying to chronicle the tortures of the Pontian Greeks. The eye-witness accounts of abuse of every kind are countless. Thousands were slaughtered. And as for the survivors? Every living breath they drew was paid for with great struggle, deprivation, and, all too often, the despair which led to derangement. There is no torment for a woman that the Greek women of the Pontus did not endure. There is no torture against the old that the aged Greeks of the Pontus did not suffer. There is no emotional or physical child abuse that the Greek children of the Pontus did not experience.

Our holocaust is still downplayed by the Greek government. Despite its official recognition in 1994, the state has taken a hostile stance toward

---

17. A town in southwestern Greece, known as the site of a dramatic siege during the Greek War of Independence. Kelekides refers to the desperate attempt on the part of the soldiers and townspeople to break through the siege forces and gain their freedom. The famous British poet and philhellene Lord Byron, who supported the Greek struggle for independence, died in Messolonghi in 1824.

18. Demosthenes Kelekides, *To Antartiko* in *To Antartiko tou Pontou*, Gordios, Athens 2006.

the Pontian issue. The heroic resistance of the rebel captains of that period has yet to be recognized. One by one they died in the places of their resettlement, without being given the slightest compensation.

The rebel associations which were founded in Drama and Kavala, with presidents Istyl aga (Stylianos Kosmides)[19] and Pantel aga (Pantelis Anastasiades) respectively, broke up without achieving even the minimal moral vindication which these dauntless fighters deserved. During the Bulgarian occupation, the government registers of the rebel members who lived in Drama and the photographs of them wearing *zipkes*[20] were exploited to more easily arrest and execute them in the central square. Valorous and dutiful Pontians, they died unrecognized, though they were of the same mettle as Kolokotrones[21] and Katsantones[22].

Santa of the Pontus ceased to exist in 1921, after four and a half centuries. They burned all its seven villages. They looted, raped, killed. The approximately 2,000 women and children who survived were exiled to Erzerum.

With the so-called population exchange of 1923, Uncle Christoforos came down from the mountains. He found the village of Skopia utterly plundered. Not a soul was to be seen. He left the ruins of the village behind, shouldering the burden of his ravaged past, and moved on. He headed for the parish of Daphnunta in Trapezunta, in whose schools and churches could be found the former residents of the Matsouka district. They were forbidden to enter the city.

His family was there. Disguised in women's clothing, his moustache covered by a scarf as he could not bring himself to shave it, he finally made it to them: Anasta, his parents, and his children, who by now were three. In the midst of turmoil and violence, nature continued to demand

---

19. Born in 1886 in the village Kovtsapogar, near Samsunta, he was the rebel leader in the Agiou-Tepe area. He died in Drama, Greece in 1940.
20. Distinctive, form-fitting, Pontian soldier's outfit.
21. A valiant Greek general and a great leader in the 1821 insurrection against the Turks.
22. A famous Greek klepht, who fought against Ali pasha of Ioannina.

her due share, and one more little girl had come into the world. In a short time, they boarded a ship for Greece. The Turks had already killed Anasta's father, by the bridge of the Zygana River, as he stepped out from the file of exiles he was in to drink some water. The armed guards had forbidden them to approach the river, which flowed so tantalizingly beside them. That is how yet another tyrannized Greek of the Pontus lost his life: at the moment when his unbearable thirst would have been quenched with a little coolness.

Anestes Papadopoulos writes in his book *Memories and Longings of our Pontus*: «The country teacher Giorgos Mylonides from Agourzenon, unable to bear his thirst any longer, dashed to the river, but a tirade of shots killed him on the spot.» As if widowhood had not been enough, or the loss of his four sons to the plague, there came exile and this senseless death. Would it serve any purpose to remark that even the snake is respected while it quenches its thirst, or to draw other similar comparisons? A thousand times no. For shame, respect, and basic human decency had long lost their meaning. Supreme evil had been unleashed on the world, unbridled, brash and catastrophic.

When my own relatives, on their voyage from Oinoe to Constantinople, were forced to lock up the Turkish crew who had been planning to attack them, they shared with them whatever little water they had left. They knew they were not going to find any more while at sea and their own mouths were parched with thirst. Nonetheless, they could not find it within themselves to deprive even their enemy of water. We may not always feel proud of being Greek. But we are those same people who, no matter how dire our condition was, did share what little water we had with those who brought us to that state and who have themselves actually used thirst, among many other means, to eradicate us.

As soon as they boarded the ship, Anasta's hair had to be cut off for reasons of hygiene. She fought, she begged, but to no avail. Pleading over so trivial an issue may sound absurd amidst such great bitterness, though long hair was a basic criterion of beauty for Pontian women, and the violent cutting of it amounted to an act of humiliation. For such tortured souls, however, even one tiny drop of further humiliation could bring on torrents of grief. No doubt she was aware that numberless other Greek women had suffered much worse. But gazing at her long braids floating on the sea as their ship was sailing away, she was overcome with emotion and cried mournfully; all her losses and violent separations, all the uprooting and cruelties, became intertwined into one. Unconsciously, her hair had become her homeland.

Upon their arrival in Piraeus, Uncle Christoforos's mother, Sophia Tsachiridou, died and her body was thrown into the ship's boilers. They disembarked at the quarantine station on the island of St. George. Three-year-old Anna died there, while the newborn survived because she was feeding solely on mother's milk and did not get infected. Uncle Christoforos could not get over his first wife's death. He later gave her name to three little girls he became godfather to, but none of them survived. When one died, he would name another one Anna. That one would die too, only for a third Anna to take her place, also short lived. A tragic obsession, but Christoforos Tsachirides was not destined to have an Anna by his side.

There is, of course, a more subtle issue here, which has to do with Anasta. How did she cope with the presence of that idealized shadow of his first wife in her life? How did she handle her irrevocably inconsolable husband? Did her harsh daily reality leave room for such emotional demands? In all likelihood, it did not.

After a brief stay near Piraeus, they left for the mountain villages of Kozani[23]. Along with refugees from Matsouka and various other Pontian areas, they founded the village of Komnena, near Ptolemaida. Thus, the glory of the Pontian dynasty of the Komnenoi became a counterweight, at least in name, to restore their wounded pride.

Uncle Christoforos never found mountains like the mountains of the Pontus, because they are not easily found elsewhere. But he did breathe the fresh air of Mount Vermio, and was at least partially consoled. These mountain pastures, where he would herd his flocks in the summer, revived in his memory the Pontian *parcharia* and, with the passage

---

23. A prefecture in northern Greece, located in the western part of Macedonia, in the northern section of the Aliakmonas River valley.

of time, he slowly adjusted. There were difficulties and deprivation, of course, but they were all used to that from their life of poverty in Skopia.

More children were born. The last one, a little boy, died in 1934 at a very young age. They endured this, too. But in 1937, the blow that struck was like a nightmare. Two of Uncle Christoforos's children died of tuberculosis: his firstborn son, aged 24, the only child he had from his first wife, and within six months one of his daughters, at the age of 17. Thus, of the nine children he had in all, he was left with five.

During the German occupation, Christoforos Tsachirides and his two older sons enlisted and fought with the Greek People's Liberation Army (ELAS). Though his son Yannis was barely 16 years old, he took part in a total of 72 battles against the invaders. He was with captains Stathes and Katsones. Once, risking his life, he was the first and only soldier to climb onto a train carrying the First Division of the Mountain Rangers of Wehrmacht to Germany. In August 1944, at Moucharem Khan, in Arnissa, three ELAS battalions blew up the track, and the entire train, with its 28 cars and two engines, was immobilized. A fierce battle ensued. There were dozens of hostages and several casualties. The large baskets that local farmers had intended to use for their grape harvests were filled with the medical supplies that had been confiscated from the Germans and were sent to the free Greek territories.

Many times the resistance against the occupation forces was borne on the backs of the Pontians. There were dozens of Pontians who either fell in battle or were executed. Austere marble slabs at the memorial sites of Macedonia are full of surnames ending in the suffix -ides. The Albanian offensive and the massacre by Nazi troops at Messovouno of Kozani (the first village of northwestern Greece in which the Pontian residents set up a resistance force) are typical examples of Pontians giving their lives for their country.

After the withdrawal of the occupying forces in 1944, Yannis's battalion made the unbelievably harsh trek from the mountains of Kaimaktsalan, in northern Greece, to Mount Penteli, outside Athens. They crossed Vitsi, Askio, Chasia, Antichasia...

Yannis was barefoot, like most of his comrades. When they reached Karaouli, facing Athens, they set up their machine-guns and awaited orders. Spreading before their eyes and boiling like a cauldron was the basin of Attica, the place where they expected the great social change to take place. At last, their struggles would be rewarded. Yannis's uncle, my grandfather Thodoros, who lived in Melissia just a few meters down the hill, was busy constructing street barricades, little knowing that his young nephew was so nearby. Both at the peak and at the foot of the mountain, two relatives waited in coordinated readiness for action—entirely in vain, as it proved.

When Yannis and the ELAS fighters received the order to lay down their arms and return to Macedonia, they felt vastly betrayed. As they turned back, Yannis was sobbing. Why had he fought? The reversal that the resistance fighters had planned was being reversed, and just a few days later, the Treaty of Varkiza sealed their fate (see Chapter 6, footnote 7). Matters had been decided. Indeed, regardless of the varying opinions which have been expressed repeatedly since then, one thing is certain: the disillusionment suffered during that period reached the ultimate limit of genuine tragedy.

Fierce persecutions followed. The victims were the resistance fighters of the Left and their families. The German collaborators now became the official assessors of patriotism, resorting to raw violence and terrorizing the people in order to avoid the consequences of their betrayal. These latter-day patriots turned against all those who had mortgaged their youth in the war against the German occupation.

Uncle Christoforos and his two sons were subjected to frequent humiliation, attacks, threats, the phalange[24] and other ruthless beatings. In Komnena, as in the rest of the country, accounts were being squared and alibis constructed. After brief detention in the jail at Ptolemaida, where Uncle Christoforos escaped certain death from intense beating only by the intervention of a Pontian acquaintance, they returned to the village. The same acquaintance sent warning the next day that they

---

24. Being tied down and having the soles of their feet beaten mercilessly.

would be coming to arrest them again. They were forced to hide in the mountains that very day. These were times of horror, which demanded that a man join either the one side or the other.

The subsequent political climate and the emergence of either equivocal figures or sheer traitors in the role of governance, as up against the enticement offered by the communist vision of a just society, brought about the second resistance movement. Of course they were influenced by ideology, but their life in the village had become unbearable.

Yannis was arrested and sent to prison in Veroia. He was later sent into exile in Yioura and from there he was conscripted and sent to fight at Grammos. Still loyal to his convictions, he deserted and joined the resistance army again. At the end of the Civil War he was forced to leave the country, as he was in the camp of the defeated. He wound up in Taskend[25], where he married a Greek girl who had been there since she was 15 years old. She had been arrested by leftist rebels while she was tending her flock of sheep, and ended up in the Soviet Union. They returned to Greece together in 1957, but they did not stay. Poverty and deprivation forced them to emigrate, first to Germany, which was a pole of attraction for workers in the industrial sector, then Australia, where Uncle Christoforos's youngest daughter lived and was married, and finally the U.S. They did not put down roots anywhere, unlike their two children, who still live outside New York to this day. Eventually they came back, and now live in Komnena.

In answer to the question I recently posed as to whether his struggle was worth it, Uncle Yannis replied: «With such a heart, would I have stayed in the village?»[26] He never condescended to accept a pension for his role in what is now referred to as the National Resistance, saying: «I didn't fight for money or for certificates.»[27] My uncle is a true *leventis*[28]. I do not share all his beliefs, nor do I expect victories by the people, and

---

25. Then a city the Soviet Union, now the capital of Uzbekistan.

26. *«M'aeikon kardia tha esteka apes''s so xorion?»*

27. *«Ego 'k' epolemisa gia ta paradas kai ta chartia.»*

28. Brave, proud and manly all in one.

I certainly would never have done most of what he did. I do believe, though, that these days it is rare to encounter such a dignified warrior.

Uncle Christoforos's other son, Giorgos, who had also fought the occupation forces from the ranks of the Greek People's Liberation Army and was cruelly persecuted upon the liberation of Greece, chose to take refuge in the mountains. After the Civil War ended, he crossed into Albania. Conditions there, however, were anything but a socialist paradise: hunger, mistreatment, imprisonment, torture, executions. When he organized a protest with the men who were in the same encampment as he was, they put him in prison. There, he suggested sharing their meager rations with the starving Albanians. In fact, one time they improvised a slide out of a large sheet of metal and threw bean soup down it, into the courtyard outside, where the hungry ones were. This move was considered suspicious and he was sent to do forced labor. He dug ditches and built roads. The beatings were endless. A man who shared a cell with Giorgos for eight years, later had this to say about him: his persistent refusal to work on the Albanian airport, which was under construction at the time, had resulted in extreme corporal punishment. They hit him everywhere–on the back, the legs, the arms, the head. A tumor he developed in his cerebellum was a reminder of that time.

Giorgos remained in Albania for eight years, forgotten. His Greek relatives believed him dead. When he was accidentally discovered by U.N. inspectors, unrecognizable on account of the years of torture, and returned to Greece, he was court-martialed.

I myself witnessed the drawn-out legal battle which he fought. At the time, he was staying at my grandmother Chrysoula's house, where his legal proceedings were the subject of discussion day and night. I still remember my good-natured, conservative father, Savvas, showing his wife's cousin support in a most moving manner, despite their major political differences. At the end of his trial, Giorgos thanked his judges, who, to his good fortune, were able to discern that the defendant was a victim of circumstance rather than a traitor.

His words were: «Thank you for the golden road you have opened up for me.» His poor family became all the poorer after shouldering the legal expenses, but Giorgos was saved. Some time later he had an operation and had the tumor removed from his brain. In time he married, had children, emigrated to Australia, and several years later returned to Komnena. He died at age 55 from a new brain tumor in the same spot, a further remnant of the companionable hospitality he enjoyed in Albania.

Uncle Christoforos's youngest daughter was not able to go to teacher's college in Greece. She had finished high school in his absence, making great sacrifices along the way, but still was not able to procure the necessary legal certificate identifying her political affiliations. With few other options, toward the end of the 1950s she left for Australia. That country was looking for workers and housemaids. The only items in her suitcase were a pair of shoes, a dress and a comforter–nothing else. She married a Pontian, whom she knew only from a photograph, and she still lives in Australia with her children and grandchildren.

Uncle Christoforos's youngest son also emigrated to Australia and later on to the U.S., where he lives with his family today. Growing up in the midst of hunger and fear, he had become the only «man of the house» at a very young age.

Uncle Christoforos's other daughter, the baby who had survived death in exile because she happened to be breastfeeding at the time, married, had children, and emigrated like the others. She worked for years in the factories of America and retired there. She died recently and was buried on the outskirts of New York, where her children and grandchildren live permanently.

Anasta ended her turbulent life in Komnena at a ripe old age, near Giorgos's widow and children. She had suffered many sorrows. A number of non-Pontian villagers, former German collaborators and then fervent nationalists, did not miss an opportunity to taunt that tormented soul.

Uncle Christoforos himself escaped to Hungary after the Civil War, where he died eight years later. The fateful year 1957 found one of his sons returning to Greece from the U.S.S.R., another who had been thought dead, discovered alive and on his way back from Albania, and the father departing from this life in the aftermath of surgical intervention, ill, alone, and desolate. In the hospital bed next to him, a patient was eating yoghurt. He longed for some, but his request was denied. His last wish was not granted, and no relatives were by his side. His son Yannis, who had not left Taskend yet, was not allowed to take him to live with him, in spite of his persistent efforts. There had been no place for his father in this world.

Paradoxically, both the son and the brother of Captain Eucleides, the rebel chief of the Santa mountains, were killed fighting on the side of the Greek national army, against the resistance forces that Uncle Christoforos and his sons had enlisted with during the Civil War. The indomitable comrades of the Pontus had become instruments in the fratricides in Greece.

At first glance, this strange turn of events seems unrelated to the persecutions of the Greeks in the Pontus. How could the past play a role in determining their decisions so many years later, in a different land and under different conditions? A deeper look into the events, however, obliges us to admit that life experience, as the foundation of character, played a decisive role. They had suffered persecution through no wrong of their own. They had lost their fortunes, their homes, and above all their families, their own people. They became experts in armed combat. Arriving in Greece, physical and emotional wrecks, they were received with suspicion and, all too often, outright hostility–anything but a brotherly welcome. They met with deprivation and illness, war and conflict. The wrong done to them was never righted, and each of them searched for justice in a different place.

Also curious is the fact that people who had known the living Christian tradition in the monasteries of the Pontus later fought on the side which adhered to ideals thoroughly hostile toward faith, but that constitutes yet another tragic chapter in the Pontian genocide and its eventual consequences. They were consumed, mind and soul, by a burning desire for justice. True, many did not dare give voice to it. The feistier ones, however, became actively involved. Besides, the socialist experiment had begun in Russia, a country they knew well and felt akin to, and it promised a perfect world. For this reason many of them, instead of waiting for retribution in the hereafter, opted for a radical redistribution in this life.

The challenging question of whether the evolution of Uncle Christoforos's family did justice to his struggles has no easy answer. It might be easy to say no, but the incessant changing of right to wrong confounds the criteria and disorients us. Nowadays, the boundary between genuine patriotic struggle and raw intervention under a patriotic façade is hazy, and the concept of sacrifice is obsolete.

And yet, could the dispersion of Uncle Christoforos's children and grandchildren all over the world, the repeated emigrations and the long search for a place to settle down, have as a deeper cause the search for their lost homeland? Is the search for work and financial security sufficient to justify such mobility? Spread over three continents today, they have each found their haven; the younger ones, especially, feel that that is home. What could they understand and why should they care about places they never lived in, or about persecutions they could never imagine, even in their worst nightmares? No matter how Greek they may be, what could a distant grandfather of the previous century possibly mean to them?

In the late 1950s, Christoforos Tsachirides fought his greatest fight in the Yannos Korchas Hospital in Hungary. He had always done what he considered to be his duty. He was never a coward and he never submitted. In the middle of Europe, far from the Pontus and far from Greece, irrevocably expatriated, exhausted and a victim of injustice, it remained for him to show his courage and bravery one last time: to deal with his own end in greater desolation than any he had known while escaping from Erzerum. There he was, in the sheer desolation that a single hospital bed in post-war Budapest represented, without any care from his family, without the solace of a tender gaze, without the warmth of an embrace. Perhaps life tries the limits of the strong so that they may focus more single-mindedly on the meaning of the last moment.

Skopia nowadays, the village in the background with the minaret.

Tsevisluk, the largest village of Matsouka, a few decades ago.

A Pontian shop in the marketplace of Trapezunta (archive of A. Mailes).

Four village girls at work (archive of Anna Theophylactou).

267

The «melodious chanter», mentioned by Chrysanthos of Trapezunta in his *Biographical Recollections*, Hieromonk Jeremiah Tsarides, who rescued the relics of the Monastery of Panagia Soumela (the Tsarides family archive).

The earthquake at Ierissos. During such a disaster, Jeremiah completed the liturgical service unruffled.

Monks of the Monastery of Soumela. Also present, first on the left, is Panaretos Topalides, next to him is probably Gerasimos, sent by the patriarchate, and third from the right is Jeremiah.

Chrysanthos, Bishop of Trapezunta, on a visit to the Monastery of Our Lady of Soumela.

The sons of the Triantafyllides family from the village Giannanton of Matsouka. The first one on the left was killed fighting in a rebel band (the Triantafyllides family archive).

The brotherhood of the Monastery of St. John Vazelonas at the beginning of the 20th century. Center, Panaretos Topalides. Among them the Triantafyllides brothers (archive of Theodora Ioannidou).

Cultural genocide. Desecration of frescoes at Our Lady of Soumela.

Cultural hypocrisy. Shirking responsibility behind a façade of care.

The Monastery of Our Lady of Soumela before the Turks came...

... after they had passed.

The Monastery of St. George Peristereotas before the Turks came...

... after they had passed.

The Monastery of St. John Vazelonas before the Turks came...

... after they had passed.

Women and children outside a cave, trying to escape the slaughter. Countless similar scenes unfolded all over the Pontus (Historical and Literary Archive of Kavala).

Eucleides Kourtides.

Armed fighters of Santa.

Lazarus Tzaferides, rebel from Kerasunta. He was the only one to survive of the nine stalwart men commissioned to swim to the American war ships to beg for help in their struggle. The other rebels had been preparing them for months before, feeding them well in order to strengthen them for the battle against the waves. They strove for hours. One by one, his eight companions were lost. He alone endured, driven by the strength of his hope in the likeminded Americans. They dragged him out of the water and onto the ship, half dead. They next day, the captain handed him over to the Turks, who imprisoned and tortured him. He escaped, and after many trials he reached Greece.

Labor battalions of the Turkish army. The Pontian lyre is present, as it was at every expression of joy or grief (archive of an unknown English diplomat).

The port of Daphnunta in Trapezunta (archive of the Committee for Pontian Studies).

The church of St. Eugenios of Trapezunta nowadays. One is left speechless. It is a mosque.

Ptolemaida (Kailaria) in the 1930s. A party of Pontians with a lyrist, at the feast of Our Lady the Life-giving Font. Two of the refugees on the left are pointing to the Pontus. The wound is still raw.

Giorgos Tsachirides.

Yannis Tsachirides.

«IN RUSSIA THEY WERE NOT RED, THEY BECAME RED IN DRAPETSONA»

THODOROS TSACHIRIDES
[1902-1944]

«Mana, parakal' ton Theon soltatos na min pao,
sapkan na mi skepasoumai, talin na min ephtao.»

(Mother, pray to God that I may not go to the army,
that I may not wear a soldier's cap, that I may not serve.)

Thodoros Tsachirides was my mother's father. He was killed quite a few years before I was born. Though few accounts have reached me, they are sufficient to discern what a gifted man he was. I remember how his three fatherless children and his widow, my grandmother Chrysoula, used to speak of him with pride. «We didn't go hungry during the Occupation because Father took care of everything,» they would praise him.

Indeed, his foresight and adept handling of situations were truly a life-saver in those tough times, despite the fact that his untimely death would soon bring them to the point of having to permanently face the hunger that they had avoided during the German Occupation. At the same time, the manner of his death constituted an additional cause of misery. For some, what he did was an act of honor, for others, a sheer waste of his life; a cause for compassion in the good-natured, but a chance to grab anything and everything for the greedy.

He was born in the Matsouka area, in the village of Skopia, which probably got its name from an *episkopi*, i.e., a bishopric, which existed there during the time of the illustrious Pontian dynasty of the Komnenoi, one of the last bastions of the Byzantine Empire. The village was situated near the monastery of Panagia Soumela and the old caravan route, known in Roman times as Eliyieri, which connected coastal Trapezunta with the region of the Euphrates River and the interior of The East. This was the same route that Marco Polo took. Only during the summer could the road be traveled by the caravans, or *kervania*, as they were called by the locals, which consisted of 49 or 69 loaded camels and one more for the driver. The rest of the time, it was totally blocked by snow. Near Skopia, camel-drivers who were carrying goods to and from the western markets would stop and rest. At the beginning of the 20th century there were about 150 inhabitants, living in 35 homes. The poor village folk managed to survive by cultivating the lands belonging to the monastery, as their own soil was quite barren. There was nothing green near their houses, and the ground was so steep that there was no village square. As a result, they had to hold dances and celebrations on the threshing floors. The village was made up of small bunches of houses, which constituted the neighborhoods. My grandfather lived in the one called *Avleas*, meaning «yards».

The Ormin, the flowing ravine which passed right through the village, poured into the river in Larachanes[1] before the latter joined the river Piksites[2] in the nearby village of Kouspidi[3]. Only those who have seen this complex system of waterways with their own eyes can grasp the exceptional beauty of the scenery.

The mountains, ever so tall, are crossed by countless branching streams of abundant, majestic waters. The steep slopes plunge nearly perpendicular to the river beds, whose torrential waters rush noisily between them. Does our natural environment affect our countenance? For me, the answer is self-evident, for I have encountered the ancient pathways of Matsouka in the primitive look of my relatives, some of whom I have seen in photographs while others I have met in person. Their appearance seems to have been stamped with a wildness often greatly disproportionate to their innocent natures. In fact, my mother's brother, because of his especially dynamic appearance, acted in both Greek and foreign cinematic productions in roles which required a fierce look.

The region had been struck by epidemics of *gourzoula* a number of times, losing many victims to it. The naïve villagers were essentially alone in the face of various dangers and they had developed primitive

---

1. A village in Matsouka, with 1,500 Christians and 500 Muslims.
2. Also known as the Daphnopotamos, it is formed by three rivers that join at the town of Tsevisluk, one of which is the river which passes Panagia Soumela. Its source is on Mt. Zygana.
3. An all-Greek village in Matsouka, with 450 inhabitants, which boasted the convent of St. John the Baptist. According to tradition, this village hosted the founders of Panagia Soumela Monastery, Barnabas and Sophronios, in the 4th century AD.

ways of suppressing their fears and insecurities. Most of the time they took refuge in simple prayers, such as «Jesus Christ is victorious, all evil be scattered,» or in ritual blessings, such as were performed at the annual feast of St. Vlassios for a bountiful supply of animals' milk, and for their ropes, the *zoskoina*[4], so that the animals would not get tangled up in them! At other times, they were quite at ease combining prayers to saints with invocations to mythical healers and supernatural powers.

One of my grandfather's relatives, Aunt Elizabeth, the local folk doctor and midwife, was a distinguished figure in their small community. She had the proper charms to exorcise any possible illness: sunstroke, backache, the bite of a scorpion–they were all the same to her! This good-hearted woman later continued her healing in a suburb of Athens, where exile landed her, assisting the women to give birth without charging the slightest fee. Many of the people of that area still remember her with gratitude. She did not desert them even when she was offered a paid position as midwife at an eminent maternity hospital in the area.

A typical charm she would use for eye pain was the following: «Each of seven children took each of seven pickaxes and went to the forest. They found a hollow piece of wood, and found a cloudy eye. They cut away rheum, they cut away tears, and made the eye like the sun.» Here, the secret number symbolism of the tale, the pickaxes, the sun and reality all blend together, to relieve the eye and the soul simultaneously. The rhyme includes both supernatural appeasement of fear and a poetic foreshadowing of antibiotics. In its innocence, it embraces the fear and soothes it. With such rhyming concoctions did Aunt Elizabeth provide medical succor in that terribly isolated place. Hers was charity of a special kind and in special circumstances. Her quackery usually offered comfort and not physical treatment. From our contemporary standpoint, we are obliged to approach the matter respectfully, regardless of the comparative effectiveness of the medicines available in drug stores nowadays.

---

4. Literally, animal ropes, used to tie them up for grazing, etc.

My grandfather Thodoros lived his first 18 years surrounded by towering mountains. His small world was isolated from anything at all foreign to its traditions, uninterruptedly the same for centuries, just like all the mountain regions of the Pontus. The inhabitants lived according to their own customs and spoke their own dialect. In church, the liturgy had to be translated into the local Pontian Greek in order for it to be understood by the parishioners, an opportunity that arose only when the metropolitan bishop from nearby Livera held a service in Skopia. The rest of the time they could not understand the words. They certainly must have felt their meaning, though, or there would not have been over 15 small churches in and around the village, some in use, others *anapamena*[5].

In 1916, when the district of Matsouka found itself in the epicenter of the Russo-Turkish war, Thodoros was just 14 years old. With their eye on the advancing Russians, the Turks recklessly seized whatever they could before yielding the eastern part of the Pontus to them. The monasteries of the region were looted and burnt. The religious treasures of Panagia Soumela monastery were either stolen by German officers, replete with the conceit that they were the saviors of civilization, or simply destroyed. The village houses were burnt down, the women were raped, the churches were desecrated, and the Matsoukans were either dying of starvation or roaming the forest, hunted, so as not to be sent into exile. Each village counted an estimated 15 deaths a day from starvation, and many women, who had already been defiled by rape or wanted to escape such a fate, resorted to suicide by throwing themselves in the river, along with their children. Thodoros, a young boy still, lived in poverty in his ravaged village, where many of the proud people reached the point of having to beg. Whether Grandfather did too, I never learned.

As the Turks abandoned the area and the Russian troops took over, order was slowly restored and the Greeks could breathe freely again. They hoped that their country wouldn't meet any other disaster. Nevertheless, in the nearby town of Tsevisluk[6], a concentration-extermi-

---

5. In the colloquial usage of Skopia «at rest, deserted, unused».
6. Ancient Dikaisimos.

nation camp was soon to be set up for the Pontians. Officially, it was known as a camp for the resettlement of exiles. Vali Ebu Bekir Hakim and Mayor Hussein, under the strict observation of government officials, were powerless to protect the ethnic Greeks. According to testimony by American witnesses[7], whoever went in never came out, a fact that made the planned transfer of 300 boys aged 11 to 14, from Trapezunta to this particular camp, a waking nightmare. Many people were placed there under the pretense that they were suffering from the plague or cholera. Conditions were atrocious, and they were not given food. Even infants were sent there with their parents. And when certain leading Turkish citizens of Tsevisluk protested these crimes, their fanatic fellow countrymen beat them viciously. One of the protestors had cried out, aghast, against the inevitable historical vilification: «We will be condemned by all the nations!»

The time came when Thodoros would have to serve in the army and face all that enlistment entailed: exposure to deadly conditions, hunger and hardships. In order to avoid such a fate, he went to densely populated Constantinople. In that melting pot of nations, the *Skopanit*[8] dwelt together in a community of substantial size, which provided mutual support and solidarity.

The preferred trades were those of the tinsmith or the mattress maker, and my grandfather chose to be a tinsmith. Why did he not become a mattress maker? Perhaps because his father, Nikolas, and his father's brother, knew the tinsmith's trade and could teach him its secrets, or possibly because the softness of the down for the mattresses and the gentleness with which it must be handled were not compatible with his dynamic character.

The Skopanit who lived in Constantinople would send home money to pay the salary of the teacher, and to cover the needs of the school, the church, the imprisoned, the exiles, and their relatives. These villagers

---

7. Herbert Adams Gibbons, Greek Massacres by Turks Continue, *Christian Science Monitor*, Boston, May 31, 1922. The author was an eyewitness in Trapezunta at the time.

8. Pontian for «the residents of Skopia».

working abroad may not have known how to read or write, because they had never had the opportunity to learn, but they loved education and progress, and they believed that the children of the village should have the opportunity to advance in life. The teacher lived next door to the school and the villagers saw to his board and daily needs.

Upon the withdrawal of the Russians from Trapezunta and the surrounding area in 1918, a new, murderous scene mounted the stage once again, with the unarmed residents in the villages and the Pontian rebels in the mountains. The resistance forces of the area, with the Santa rebels playing the leading role, were renowned for their effective action. Under their protective shield, the villages of Matsouka were never completely emptied. By contrast, the villages of Chaldia, such as Tantourlouch, were deserted immediately after the Russian withdrawal, relatively cut off as they were from any nucleus of resistance. Of the original 25,000 inhabitants of the Matsouka region, 3,500 died in exile, over 1,000 were slaughtered, and 8,000 sought refuge in Russia and the Caucasus. This left over 10,000 residents to be «exchanged» in accordance with the Treaty of Lausanne a few years later.

Thus, in October 1923 Thodoros and his parents reached Piraeus as refugees from the Pontus, numbered among the «exchangeable». After being temporarily housed in a school, they soon settled in Drapetsona, a municipality in western Piraeus where the refugee shacks were built of tar paper, gunny sacks and gasoline cans. Conditions were unbelievably crowded, with people jam-packed against each other. They built a shack themselves, and lived there as best they could.

Regarding my grandfather's mother I was unable to discover much. Was she also from Skopia? Did she have siblings? Who were her father and mother? She is the only one of my parents' grandmothers who has been forced to remain in the margins due to lack of information. The only thing I found was a death certificate in the Piraeus County registry office with the entry: «Tsachiridou, Despoina, wife of Nikolaos, year of death: 1926.» Much more should be said of a woman who lost all but one of her six children, my grandfather, and who, for nine months before she died, was an invalid in the hands of my newly-married grandmother. How did her four boys and one girl die? In exile, in the labor battalions, of famine, of the plague? What pain weighed on their shoulders and darkened their gaze? Whatever the cause of death, there was every likelihood that if they had lived to make the voyage to Greece, they would have succumbed to some other deadly fate before long.

Life in Drapetsona, with its population of around 30,000, turned out to be a perpetuation of trials and tragedies rather than the promised land the refugees had been seeking. Before settling there, most of them had lived through nearly every kind of hardship. They had finally been delivered from the knives of the Turks, only to confront death once again on the ships which they had crowded into to travel to Greece. They lost family members and were themselves in danger, largely from the contaminated water in the ships' holding tanks. This absolutely indispensable staple had become a death trap. The direness of the situation is illustrated by the case of an orphan aunt of mine, who, being a small child at the time and having no one to help her drink, collected water in the lid of a sauce pan whenever it rained. That water saved her, while all around, dozens were dying from the contaminated tank water. Then, at the quarantine stations, instead of providing the relief which the refugees so desperately needed, the situation was exacerbated by a severe shortage of water, which they then continued to face in the shantytowns of Drapetsona. Its wells were few and all were contaminated, while the tank trucks which the residents bought water from were not sufficient for the needs of the extensive population. They had gone from the abundant waters of the Pontus to the miserable lack of water in Piraeus. And how could there be enough water for household needs, when there was not even enough to drink? Every drop was a precious treasure. Maintaining cleanliness on an everyday basis was a major feat.

I wonder how those downtrodden refugees were able to tolerate the pushing and shoving around the barely 17 outdoor toilet facilities, each of which had to be shared by 1,750 people. How could dignified people, brought up in scrupulous cleanliness, endure the stench from the carts that emptied the waste?

Several years later, the Mayor of Drapetsona would write in a letter to the Mayor of Piraeus: «The children of Drapetsona know that spring has arrived by the odor of the common outhouses, which becomes more intense in the summer.»

Added to the already polluted atmosphere was the suffocating dust from the nearby cement factory and the gypsum factory next door. Stifling clouds choked the air, and the fresh air of the Pontus became a distant memory. Also nearby was the electric power plant, which burnt *mazout* (crude oil), and a little further on were the fertilizer factory and the fuel and oil reservoirs belonging to Shell. Finally, there was the neighborhood called *Tabakika*, where the tanning factories with their harmful waste were located.

At the glass factory, which operated on the premises of the fertilizer factory, there were jobs for quite a few refugees, as well as accommodation in newly-built housing. Of course they paid rent, but they were far better off than the residents of the nearby shantytown. However, an 8-hour work day was not yet in place, and the daily wage for the underage employees was only enough to buy two *okades*[9] of bread. In July 1929, in my grandfather's small yard, policemen mercilessly beat a young man before their very eyes, because he had participated in the big strike demanding an 8-hour day. The victim, in a hopeless attempt to evade the policemen, had rushed into their small bedroom and tightly embraced a chest. The police dragged him out, chest and all, and beat him ruthlessly. It was an experience they could never forget.

In 1928 the ghetto was struck by an epidemic of dengue, an infectious disease also known as «breakbone fever» because of the high fever and severe pain in the joints, thus torturing the already suffering residents. The outbreak was most likely caused by the squalid condition of the sewer system and the contaminated water. Unlike the center of Piraeus, which got its water supply from Lake Marathon, the district of Drapetsona was excluded. Were the government authorities aware of how many brave Pontian Greeks were afflicted by their indifference? Did they have

---

9. About two and a half kilos.

any idea of the torment and hardships they had endured, on top of which were now added thirst and illnesses?

It seemed that there would be no end to their suffering. On Assumption Day of 1933, in the dead of summer, a huge fire broke out in the vicinity of Anastasi and many shacks burned down. A year later, the district was flooded in a severe November rainstorm. The residents ran frantically through the narrow alleys, full of mud, dirt and floodwaters. The danger of drowning was great. The ramshackle shanties were impossible to live in for some time afterwards, so the people had to be housed in schools and other public buildings. Taking advantage of their desperate need, successive governments made generous promises, especially before elections were due, but fulfilled them only parsimoniously after the elections were over.

And no matter how vital the input of hashish junkies was in the birth of *rempetiko* music, the housing of refugee families with small children in the same neighborhoods as them was one more proof of their being treated as second- or third-class Greek citizens. In the dingy taverns of Lipasmata, all sorts of knife-carrying lowlife resolved their differences right next door to hard-working family men. People who could not believe their ears the first time they heard their neighbors swearing and blaspheming the divine, now had to coexist with every type of wretch, and face situations that, though they may have been justifiable in some way, were nonetheless base in nature.

Somehow, the Pontians endured. Doing his best to support his family, my grandfather opened a stone quarry and became a model employer. He was prudent and cautious in his transactions rather than open-handed, which was quite reasonable considering the circumstances he had lived through, but not a single worker of his ever went unpaid. As a matter of fact, the week's wages were always paid on Friday, in plenty of time to do their shopping for Sunday.

The first child my grandmother gave birth to was a boy. The couple experienced immense joy, only to lose the baby six months later. The infant mortality rate was extremely high in those days. Later on, their other three children were born: my beloved Aunt Despoina, my mother, Ourania, and the pet of the family due to his gender, Nikos.

My grandfather's evenings at a local café, owned by his wife's brother, the enterprising Yangos Sidiropoulos, were often sweetened by my mother's young presence. About eight years old at the time and gifted with an exceptional voice, she would stand up on a table and sing songs from the homeland, soothing the refugees' pain over their uprooting. «The daughter went to the summer pastures», «Though Greece has waned, she is blossoming and will bear fruit again», «My Imera, I long to see your little castle» and «Tsampasi has been burnt»[10] were but a few of them. The audience at the café, for the most part friends and relatives, must surely have returned to their poor shacks feeling stronger to face the next day's struggle. A representative of the next generation, a little girl, was upholding the Pontian tradition on her tiny stature. In just those few square meters of the café, many a hope for a better life was born, at least for the little children.

This same haunt was a gathering place for the leftists of Drapetsona and, during a strike, it once had its windows smashed in by the police. My grandfather Thodoros was held in high esteem there. He would advise its patrons, update them regarding political affairs and, often enough, would loan them money. He had what they called «good command» of his finances, which was sometimes a polite epithet for stinginess, but such was undoubtedly a lifesaver in those difficult times. They did not discuss advanced politics; but the urgent needs of their municipality and of their new homeland imposed on them common problems and the need for decision making. Grandfather was known for his homespun axioms, such as «the Greek miracle lasts three days»[11], by which he expressed not only the fickleness of the Greek populace, but also the lack of accountability on the part of the government regarding its broken promises. Such succinct remarks resulted in general appreciation of his discernment and political acumen, so that his words gradually took on the grandeur of special wisdom to the innocent, weary Pontians.

---

10. *«H kor' epien 's so parchar»*, *«H Romania ki an perase, anthei kai pherei ki allon»*, *«Imera, erothymesa na elepo t'ospitopa s'»* and *«Ekaen kai to Tsampasin»* (Tsampasi was the summer pasture of Ordu).

11. *«To ellenikon thama tria meras kratei»*.

289

Moreover, it was during this period that their political awakening began, amidst the harsh reality of their daily labor. In those days, the Piraeus area was a hotbed of politicized workers and leftist fomenters. I can still hear the low voice of my grandmother's sister's husband echoing in my ears, during some elections of the 1960s. «Hush! The results from Kremmydarou haven't come out yet!»[12] Hearing the disappointing vote count for the Left, he comforted himself with the thought that that particular district of Drapetsona would turn the tables.

Grandfather, ensconced in the misery of a refugee ghetto in an impoverished and ravaged country, where the local Greeks were not only suspicious of the refugees but often condescending towards them, and fully aware that he was a victim of circumstances which he himself had not brought about, was naturally attracted by promises of worldwide justice. He subscribed to the new, leftist newspaper *Rizospastis*, which was in illegal circulation at that time, and he was convinced that the time had come when all the downtrodden of the world would rise up and build a better society. My grandmother wholly supported him in the struggle to build a new world.

Aunt Maria Sidiropoulou, Yango's wife, a clever, prudent woman, says pointedly in a significant recorded interview regarding our family's experiences as refugees: «In Russia they didn't become Red–they came to Drapetsona and became Red!»[13] While this is absolutely true, the reasons are obvious.

Their hope that in Greece they would find justice and restoration of their rights had been alive ever since they left the Pontus.

Upon arrival, however, exhausted from the travails of their journey, having lost many family members, in ragged condition, and unable to communicate easily due to the Pontian dialect, they realized that life in the destitute mother country would be far more difficult than they had foreseen. At the same time that their children were suffering eye problems from trachoma in squalid Drapetsona, they learned that somewhere

---

12. *«Sous! Kremmydarou 'k' ekseven!»*
13. *« 'S si Rousia 'k' eyenten kokkinoi, erthen 's si Drapetsona ki eyentan.»*

else a society was being built which would provide equal opportunity for all children. Many of the refugees were filled with hope by this vision, despite the fact that the charm of the communist ideas which determined their course was disproportionately large in comparison to the bitter truth of Lenin's undivided support for Kemal. Though this support ceased to exist after Kemal grew closer to the West, the crime against the Greeks had already been committed[14].

My great-grandfather, Nikolas, wavered between caution and absolute disapproval of his son's political activities. This negative stance was largely determined by grandfather's irreligiousness. Skopia was home to a deeply rooted faith and Nikolas had been raised accordingly. Quietly and humbly, without need of advanced theological analysis, he apprehended that his son had changed course. He tried to reign in the impulsiveness of my then young grandfather, but Thodoros was fast evolving into an ardent ideologue. This difference burdened their weary souls, for they had no previous experience of such a dichotomy, and their family cohesion was sorely tried. The one would take his grandchildren to church, while the other would barely tolerate it or even forbid it outright.

In the narrow alleys between the shacks of Drapetsona, the winds of change blew persistently. A new world was making its debut on the historic stage, and the youth among the refugees composed its citizens. Overwhelmingly downtrodden, they believed that the hour of the great reversal had come. Their exploitation would end. The old world would vanish, along with its injustices. They would even give their lives for such a cause. My grandfather was absolutely determined to fight for the overthrow. By now, his driving force was wrath.

After Piraeus was bombed by the Italians in 1940, he loaded the family and their belongings in a cart and moved to Melissia, where other relatives already lived. His father had died. Along with their other belongings they packed essential provisions: flour, oil, raisins and yard goods.

---

14. On Jan. 13, 1918, the *Pravda* published the dogma of the integrity of Turkey. However, at the 4th World Congress of the Communist International, Lenin characterized the Ankara government as traitorous because it had entered discussions with the West.

After staying briefly with my grandmother's sisters, they moved into a one-room house they built themselves. Every night they brought the goats and the chickens inside, to prevent their being stolen. They also dug a bomb shelter next to the house. The hunger which thousands of people experienced during the Occupation was unknown to them. My grandfather always made sure the children had their fill before he ate a morsel, an occurrence which, though typical for parents in those bleak years, was nonetheless touching and worthy of respect. They earned some money from the charcoal kiln they built on Mt. Penteli, drank milk from their *aigidia*[15], and ate vegetables from their garden. Today our family still eats figs from the trees they planted those 70 years ago, basically indifferent to the fact that grandfather never tasted them himself.

Because there was no school at that time, my grandfather and fifteen other men started the building of the first elementary school in Melissia. This did not in the least impress the fanatic right-wingers of the area, who upon learning that he was a leftist attacked and beat him viciously.

In January 1944 the Allies bombed Drapetsona and the surrounding area. Their target was the leadership of EAM (the National Liberation Front) rather than the Germans, of whom they killed only eight, whereas 5,500 Greeks were killed. A few months later, on the first of May, the Germans executed 200 leftist Greeks at Kaisariani. On August 17 of the same year, 174 leftists were executed and thousands were taken prisoner at a road block at Kokkinia. On October 12 the Germans left Athens and on October 18 a government of national unity, supported by the British government, took over in Greece. The talks with EAM failed, however, and on December 3 the *Dekemvriana*[16] broke out.

---

15. Goat kids, from the ancient Greek word *aiks*, which in Modern Greek has become *katsikakia*.

16. «The December events» refers to a series of clashes fought during World War II in Athens from December 3, 1944 to January 11, 1945 between the Greek left-wing resistance forces (EAM-ELAS) who were supported by the Communist Party (KKE), and the British Army, supported by the Greek national government, the Athens police and the far-right Organization X. The conflict ended with the defeat of EAM-ELAS, leading to its disarmament, as officially agreed in the Treaty of Varkiza.

The U.S. ambassador to Greece, Lincoln MacVeagh, in a letter to President Franklin Roosevelt dated December 8, 1944, is critical of Churchill's «blundering» of the situation: «But at bottom, the handling of this fanatically freedom-loving country (which has never yet taken dictation quietly) as if it were composed of natives under the British Raj, is what is the trouble.»[17] That was the climate which my grandfather and the entire Attica basin lived in nearing the end of World War II.

It was on Sunday, December 10, when, heeding the call to resistance against the British by the Communist Party of Greece (KKE), my grandfather was building a street barricade and was mortally wounded. Three other comrades were killed outright, one of whom was a Pontian refugee boy only 14 years old. They were bombed by the Spitfire planes of the British air force, which had amazing maneuverability and were capable of sending their deadly machine-gun fire even under the small bridge nearby, where they were trying to take cover. Just a few hours earlier, a relative of Grandfather's had met him making his way down from the kiln on Mt. Penteli, ready for the great battle they were preparing to fight. But once again, British politics, so well known to him from the Asia Minor Catastrophe, rose up in opposition to his yearning for an independent homeland. He died about one month after he was wounded. He was 42 years old.

«If only he had gotten killed by the leader's side, if only he was taken by an Englishman's shot or a hunger strike in prison, I'd have cried with pride to have lost my laughing boy» goes the Irish song. My grandfather was neither a smiling lad, nor was he at the side of some leader when he was killed, and he did not die of starvation while on a hunger strike. Yet, unlike the boy of the Irish song, he was indeed killed by an English bullet, which was the reason his wife and children were never eligible for the pension normally received by the family of a soldier killed in action. As to whether Grandmother took it as a point of pride that her husband

---

17. Series 2: Correspondence, 1932-1945; Lincoln MacVeagh Papers, Public Policy Papers, Dept. of Rare Books and Special Collections, Princeton University Library.

had died fighting, I would say without a doubt that she experienced the loss as a total calamity. In response to her pleading that he not go to the battle, he had been unyielding. A funnel, for lack of a megaphone, was calling the Melissians to resistance. She barred the doorway with her petite body to prevent his leaving. She reminded him that he had agreed to go to the mountain with a nephew to get charcoal. She warned him that many had already been killed in the Greater Athens area. She begged, she cried, she shouted. He pushed her aside roughly, and went out. No force in the world could have kept him back from his rendezvous with death. Their last tragic dialogue was as follows:

«Thodore, don't go! You'll be killed!»
«If I don't get killed, my children will never see freedom.»[18]

That is how my grandfather lived the 22 years of his free life, after leaving the Pontus. He never learned that the Balkans had already been divvied up in Moscow that October, and that the division was officially signed and sealed in Yalta during the very same days that he was languishing in the hospital. Neither did he learn that the freedom which his children were to see was precisely, and only, that which was fashioned and meted out by the same people who had killed him, and by their successors, with the consent of those whose promises for the eradication of injustice had inspired him, unto death. It is indeed a consolation that he never learned that the great experiment which he envisioned was to fail, and that he was not left bankrupt of hope.

Immediately after his death, two neighbors, armed and under the cloak of patriotism, came to the home of the bereaved and threatened my grandmother at gunpoint to pull back the boundary of her field for their benefit. Those were difficult times, hard times. From that point on, Thodoros's wife and children held that two-hour ordeal and his uncompensated-for death as the criterion for their political choices in every

---

18. *«Thodore, min pas, tha skotousai!»*
   «An 'k' skotoumai, ta paidia m' eleftheria 'k' tha elep'ne.»

future hardship they faced, believing that any view which diverged from his would constitute a betrayal of the dead.

At this point I am obliged to reflect on grandfather and granddaughter. The generation of the Polytechnic uprising[19] (to which I belong and which could easily have raised me to the status of a resistance fighter, during the mere nine hours I was held in detention after a random group arrest) let down the entire Greek nation. With victory in our hands, we let down our guard. Most of the leaders of the uprising eventually cashed in whatever fighting prestige they had. A great deal of wood from Circe's rod–the one she used to turn Odysseus' crew into pigs–was used to make the chairs they chose to sit in. The rest of us took refuge in political indifference. Many of us told ourselves that professional and family accomplishments constituted adequate social contribution. We relaxed, sinking into the comfort of our armchairs, from which, as everyone knows, no confrontation, struggle or overthrow can ever originate. The present plight of a proud people, as are we Greeks, is to be blamed on the generation of the Polytechnic, including myself. Part of the responsibility is mine, too. What social struggle did I serve in? Did I risk anything important for my ideals? Did I ever have high aims for the general good?

In the midst of this self-questioning, the figure of my grandfather Thodoros emerges, in the dignity of his sacrifice. He ceases to be the naïve ideologue, who ignored the fact that he had a family to feed and obeyed his party's call to arms, even as the game was already up, for they had been sold out. He becomes a courageous person, who did not give thought to his kiln and its coals, whereas I cared mainly about my personal affairs; who tried to give his children a just society, while I tried to give mine the qualifications to survive in an unjust one; who died for his ideals, whereas I would not have done so. The response to the self-evident question which arises from the comparison of grandfather and granddaughter casts its unfavorable shadow over me, even in light of the mitigating fact that ideals, in general, have been abandoned worldwide.

---

19. See *Chapter 8*, footnote 14.

On the grazing land outside my grandfather's village, in the summer pasture Mezeren, innocent animals still graze today, unaware of the blood which once drenched the land where they now feed. Luxurious villas belonging to Turks from Trapezunta have taken the place of my ancestors' poor Pontian homes in Skopia. The ruined and looted monastery of Panagia Soumela hosted a liturgy in 2010, giving credence to the European façade of a Turkey that is endeavoring in every possible way to erase its barbaric past acts.

My grandfather, far from that place, with the bitter taste of refugee life on his lips and the wrath caused by injustice stirring his soul, was sacrificed in the December Events for dreams that never and nowhere materialized. People continue to mistreat and abuse those who are weaker and poorer. The world is a permanent theater of war and the unprotected continue their lives in the middle of persecution and deprivation. His children, who have grown old, never experienced the world he had envisioned. As for his grandchildren and their children, they are now subjected to the most insidious kind of enslavement, by means of globalization. A prison has been constructed, with the entire planet as its cell.

Scene from daily life inTsevisluk at the beginning of the 20th century (archive of Anna Theophylactou).

Camels loaded with goods on the caravan road, Eliyieri (archive of the Committee for Pontian Studies).

Does nature affect one's physiognomy? The answer is clearly shown by the face of my uncle Triantafyllos Tsachirides, now an emigrant in the USA.

Nikos Tsachirides, the actor, my mother's brother.

Women from the Matsouka region at the beginning of the 20th century. Though heavily laden, they are knitting as they walk (archive of the Committee for Pontian Studies).

Pontian refugees in Piraeus (Historical Archive of the Municipality of Piraeus).

Refugee shanties and tents (archive of the Center for Asia Minor Studies, Manolis Mega-lokonomos collection).

Tank carrying water to be sold to the refugees in Drapetsona (from the book *The History of Drapetsona*).

An elderly refugee drawing water from a well in Drapetsona (from the book *Certain Samaritans*).

Line of refugees outside the American volunteer doctors' office in Drapetsona (from the book *Certain Samaritans*).

Family photo in Drapetsona. Thodoros Tsachirides with his father, his wife and their three children in 1936. On the right, barefoot, my sweet-voiced mother at the age when she sang the Pontian songs with wondrous perfection. Left, my beloved Aunt Despoina, and in his father's arms, Nikos, the family pet.

Athens, a street barrier during the December Events (archive of the War Museum).

The December Events. British parachutists against the Greek resistance fighters in the center of Athens (archive of the War Museum).

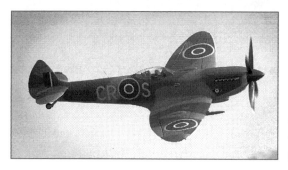

Spitfire of RAF. Highly maneuverable and effective, unfortunately for my grandfather.

«EH, POOR TANTOURLOUCH...»

CHRYSOULA TSACHIRIDOU
[1906-1986]

«Anathema kai ta makra, othen ki paei e lalia,
t'ommata m' eskoteinepsan as 's sin arothymian.»

(Cursed be all distant lands where my voice can't reach,
darkness has fallen upon my eyes from that incessant longing.)

Chrysoula Tsachiridou was my grandmother, my mother's mother. She and her twin sister were the youngest of the eight children of Isaac and Maria Sidiropoulou.

If I were to choose among all the adjectives in the world one which would characterize her completely, it would be the word authentic. If I named only one that would describe the influence she had on my life, it would be the word irreplaceable. If I were allowed to say only one thing about her, it would be that she lived and died inconsolable over having been uprooted from her homeland. Any and all visions of a world without borders, of the abolition of countries, were dashed to pieces before my grandmother. That little part of the mountain where she was born had lodged in her heart for a lifetime. She would not exchange any place in the world for it. No beauty in the world could compare to its slopes. Nothing could hush the sound of its waters. It didn't matter that it was hard to reach, that it was at the edge of the world, that they lived there like hermits. She wanted that, and nothing else. And the belief that time heals all? Dashed as well! Instead of being comforted with the passage of time, the longing within her grew stronger, and never shrank.

It was around 1970, I remember, when in a primitive outburst of grief she tried to express the incurable pain she felt for Tantourlouch, her village: «Eeeeh... poor Tantourlouch and again Tantourlouch and again Tantourlouch and again Tantourlouch and again Tantourlouch and again Tantourlouch! With your cold waters... poor Tantourlouch, and again Tantourlouch and again Tantourlouch...»

For us, her three granddaughters, this utterance didn't mean much. In fact, I remember we laughed. We focused on the foolishness of the expression and laughed our hearts out as she said the same thing over and over. We were immature. We did not have even an inkling of the longing she was giving voice to with that monotonous repetition of the name of her village. We could not possibly fathom the sacredness of a pain that lasted over half a century.

My grandmother was never assimilated into mainland Greece. She adopted no new habits, no new ways of life or of expressing herself. She was not interested in trying new experiences, learning different songs, enjoying other kinds of celebrations. She did not even want to taste new dishes. She had everything she needed–she had her own ways. Her whole being was Pontian, her life revolved around the Pontian, her daily routine was given meaning only by things Pontian. Whenever she heard a last name ending in the Pontian suffix -ides, or noticed a *katsi*[1] that reminded her of a fellow countryman, she would ask, with searching eyes: «You there, tell me, are you Pontian?» She was like the miser who needs to count his gold in order to feel reassured. When the answer was yes, she was happy. Automatically, the stranger became her acquaintance, her own, one of her people. Just as the legendary mermaid, sister of Alexander the Great, was appeased when anyone answered yes to her perpetual question, my grandmother needed this reassurance[2].

There would follow other questions to the stranger who happened to be a compatriot: which part of the Pontus they were from, when they had come to Greece, and how. For the most part she would never see them again, but that was not necessary. It was enough that she had made certain that the Pontians endure, are recognizable, are not lost, that they are hardy stock.

I remember how, when I introduced her to the young man I was going to marry and announced that his name was Karakousoglou, she remarked

---

1. face.
2. According to legend, in a rage Alexander cursed his sister Thessaloniki to become half woman and half fish. But she bore him no grudge. She traveled the seas and asked the sailors if King Alexander was still alive. Wise sailors would answer «He is alive and reigns over the world», so that she would let them continue their voyage. But if they made the mistake of answering that he was dead, she flew into a fury and sank the ship.

instantaneously, directly and impulsively «If he were a Karakousogl*ides*, it would have been even better.»[3] For her, a Pontian husband meant an indubitable guarantee of happiness for her granddaughter. It was with such consolatory practices and naïve stereotyping that my simple grandma dealt with her uprooting.

Her endearing behavior could easily be regarded as quaint, especially in light of today's standards, by which the tendency to become colorless, odorless citizens of the world is rapidly gaining ground. My grandmother, however, with her fanatic fixation for place of origin, gave color and fragrance to every single minute of her troubled life. The mere twelve years she lived in the homeland had become for that innocent woman an inexhaustible source of strength. In fact, they proved to have been enough for the remaining sixty-eight years of her octogenarian life, so that, though her body might tread upon Greek land, her soul breathed in the Pontus.

Her village, Tantourlouch, which was also called St. George, took its name from the *tantouria*, the underground ovens. A tantouri, or *klivan*, was a hole about half a meter deep, usually in the kitchen floor of the homes. The inside was lined with baked red earth and it had a lid. The base, where the fire would be lit, had a tunnel, the *physoun*, whose mouth was located in the yard. In it they baked special pies, the so-called *lavasia*, bread, and main dishes. Moreover, during the harsh Pontian winters they would put a table on top of the tantouri and spread a blanket, which would cover the legs of the people who sat around it, thus making a *saga*[4]. Such ovens existed in other areas of the Pontus, of course. Perhaps the name was given to this particular village because they were first made there, or because renowned artisans who built them lived there.

Tantourlouch lay at an altitude of 2,400 meters in the foothills of Mt. Chatsar, itself a cone-shaped, bright green expanse which was part of the

---

3. «*An eton Karakousoglides ato tha eton ki allo kallion.*»
4. A method of keeping warm in the home. By placing a brazier under a table and covering this with a blanket, the family and friends sitting around it could drape the blanket over their legs and warm themselves. Instead of a brazier, in Tantourlouch they positioned the table over the tantouri.

mountain range Theches, with a handful of houses at its feet. That was her village. It belonged to the precinct of Yiagmour-Dere in the county of Erzerum, or Theodosioupolis, which had a total of 45 villages, some Muslim, some Christian, and others mixed in population. The nearest all-Christian village, Yetourmaz, was four hours on foot from Tantourlouch.

The first years of grandmother's life went by smoothly. It was a time when emigration to czarist Russia had granted financial ease to the residents of these once poor areas. The northern side of the Black Sea enriched the southern side. Little Chrysoula knew only childhood pleasures and had no cares. The village was full of children–cousins, neighborhood children, her twin sister–with whom she could play and fill the hours when she was not in school. Even the six winter months they spent isolated inside their homes were beautiful, for young and old alike. They did not have to tend the garden or the fields, or take the animals out to pasture; over the summer they had stored up plenty of feed for the animals, and for themselves there were abundant salted meats, pickled vegetables, butter and whatever else they needed. The land lay quiet under the snow and they spent their time at home with *parakathia*[5] and *kalatsias*[6]. Those may have been days of idleness and stagnation, which did little to broaden their minds or develop their potential. Nevertheless, the villagers held fast to already-existing ways and practices, unadulterated by new influences and capable of preserving unchanged for centuries the continuation of our race in the region. These isolated bastions of Hellenism on the snows of Theches faithfully guarded ageless traditions against fashions and trends foreign to their solidly structured small community. Without realizing it, they were the genuine continuation of the ancient civilization, whether they were singing, dancing, playing the lyre, or talking. Their village was not a main thoroughfare; rather it was the most remote inhabited spot on the Pontian mountains. Only one or two passages united them with the outside world.

---

5. From the ancient Greek *parakathemi*, I sit nearby, it meant a gathering for discussions, meals, songs or even work. It usually took place during evening hours.

6. Chatting or discussion.

Did this geographical isolation among steep mountainsides, with their dense forests and plangent rivers, give them some sense of safety? Probably so, because they were innocent. But when they found themselves in front of the gates of Hell, chased out of their Paradise, they would certainly realize that they had been deceived by the magnificent mountain ranges surrounding them. How easily they had been transformed into a chilling death trap. Did they hate them for that? On the contrary! They died with the eyes of the soul gazing on their ridges.

According to the theory of Charilaos Andreades, it was in the vicinity of Tantourlouch that Xenophon and the Myriad arrived and the famous cry «The sea! The sea!» was heard from some slope. He notes, after careful study of Xenophon's writings and the geography of the area: «Therefore, according to all this, Theches is located where the Greek village of Tantourlouch now lies, that is, where the plains come to an end and the mountain regions of Govas and Gumushane begin.»[7]

My grandmother traced part of the same route that Xenophon and the remaining soldiers of the Myriad took, holding a little white flag in her hands so she would not be shot. However, she was not following the ancient pass heading towards the ports of Pontus in the north, but towards Erzerum, in the east. Was the difference in direction crucial, though? Was that the important thing? Definitely not. What made the situation totally different was that she was being uprooted, she was leaving her homeland, whereas the Myriad were returning to theirs. Against her will she was leaving the school where she had first learned to read and write, the neighborhoods, the pastures where they used to summer their flocks, the forests and the cold waters of the rivers. She was forced to leave, while the Myriad had chosen to go on their campaign. She was not a hardened warrior but a weak child; on the same paths, but with so many differences. She was too young to understand the meaning of what was happening to her, but she was old enough for the fear of slaughter to remain unforgettable. She knew very well that there was no time for

---

7. The researcher gave this opinion to Konstantinos Papamichalopoulos, who included it in his book *Travels in the Pontus*, Athens, 1903.

her to stop, to complain, to cry, or to collapse. She had to keep moving continuously so as not to freeze. Let the snow pelt her, the wind whip her, let her hands and feet hurt from the cold. She had to keep moving.

At the time of the upheaval, everyone in the village had been openly practicing Christians since 1856, when the Hatt-i humayun (the Reform Decree of 1856)[8] was issued and many of the secret Christians officially declared themselves. Nineteen villages in Chaldia are mentioned by name in the committee letter which was drawn up for acknowledgement by the ambassadors of the Great Powers, requesting recognition of their religious identity. Among them was Tantourlouch. Chaldia, a region with approximately twenty monasteries, half of which were devoted to the Holy Virgin, sought its rights. In an audio recording of my grandmother's reminiscences, she refers to the «under» Christians, who are the better ones, who hold secret *charandas*[9], and who secretly climb above ground via steps. Is this an unconscious description of the secret Christians, or a simple-minded notion of elves? Whatever the meaning of my grand-mother's words, the matter composes yet another dramatic aspect of the suffering of the Hellenes at the hands of the Turks. It is to our credit as Greeks that our treatment of Muslims has never forced them to practice their faith in secret. Free will is a basic presupposition of Christianity.

To what extent the decree was actually complied with by local Turks can be seen from a few examples. In the 1950s in Constantinople, the Athonite Gabriel Dionysiates baptized, heard confession and gave com-munion to a number of the remaining secret Christians of the historic Pontus. These people had been exempt from the population exchange because they were registered as Muslims, and according to the Treaty of Lausanne, religion was the single criterion for the exchange. Afterwards, they asked him to perform the funeral ceremony over some soil they had brought to him from the graves of their relatives. Then followed some-thing still more poignant: although it was not Easter, they begged him

---

8. Decree signed by the Sultan Metzit on February 18, 1856. Largely due to pressure from Russia, the High Porte was obliged to issue the Hatt-i humayun, which enforced respect for all religious convictions in the empire.

9. Weddings.

to chant the Easter service. «Do the Resurrection service for us, Father, so we can hear the "Christ is Risen" hymn, and then we don't care if we die.»[10] So he did.

One wonders how many indigenous Greeks of the Pontus were never able to fulfill such a yearning. How many never experienced what took place in a basement in Constantinople in 1957?

In 1915 my grandmother was only nine years old, but the figures and the lamentations of the young Armenian girls being beheaded by the dozens on the mountain ridges around the village left an indelible memory. The Turks would undo their beautiful black hair and then behead them. For the rest of her life, every time there was a fuss around her, she would liken it to that horror: «Come now. Don't carry on as though the Armenians were being slaughtered.» To describe a recent quarrel she would say: «It was just like the Armenian slaughter!» And in anticipation of an imminent event, she might proclaim: «It will be the Armenian slaughter all over!»

Stathes Christoforides[11] mentions in his memoirs a scene he witnessed with his own eyes. The Turks stoned to death six hundred little Armenian children with rocks they had brought in sacks. The hungry little martyrs, seeing the soldiers on horseback and believing the sacks to contain bread, quickly ran to get something to eat. They murdered them with those stone loaves, without the slightest hesitation. They had raped many of them, both boys and girls, beforehand. Afterwards, they divided their pretty clothes among themselves. «They divided his garments among them.»[12]

In 1918, when the hills around Tantourlouch seemed to have blackened with the scores of enraged Turkish vigilantes, my grandmother, like

---

10. «Na eutas, Pater, einan Anastasin, na akouomen to "Christos Aneste" k' epekei as apothanome.»

11. Born in Kounaka, in the Matsouka district, he arrived in Greece at the age of 17. With only a sixth-grade education, he preserved fairy tales, anecdotes, and memories in the idiomatic Pontian dialect of upper Matsouka. The event in question is described in his book *Mavra Kairous kai Mavra Meras (Black Times and Black Days)* in the chapter entitled «The Little Armenian Children».

12. Matthew, 27:35.

all the other little children in the whirlwind of war, felt absolute terror for herself and her family. She was overwhelmed by the fear that she might have the same fate as the Armenians. They were held hostage for hours in her own school, before they were pushed out into the freezing cold. Father Gior's, the last priest of the village, and Damianos Papadopoulos, the last of the *mouchtares*[13], with the few men who were not abroad, would have to lead the women, children and the elderly to safety. But where to? Where would they be safe? Without a doubt, the only escape route was to Russia. Once again, off to Russia. In this way, yet another large-scale emigration-exile set out for that destination. It was the fourth in a row, and involved a total of 150,000 Greeks from the Pontus[14].

What did the girls, Chrysoula and her twin, feel as the village was burning? Certainly they were scared, and they may have cried, but it was somewhat later that things got much worse–after they had walked for several hours and darkness had settled over everything, after the white and the black, the snow and the darkness, united in a deadly combination that froze not only their little bodies but also their frightened souls.

I wonder if those little Greek children, the thousands of underage Christians that died of hunger, of privation or by the knife, or who were forced to become Muslims, or who simply disappeared, will ever take their rightful place in the roll of the world's martyrs. It may be the case that none of them left a diary behind as Anne Frank did. Yet the evil that aims at children's souls will always and forever be the worst kind of crime against humanity, whether it concerns a young Hebrew girl in a Dutch attic, or the little Christian orphans who wandered alone, ragged, hungry and ill, from one end of the Pontus to the other.

There is a well-known photograph of a naked child running in a village street in Vietnam to escape the napalm bombs of the Americans. The same terror filled the children of Tantourlouch when they were thrown

---

13. The word *muhktar* means «chosen» in Arabic and refers to the head of a village.
14. Large-scale emigrations from the Pontus to Russia took place in 1829, 1875, 1886 and 1918.

out and they started their journey in two meters of snow, while behind them their houses were burning. Thousands of similar dramas have unfolded with the children of the Pontus, only that there was no lens to record them. There is also another photograph, in which a vulture sits beside an emaciated little child in Africa, awaiting its death in order to devour it. Again the lens was absent which could have recorded like events during the Pontian slaughter. Thus, it is difficult to comprehend that skeletal Pontian babies still sucked at their dead mothers' breasts before they themselves died, and vultures stood by to eat them. For such crimes, and many others, did take place in our own infanticide. Since the time of the *ic tsoglan* in the 16th century, when small boys from 6 to 9 years old were abducted for the harems of the *agades* (wealthy Turkish administrators), up until the Asia Minor Catastrophe in the 1920s, there is no misery that the children of the Pontus have not undergone.

The American nurse Theda Phelps[15], serving as a member of the Near East Relief Committee[16], reports:

«On leaving Sevasteia, I passed a group of about 200 women and children. Every day I saw on average three dead bodies along the road-side. There was a skeletal little child practically without flesh, and a huge eagle sat on its chest and finished off the little flesh that remained. Another small child with its head turned to one side had just died and another bird of prey had begun its work. A small child so pale and thin that its skin was transparent, with teeth that showed through the skin, with huge black eyes, awaited the fate of the other two, and we were forced to leave him all alone on the mountain.»

---

15. In her work in the Sevasteia region, where she was forced to beg the Turkish officers to allow her to treat the ill and shelter the weakened exiles, Ms. Phelps came down with typhoid herself.

16. The Near East Relief is an international social and economic development organization based in Syracuse, New York. Founded in 1915, under the name Near East Foundation, it is the United States' oldest nonsectarian international development organization. Near East Relief organized the world's first large-scale, modern humanitarian project in response to the Armenian Genocide in the early 20th century.

Ethel Thompson[17] gives further testimony to the heartless abuse of small children being exiled:

«During my stay in Amison (Samsunta), in early July 1921, the surrounding Greek villages were burnt down and the residents were displaced, including women and children... On approaching, we saw 300 children inside a circle formed by 20 gendarmes, who were hitting them with their swords. One mother who rushed in to save her child suffered the same fate and was thrown out. The children bent down to the ground or raised their little arms in order to avoid the blows. We couldn't stand any more.»

Turks, oh, you Turks, how can you sleep peacefully at night?

Grandma Chrysoula's trek all the way to Russia has already been described by her then future brother-in-law, Panayotes Spyrantes (see Chapter 4). Her family, however, went to the village of Alisophe when they reached the Kars region, whereas Uncle Patzos and his family went to nearby Moulamoustafa. Other fellow villagers headed for Pelikpas, where there was an entire neighborhood by the name of Tantourlouchet.

They had traveled to Kars by sleigh, which Chrysoula's older brother Yangos hired. At Baipurt they had dared to hope that the evil of the initial fifteen-day persecution through the snow was over, but in vain. They had not considered what it meant to face Mount Kop-tagou in the middle of winter. And if they had known, could they have chosen to stay in Baipurt? The tsetes were chasing them relentlessly, and by comparison the 3000-meter altitude had seemed to them a lesser evil. But it proved to be a horror of equal dimensions, where nature had taken over the role of the butcher.

---

17. An American from Boston, Massachusetts, who worked for the Near East Relief Committee from August 1921 to June 1922. On her return to the U.S., she boldly denounced the Kemalist atrocities which she had witnessed, in an effort to prevent such crimes against humanity from happening again. The quote is taken from the archives at the Home Services of the Greek Ministry of Foreign Affairs. The incident occurred at a water reservoir on the outskirts of Mezere on February 5, 1922.

We usually imagine hell as being full of fire, with enormous flames, boiling waters, and burning irons. We think of it as symbolism of punishment, always associated with unbearable heat. Are we aware of the frozen version of hell? Can we imagine the blizzard aspect of it? Have we ever felt the whipping of the freezing wind on our faces, the hail and the inexorable snow? And the huge avalanches that roll down? Have they frightened us? No, for we did not have to pass through the homicidal Kop-tagou. The thousands of Pontians, however, who had to struggle for 13 days to cover the 100 kilometers to reach Ilitse, found themselves in a true hell. They moved forward unceasingly, for otherwise they would freeze to death. Not even in our imagination could we endure such agony, the frozen breath of death itself whipping the snow in our faces. People began to lose their minds. Let us not be in a hurry to condemn, from the comfort of our homes, mothers who abandoned their children. Let us not wonder why the sick and the old were left to die helplessly. Do we know what tragic deliberation went on in their desperate minds? Can we understand what they weighed in the balance in order to make such tragic decisions? «If I die, it will die with me. If I leave it, I will survive and save the rest of my children.» This is the most likely line of reasoning. Suppose nothing like that actually happened, and they simply went insane? Instead of judging without any right, instead of focusing on results, perhaps we should go back to causes. Should we perhaps ponder the fact that innocent people were left to be slaughtered by the Turks, and that this policy was condoned by the heartless world powers? Could this be the most important thing, rather than the way in which they handled their own utter despair?

In the film *Sophie's Choice*[18], the lens focuses on the drama of a Polish Jew, a young mother in a Nazi concentration camp, who is forced to decide which of her two children will live and which will be executed. Mothers of Kop-tagou, who will take an interest in your pain, and when? Pontian women, frozen and weary, what choice were you forced to make? What about the woman among you who moved to the side of the

---

18. *Sophie's Choice* (1982) directed by Alan J. Pakula.

path and laid her little infant on the snow, so that her two older children, clinging to her skirts and whimpering, could lean against her? Could she ever have imagined, in her early days, that she would be so violently chased by men and nature? Or that the little child she had brought into the world with a mother's thrill of anticipation, with only its tiny weight, would end up being such a heavy burden that it nearly dragged her and its siblings to death? Our very own Tsofa (Sophie in Pontian Greek) represents the living and yet to this day unvindicated Pontian woman who was driven to the brink of despair by the Kemalian horror. Respect for the relationship between mother and child is nonnegotiable, and defamation thereof is an atrocity. Only souls guided by demons could violate the basic tenets of human existence in such a way. Thus, instead of concentrating on the manner in which the calamity was faced, let us focus on the fact that in the genocide of the indigenous people of the Pontus, mothers were psychologically looted and devastated more than any other group, to the point where, particularly on Mertzan Lithar and Kop-tagou, the outrage utterly crushed the sacred.

One of my grandmother's cousins stayed behind the refugee procession along with a few other strong young men, because an avalanche had come crashing down on top of a horse-drawn cart full of women and children. They saved them only after terrific efforts. The minutes of agony were indescribable as they tried to open a hole in the enormous pile of snow and extricate them, lest those trapped underneath die of asphyxiation. Would they be in time? Were they still alive under there? Would not the trapped people, all of whom were women, children and the ill, be paralyzed with fear by the likelihood that the snow would become their grave? Before my grandmother moved on, she saw the snow cover them, heard their shouts and panting. She stood stock-still, wordless, both from her fear and the cold, while the blizzard raged on. Ten-year-old Magdalene Tornikidou, or The Big One, as they called her, being the oldest of four orphans, though she was not at all big but quite small, suffered serious frostbite. One finger shorter than the others and an indentation in her heel were the badges she earned on Kop-tagou and wore for a lifetime.

Mrs. Despoina Michaelides was some years older than my grandmother. Years later I knew her as a friend of the family when I was growing up. When they started to climb Kop-tagou she had each of her two little children by the hand, so, naturally, her position was not at all easy. Yet despite the difficulties, she willingly undertook the care of an orphaned infant about a year old who was being carried by its grandfather but whose blind aunt was in great danger in the snowstorm and needed assistance. Despoina gathered up the child and carried it in a basket on her back. Her big heart had room for the unfortunate little one, and in the midst of the freezing cold, the warmth of her love wrapped it up. That little girl eventually survived, and passed away in her old age just a few years ago. By contrast, the two little children of the good-hearted Despoina did not endure until the end. They did reach Greece, but they died in the quarantine station on Makronissos. When life grows sarcastic, there is nothing we can say.

In Pourna-Kapan[19], bandits from Tatar took my grandmother's brother Yangos hostage and demanded ransom to release him; otherwise they would kill him. In spite of the trials he had been through, his countenance and clothes betrayed a man of means, and he stood out from his villager relatives. Perhaps word had spread that his wife, in a moment of insanity, had thrown away a sack of gold coins which she could no longer carry, and that he had found it after searching in the snow. They imprisoned him in a muddy stable. Outside it was snowing hard and the wind was raging. Inside it was bitter cold. The horses stood quietly by as Yangos awaited the decision which would determine his future, while his twenty-year-old wife cried her heart out a short distance away.

He was saved in the nick of time by an aunt of his, a dynamic, courageous woman of the Pontian villages and also a daughter of Trechtes, who barged in, screaming in Turkish that they should be ashamed of treating refugees like that, and determinedly dragged him out before they could react. Did they have a sense of honor? Did they think that they probably would not have gotten much ransom? We will never know.

---

19. A village in the foothills of Kop-tagou, 7 kilometers from Askale. In Armenian it is known as Pertekian.

318

Yangos, everyone's protector, was saved. He would find himself in danger once again, when the Armenians subsequently ordered the conscription of the Greeks. That time, his sister dressed him up as a woman and hid him on the train which was taking the unarmed to Pot.

They had left their village on January 6, 1918 and disembarked at Theodosia, Crimea, on Easter Day, which was April 22, 1918. They had undergone over three months of fierce persecution, by Turkish tsetes, Laz, Tatars and Kurds. Recently, Gioulan Avtzi, the Kurdish MP who, ignoring the party line, tipped the balance with her vote so that the Swedish Parliament formally recognized the Armenian, Pontian Greek and Assyrian genocides, stated that with that act she lessened the shame of her people's persecution of the Christian populations of the Pontus. For it is a known fact that, before the Kurds themselves suffered from Kemal's ethnic cleansing, they had collaborated with the Turks against the Christians of the Pontus. Unfortunately for them, they have yet to see the independent state that they had been promised in return for their collaboration in the cleansing.

They traveled from Theodosia to Kerch and from there rode in horse-drawn carts to reach Sudak, where they had shops and a house. There my grandmother went to a Russian school.

In that area, however, the Russian civil war was intensifying. Anarchists, nationalists, fighters for Ukrainian independence, the White army and the Red army, Germano-Austrians and Western powers, were all in rabid confrontation. There were continual knocks on their door to ask who they were and whose side they were on. The answer that they were Pontian Greek refugees was enough to prevent them from being killed. Was it enough psychologically, though, simply to escape death after such continual frights? The streets and the squares were strewn with the corpses of men and horses from the terrible fighting.

From January to March 1919, unbelievable atrocities took place in the region of Crimea and continued later on as well. My relatives would often abandon their homes and take refuge in the fields to shield themselves from the stray bullets. Once, my grandmother's entire family stayed lying down for three days in the vineyards, not daring to rise, for the deadly shooting all around them would not let up for a minute. The successive occupations eventually ended in domination by the Bolshe-viks. New conditions lay on the horizon. What would their position be in this new reality? Once religiously homogeneous Russia was now neither united in faith nor even Russia any longer, and the campaign against the Bolsheviks, which had been aided by the Greek army, had failed. The Pontians were once again left hanging.

Grandma's parents and brothers would have to reach a consensus with the other relatives regarding their future. The hope that they would return to the place where they had been rooted for centuries had not been extinguished yet. Some considered staying put, until such a return became possible. Others, mostly young cousins of my grandmother's, wanted to stay in order to help build the socialist society, attracted as they were by the revolution's promise of justice and equality. They were the ones who later, as leftists in Greece, got to know its desert islands all too well in exile. Some of them, in fact, died in countries of the Eastern Bloc as refugees once again, irrevocably expatriated. In the end, how-ever, the decision to leave without further delay carried the day. Yangos, who had already proceeded to Theodosia to make arrangements, was adamant about it: they had to join him there as soon as possible, taking nothing but the bare necessities. They would leave Russia immediately.

The ship *Patris* took them to the island of Aegina, where they were kept in quarantine for a few days to prevent the spread of illnesses, and then they disembarked. Indeed, the decision to be in the first shipload of emigrants to Greece proved to be their salvation. In the following ship-loads, people died by the hundreds. It was mainly typhoid that mowed them down.

Having arrived in Greece, they tried to accustom themselves to the new environment. It was the beginning of a new chapter in their lives, a difficult adaptation to the unfamiliar motherland, which was undergo-ing hardships of its own. My grandmother and her twin finished the fifth grade, which they had started in Russia. After two years they settled in Drapetsona, next to the Church of the Resurrection, in two shabby little rooms.

The years rolled by, and my young grandmother reached marriageable age. In 1926, at the age of twenty, she married Grandfather Thodoros and they moved into another refugee shack, roofed with *chartomata*[20], next to the cement factory. With them lived his father and invalid mother, parents of six children, of whom only my grandfather had survived. In those days, death had far more opportunities than life did.

Beyond the traditional Pontian duties of a daughter-in-law to look after her in-laws, my grandmother had a well of respect for them, especially for her father-in-law, who always took her side and treated her as his own daughter; he had a great deal of love. My great-grandmother died nine months after the wedding, and my great-grandfather Nikolas quite a few years later, in 1937. When they had come to Greece, Grandfather Thodoros was already a widower of one year, at the age of twenty-one. If my grandmother had had any experience of life, she would have resigned herself early on to the fact that she would never be the love of his life. Somewhere back in the Pontus the girl who had held that place in his heart had gone to her eternal rest, untouched any longer by daily cares. The rest, his marriage to grandmother and the birth of his children, occurred within the framework of the conventional norms society imposes. Naturally, the struggle to raise and protect their family in such difficult times thrust emotional emptiness into the background, though I remember Grandma Chrysoula complaining often with regard to her siblings: «They gave me the widower.»[21]

The quarry which my grandfather established secured for them a comparatively stable living, though they remained poor. Their first child, a boy, died shortly after birth. Later three more children came into the world. Grandmother often went down to the docks at Perama and picked up the small fish that the fishermen would reject as they cleaned their nets. With those scorned scraps she often managed to feed her whole family, though the Pontian *chapsia*[22] would remain an unforgettable memory for her. In the meantime, grandfather's political concerns had begun to flare up. He had pinned his hopes on achieving justice. Literally

---

20. Thin boards which were used on roofs instead of tiles.

21. «*Edekane me ton seron.*»

22. An extremely tasty species of anchovy which abounds in the Black Sea.

next door, at the glass factory, agitation regarding the establishment of an eight-hour work day was simmering.

After the 1940 bombardment of Piraeus by the Italians, they moved to Melissia. Two of grandmother's sisters, Theodora and Symela, lived there. The climate was excellent. They found a patch of land to build on by encroaching on land belonging to the Monastery of Penteli, which was the common practice in that difficult period. Eventually, like all the other encroachers, they paid compensation to the monastery and were given legal titles to the land. In 1944, when grandfather died in the *Dekemvriana*, shot by the British, my 38-year-old grandmother was left penniless and unprotected, with three orphans. One of her nephews, who had become hardened as a prisoner of war in Germany up until a few months earlier, decided to take action. With incredible composure, he dug up grandfather's freshly buried body from the mass grave, removed his sixteen gold teeth, and buried him again. He gave the teeth to grandmother. Macabre as it sounds, it did actually happen. The poverty which awaited the mother and her orphans put everything in a different light, and made even this act of seeming desecration acceptable. The place was teeming with little children suffering in the whirlpool of orphanhood, and everyone knew full well what they had to look forward to. A Pontian song describes the situation perfectly: «For my orphans, a glass of water from the bottom of the jug. For my orphans, a slice of bread cut with the tip of the knife.»[23]

When grandfather was shot he was taken to the municipality of Kifissia, to a hotel which had been converted to a hospital during the Occupation. The halls were full of men who had been wounded in the street fighting. The moment grandmother set eyes on her severely wounded husband, shot in the neck and the legs, she collapsed on the floor. She realized that she would most likely lose him. In the face of the calamity which had hit her, as well as the general situation, she broke down. She burst out in an uncontrollable hemorrhage, and a short while later she

---

23. *«Ta orphana m'xouliar nero 's si mastrapa tin akran. Ta orphana m'phelin psomin 's se machairi to stoma.»* The import is that the water is minimal, and that there is so little bread that it can only be cut into slices with the tip of the knife.

swelled up under the armpits due to lymphadenitis, and was unable to use her arms for a year. She was bed-ridden for months, while the children, my mother and her siblings, did their best to get by however they could, in the midst of hopelessness and mourning. At some point she got back on her feet, and began the struggle for survival. She had no qualifications, only needs. How could she make a living?

She was forced to sell water to the residents of Penteli, carrying it on her back in German jugs. The orphaned family lived on what my grandmother earned, that is to say, on very little. She received no compensation pay as a widow, for, in an ironic twist of fate, because her husband had been killed by our «friends», the British, and not by enemies, she was not eligible.

When the Tsangare Hospital in Melissia opened, grandmother was hired as a cleaning woman. In those days it was often the case that the relatives of patients with tuberculosis would refuse to get near them. My grandmother lived and worked among them, without the luxury of being able to avoid them. Actually, in a way, her position was one to be envied. The hours and wages were stable, and she worked inside a building rather than outdoors as she used to. Like the ant, she never stopped for a minute.

We grandchildren saw little of her. Still, in her poor but always freshly white-washed home, a Pontian dish was always ready for us: *tanomenos tsorvas*[24] or *chavitsi*[25], cooked in the fireplace. She did not tell us fairy tales. Where would she find time for that? We did, however, hear her dignified commands spoken to us in the ancient speech: *«Poison ti douleia s'»* instead of the Modern Greek *«Kane ti douleia sou»* («Do your work») and *«Ak'son do tha leo se»* rather than *«Akouse ti tha sou po»*

---

24. Tsorvas is made from cracked wheat, which is boiled in water until it thickens. Then *yliston*, i.e., strained yoghurt, or *paskitan*, which is a soft cheese made by boiling the liquid left over when butter is churned, and sautéed onions are added, with a sufficient amount of olive oil. Once the concoction is cooked, it is flavored with plenty of mint.

25. A plain, traditional Pontian dish made from corn meal and fresh butter.

(«Listen to what I tell you»)[26]. She never used the word *kokalo* (bone); *stoudi*[27] was her word. *Ta karvouna* (coals) for her were *tsilidia*[28], just as she used *chalepos*[29] instead of *dysarestos* (unpleasant). As for the words *«S'agapo»* (I love you), she never said them to me. It is a very serious expression not to use the thousand-year-old phrase *«Lelevo se»*[30]. Did I realize this when she was alive? Unfortunately, it was many years after her death before I understood.

She saw her two daughters married and gained three granddaughters, but unfortunately for her, no grandson, no *agour'* (boy; in Modern Greek, *agori*). Her obsession with sons reached unnatural extremes. She never missed the opportunity to advise her married daughters and granddaughters regarding the desired object. Her «awesome» secret was that they should sleep on the right side of the bed, a sure recipe for success. That is what they thought in the Pontus, where the position of a woman was anything but enviable. We saw the humorous side of the matter, and were amused by it. After all, she was not Fragoyiannou[31].

She was innocently proud, without being egotistic. She often reminded us that she was *aftexousios*, her own boss, as if, unconsciously, she hoped to balance out the trials of widowhood with certain advantages. At any rate, a number of times she refused to trade the absolute freedom of decision-making she had for a new marriage. She had closed that chapter of her life once and for all; to her it was self-evident that that was how she should behave.

After she retired from the hospital, for a few years she served as verger at our neighborhood church, St. George's. I used to help her then. Social life for my grandmother was her unfailing presence at the celebra-

---

26. *poison* and *ak'son* are the imperative forms of the ancient verbs *poio* (to do) and *akouo* (to listen).
27. *stoudi* comes from the ancient *ostoun* (bone).
28. *tsilidia* is derived from the Homeric *kilidion* (scorching hot).
29. *chalepos* is an ancient Greek adjective (difficult, unpleasant).
30. *lelevo* comes from the Homeric *lilaiomai* (to desire greatly).
31. Fragoyiannou was the name of the murderess in a well-known story by Alexandros Papadiamantes. She would kill newborn girls so that they would not suffer as they grew up.

tions of the Pontian Fellowship of Melissia. Founded in 1954, it was the fourth such Pontian organization to be created in all of Greece. After three years, a feast was held at a relative's café, and there they raised money to build the Fellowship's first private building, essentially a small room, on a piece of land which had been bought with the membership fees. In that small space, and on its tiny porch, the Pontian refugees were able to give vent to their fervent yearning. Was there room for the musician who played the lyre? All right! Everyone else would dance, even if it was so crowded that they were on top of each other.

The most important event of the year for my grandmother, however, was the festival in Sourmena. This All-Pontian gathering was and still is held on the first Sunday after Easter, that which is dedicated to St. Thomas. My grandmother, who never missed the event, would come by early in the morning to say goodbye, with a satchel over her shoulder, all neat and tidy, and full of joy. She would return late at night, having danced all day and met with a multitude of her fellow Pontians.

My sister Antigone, who, unlike me, has been involved in the promotion of Pontian affairs for years, wrote four elegies to our grandmother. The following is one of them:

IN DRAPETSONA
The sea, that dark one,
was ours!
We sowed her without thought.
We stood by her when laboring with child.
For the sake of her waves, my grandmother
stayed up till dawn embroidering foam!
Yet she never saw her again!
In Drapetsona,
her unripened youth
her yearnings
her poisoned prayers
have all been covered in cement dust.
But she...
she kept growing and getting taller like a stem

with a black tulip at its tip.
I dare say, thousands of years
have passed since then.
Yet still my grandmother is roaming
the semi-dark alleys at noon...
Like the captive, whose tongue has been cut out,
she gestures, uttering
incomprehensible words
worm-eaten
(no words found to contain the pain!).
Cars and trucks pass by,
buses loaded to the brim,
rag-pickers
and she, a mermaid,
blocks the streets with her body
commands the passersby to stop!
Asks she: «Are you Pontian?»
seeking in the «Yes»
a wall to lean against, to rest,
seeking back the breeze
that used to come in and out
of her soul's open shutters.
Then she bends in half, like a sob
that has a sharp silence at its end:
«They've taken the Pontus!
They've taken it!» she laments...
and suddenly once more jumps up:
«Eh, my little one» I hear her say,
«We shall not vanish!
Our root is plenty sturdy!
The days roll by and the hour is coming.
Our Pontus searches and waits.»

She died a few hours after suffering a stroke. The day before, the self-proclaimed *aftexousios* had whitewashed her ceiling without our knowledge. She passed away calmly and tranquilly, to the invisible world, perhaps to be compensated for the tribulations she had undergone in the visible. Her final exit was accompanied by the sounds of the Pontian lyre. The songs of her country could be heard as we took her to the church for the funeral and also during the burial. In this way my grandmother, Chrysoula, expended even the last minute of her earthly presence in Pontian fashion.

Unfortunately, when my grandmother's longing used to choke her and she wanted to talk to me, I did not have time to listen, nor did I feel like getting involved. Just a month ago I discovered four lines she had written which say everything:

«I'm going, I can't go. I'm treading on ice. I can't stay here, to Tantourlouch I'll go.»[32]

If I had taken an interest earlier, if I had been sensitive to her pain, without hesitation I would have sacrificed my time to take her to see the adored waters of her country. Sadly, I did not do it. I needed to grow up quite a bit, which took years after the death of this simple woman, to understand the role she played in my life. She kept her humble «candle» lit and passed it on to us, her children and grandchildren, without letting the «North winds» that blew–exile and emigration, widowhood and poverty–extinguish it. She was a bridge that allowed us to meet the generations that came before us, and the ideals and traditions that they preserved and we received; generations who spontaneously and naturally honored country and faith, even though their sacrifice remained unforgivably underrated and impermissibly unrecognized.

She was not a scholar, she did not become wealthy, she did not live a comfortable life. She was an uneducated woman who earned her bread cleaning the stairs and toilets of the hospital. Nevertheless, it was from her I learned that psychological stability is not the privilege of the intellectual, the successful, or the wealthy. It is not obtained by those who demand a great deal. Nor by those who advance by looking only ahead

---

32. *«Pago, na pago 'ki poro. Pato apan' 's son pagon. Ego ada 'ki inomai, 's so Tantourlouch tha pago.»*

and ignoring what is left behind. It is not easily granted to difficult people. It is a gift, to those who face their daily struggle with simplicity and without greed. To those who are humble and satisfied with only a little. To those whose great suffering gave meaning to their small joys. To those who can feel and remember. Who did not demolish solid foundations to achieve ephemeral aims. Who loved their pains. Who respected the springs which gave them water to drink.

Turkish road sign for Tantourlouch.

Tantourlouch today.

A tantouri (also called klivan), or floor oven, in Tantourlouch.

Neighborhood of Tantourlouch today.

Many such incidents occurred in the Pontus but were never photographed. Indicative is the testimonial of the American nurse Theda Phelps (archive of Kevin Carter).

Orphans of the Armenian genocide (archive of Near East Relief).

Armenian genocide. After the international outcry against Turkey in response to photos such as these, it was strictly forbidden to photograph the underage victims of the Pontus (archive of Near East Relief).

Chrysoula's cousin Apostolos Apostolides, who stayed behind his relatives and the rest of the Tantourlouch villagers to rescue those who had been buried in an avalanche on Kop-tagou.

Apostolos Apostolides at an older age. He spent a lifetime in exile.

Kleonike Papadopoulou, the orphan who survived the ordeal of Kop-tagou thanks to the care of Poine Michaelidou.

Poine Michaelidou, a woman who faced untold hardship in her life.

The 34th Infantry division with men from the Piraeus Land Army who took part in the Ukraine campaign (archive of Voula Papaioannou).

Athens. Refugee women and children (archive of ERT, Petros Poulides collection).

Refugee soup kitchens in Greece (photo archive of the Benaki Museum).

My grandmother, proud of being able to write.

Official certificate showing her completion of the 5th grade in Aegina.

My grandmother Chrysoula's three children. Poverty in Drapetsona.

My grandmother with her children and nieces and nephews in Drapetsona. Their life seems to have improved.

Identification of the victims at the Dekemvriana (archive of Dmitri Kessel).

Pontian orphans from Melissia, working as shoeshine boys outside the Cecil Hotel in Kifissia, Athens, which the Germans had taken over during the Occupation.

Church of the Transfiguration of our Saviour in Sourmena, built by the refugees. The annual All-Pontian Festival was and still is held on its grounds every Sunday of St. Thomas, the first Sunday after Easter.

Sunday of St. Thomas in Sourmena in 1965. In the background the church of the Transfiguration of our Saviour (from state television footage).

Members of The Pontian Fellowship of Melissia in the 1955 parade honoring the 28th of October, a national holiday commemorating Greek resistance to the Axis powers. As always, the lyrist is present, immediately behind the children.

Outside the hall of the Fellowship. Grandma danced at every opportunity.

Afterword

«[...] so that our conscience may not be burdened by our heartlessness regarding this.»

Georgios Kandilaptes-Kanis[1]

Being removed in time from these bitter stories inevitably results in mitigated impressions. New misfortunes were compounded upon the older ones, and successive layers of pain buried the tragedies of the previous decades. The tendency to label one's preoccupation with such matters as a sick obsession leads to the hurried effacement of such things from our memory. Besides, any kind of patriotic affinity is not only discouraged but downright ridiculed in the face of the contemporary objective of globalizing history.

But does injustice have an expiration date? Can atrocities of such magnitude and extent be written off because those who suffered them have long been dead? And what should the attitude of the civilized world towards Turkey be, when it refuses to acknowledge that the crimes it perpetrated against the Armenians, Pontian Greeks and Assyrians are indeed well within the definition of genocide?

Does not the absence of a stern condemnation by the world community render us all accessory to those past crimes? For, if entire peoples were butchered on the fringes of Europe in the first decades of the 20th century and yet no one is ever attributed the blame, it is clear that political expediency has obliterated any shred of justice in the world.

---

1. A country schoolteacher and prolific writer on folklore and patriotic themes, born in Argyroupolis in the Pontus.

Humanity has known other peoples who have been destroyers of cultures, peoples who spread ruination. The Turkish nation belongs to that exact ilk. Because of them, the ultimate defenders of the farthest reaches of European civilization, the Pontian Greeks, were violently uprooted from lands equivalent to half the size of present-day Greece, where they had lived and prospered socially, intellectually and financially for centuries. It seems that history laid a curse on us, and our nation, that age-long bulwark against barbarism, was expelled from the Asia Minor battlements. Daughter of civilization, the West deserted Greece, the mother of civilization, during the Turkish frenzy. At the same time, the political overthrow of 1917 in Russia not only deprived the Pontians of longtime friends, but actually advanced Kemal's plans against them. Without a doubt, mankind has demonstrated appalling cruelty in other ages. The Pontian peoples, however, came up against the worst possible ruthlessness that dwells in the depths of the human psyche. The sheer degree of savagery employed and the relentless, merciless pursuit of nationalistic aims at the cost of hundreds of thousands of lives, makes the fierceness of wild beasts attacking their prey, which we so unfairly use in our characterizations, look like a mother's caress.

Our slayers came out the victors, of course, but their «triumph», drenched in the blood of innocent folk as it was, is as false as the entire façade of modern-day Turkey. Though Kemal may have been victorious, he was as responsible for the wreaking of measureless calamity upon mankind as was the defeated Hitler. The only difference lies in the fact that the former represents the primitive expression of horror, the latter, the sophisticated version of it.

We Pontians have not been vindicated yet. The admission that we have lovely dances and songs does not amount to vindication. This is nothing but a shell of who we truly are, an impressive and all too often misleading outer covering. Vindication will be brought about only by world condemnation of this premeditated crime, a crime that was directed even against infants in their mothers' arms, as well as a rigorous prohibition against the repetition of any such conduct, not only by the culprit Turkey but by any other imitator anywhere in the world.

In 1922, on the ruins of WWI, the sanctimonious West was making a financial comeback and entering a period of exceptional intellectual flowering. Proust was in search of time lost, Eliot was at work on *The Waste Land*, and Joyce was writing Ulysses. In the exact same era, far removed from that intellectual environment, the Pontians were being delivered to the slaughter. They were losing the past, present and future in their ruined land, wrecked between the Kemalian Scylla and Charybdis. Wicked suitors, who knew only too well how to appropriate a stranger's hard toil, became their land's sole sovereign.

Those few indigenous people who remained were forced to convert to Islam in order to survive, or to practice the Christian faith in secret up to the present day. During the 1920s and for decades afterwards, soldiers in the Turkish army would answer to morning roll call with Turkish first names and Greek surnames. What has become of them all? How did each "Achmet" Demiroglou, son of Demetrius, get through their daily life? Where are their children and grandchildren? Do they remember? Do they know? Our race is hardy. We endure.

The first victims of the genocide, those venerable faces amongst whom I sauntered obliviously as a little girl, have constituted a life-long debt for me. For we have a lifelong obligation to ourselves, and they are all pieces of me. My steps will forever be following their tracks in the snows of Chaldia, in the labor battalions of Erzerum, in the deportations of Amaseia, in the wards of Selimie and in the shantytowns of Kalamaria; on board the ships full of typhoid, in the thirst on Makronissos, as well as in the dust of Drapetsona. I will be following them where their exhausted bodies and courageous souls took on their backs the weight of human dignity and honor and preserved them to the end. They made up their minds once and for all, without vacillation or dilemmas. Businessmen from the city and manual laborers from the countryside, affluent, nobly born merchants and landowners alongside ordinary folk struggling to earn a living, intellectual scholars together with illiterate villagers, all formed one resounding punch of solid Greek identity, guided by their ancient heroic proclivity. The decision to preserve, at any cost, all that they had been bequeathed sprang up in them spontaneously as the only option. That was the stance from which our race traversed the centuries.

Bibliography

Alexandris, Alexis, *Pontic Greek refugees in Constantinople 1922-1923: The human cost of the exchange of populations*, archive of the Committee for Pontian Studies, Athens 1982.

Andreades, Georgios, *It was a Tempest, Memoirs of Father Prodromos Iliades,* Erodios, Thessaloniki 2002.*

Association of Pontian Ladies, *Living Memories of the Pontus, a collection of photos, letters, etc. in book form*, Thessaloniki 1988.*

Avgerinos, Dimitrios, *Erzerum 1916*, Armos, Athens 2011.*

Bakalopoulos, Konstantinos, *Modern Greek History (1204-1940)*, Kyriakides Brothers, Thessaloniki 1998.*

Bergeti, Maria, *From the Pontus to Greece*, Kyriakides Brothers, Thessaloniki 1994.*

Bouteneff, Patricia Fann, *Exiles on Stage: The Modern Pontic Theater in Greece*, Archive of the Committee for Pontian Studies, Athens 2002.

Bryer Anthony, *People and settlement in Anatolia and the Caucasus, 800-1900*, Variorum Reprints, London 1988.

Center for Asia Minor Studies, *Refugee Greece*, Athens 1992.

Charalambidis, Michalis, *Asia Minor Unites, Turkey Barbarizes*, Stravon Publishers, Athens 2011.*

—, *Aspects of the New Eastern Question - Center of Pontian Studies*, Gordios, Athens 1998.

—, *The Pontian Question in the United Nations*, Pontian Society of Thessaloniki «Efxinos Leschi», Thessaloniki 2004.

—, *The Pontian Question Today*, Idryma Mesogeiakon Meleton, Athens 1991.*

Charalampidis, Michalis and Fotiades, Konstantinos, *Pontians. The Right to Be Remembered*, Gordios, Athens 2003.*

Chatzidimitriades, Giorgos, *Diary of Exile. Erzerum 1943*, Estia Bookstores, Athens 2010.*

Chrysanthos, Metropolitan of Trapezunta, *Biographical Recollections*, Center for the Study of Greek History, Athens 2004.*

—, Metropolitan of Trapezunta, *The Church of Trapezunta*, Estia, Athens 1933.*

Christoforides, Stathes (Sarpogles), *Black Times and Black Days*, self-published, Athens 1993.*

Clark, Bruce, *Twice a Stranger, The Mass Expulsions that Forged Modern Greece and Turkey*, Harvard University Press, Cambridge, Massachusetts 2006.

Dallegre, Joelle, *Grecs et Ottomans 1453-1923*, L'Harmattan, Paris 2002

Delta, Penelope, *Eleftherios Venizelos*, Athens 1978.*

Dionisiates, Gabriel, *From Grandfather's Garden*, To Perivoli tis Panagias, Thessaloniki 1994.*

Ecumenical Patriarchate, *Black Bible of the persecution and martyrdom of the Greeks in Turkey (1914-1918)*, Constantinople 1919.*

Eddy, D.B., *Greece and Greek Refugees*, London 1931.

Efstathiades, Stathes, *Songs of the Pontian People*, Maiandros, Thessaloniki 1986.*

Erbil, Pervin, *Niovi wept for Asia Minor (Anadolu 'ya Agliyordu Niobe)*, 2nd edition, Tsoukatos, Athens 2004.*

Fotiades, Konstantinos, *The Genocide of the Pontian Greeks*, Herodotus, Thessaloniki, 2004.

—, *The Hellenism of the Efxinos Pontus*, Kyriakides Brothers, Thessaloniki 2008.*

—, *The Islamizations of Asia Minor and the Secret Christians of the Pontus,* Kyriakides Brothers, Thessaloniki 1993.*

—, *Sources for the history of the problem of the secret Christians*, Kyriakides Brothers, Thessaloniki 1997.*

Gavrielides, Antonios, *Pages from the dark national tragedy of the Pontus*, Athens 1924.*

Giarenes, Efthymis, *Those who the wind lashes*, self-published, Thessaloniki 1993.*

Gritsi-Milliex, Tatiana, *Tripoli of the Pontus-a historical monograph*, Kedros, Athens 1981.*

Halo, Thea, *Not Even My Name*, Picador, USA 2000.

Historical Archive of the Greek Refugee Population in the Municipality of Kalamaria, *Kalamaria between the wars 1920-1940*, University Studio Press, Thessaloniki 1998.*

Horton, George, *The Blight of Asia*, The Bobbs-Merrill Company, Indianapolis 1926.

Ioannides, Savvas, *On Pontus and Trapezunta*, Koultoura, Athens 1981.*

Kandilaptes-Kanis, Georgios, *Geographical and Historical Dictionary of the Villages, Towns and Cities of Chaldia*, Kyriakides Brothers, Thessaloniki 2004.*

Kelekides, Demosthenes, *The Rebel Movement of the Pontus*, Gordios, Athens 2006.*

Kiourtsoglou, Konstantinos, *In Exile. Erzerum, Askale*, Greek Institute for Historical Studies, Athens 2006.*

Kitromilides, P.M. and Alexandris, A., *Ethnic survival, nationalism and forced migration: The historical demography of the Greek community of Asia Minor at the close of the Ottoman era*, Bulletin 5, Center for Asia Minor Studies (1984-85).

Koromila, Marianna, *On The Trail of Odysseus*, Michael Russel, Norwick, 1994.

Kourtides, Konstantinos, *A Diary of the Deeds of the Greek Rebels of Santa (1916-1924)*, Kyriakides Brothers, Thessaloniki 2007.*

Koutsoupias, Fotios, *The Intellectual Renaissance of Pontian Hellenism*, Herodotus, Thessaloniki 2002.*

Ladas, Stephen, *The exchange of Minorities: Bulgaria, Greece and Turkey*, Mac Millan, New York 1932.

Lampsides, Georgios, *Topal Osman, Chronology of an Unknown Greek Tragedy*, Biblia gia Olous, Athens 1969.*

Lampsides, Odysseas, *A New Historical Source. The Biographical Recollections of Chrysanthos, Metropolitan of Trapezunta*, Bulletin 11, Center for Asia Minor Studies (1995-96), pages 239-265.*

Laparides, Nikos, *Matsouka of Pontus*, Kyriakides Brothers, Thessaloniki 1996.*

Loukatos, Dimitrios, *Foot Soldier at the Albanian Front*, Potamos, Athens 2001.*

Lovejoy, Esther Pohl, M.D., *Certain Samaritans*, Macmillan Company, New York 1933.

Mavrides, Dimitrios, *From the History of Thrace 1875-1925*, Holy Metropolis of Xanthi and Peritheorio, Xanthi 2006.*

Melanofrydes, Panteles, *The Greek Language in Pontus*, Kyriakides Brothers, Thessaloniki 1997.*

Oikonomides, Dimitrios, *The Pontus and the Rights of its Greek Population*, Association for the Distribution of Beneficient Books, Athens 1920.*

Papadopoulos, Anestes, *Memories and Nostalgia from our Unforgettable Pontus (Anamneseis kai nostalgymata apo ton alesmonito mas Ponto)*, self-published, Edessa 1962.*

Papadopoulos, Anthimos, *Historical Dictionary of the Pontian Dialect*, Archive of the Committee for Pontian Studies, Athens 1961.*

Papamichalopoulos, Konstantinos, *A Tour of the Pontus*, Athens 1903.*

Pavlides, Ioannes, *Uprooted*, newspaper of the Pontian Association, Thessaloniki 1988.*

Pelagides, Efstathios, *The Resettlement of the Refugees in Western Macedonia,1923-1930*, Kyriakides Brothers, Thessaloniki 1994.*

Pentzopoulos, Dimitrios, *The Balkan Exchange of Minorities and its Impact upon Greece*, C. Hurst & Co. Publishers Ltd; London, 2002.

Petsalis, Diomidis, *Greece At the Paris Peace Conference (1919)*, Institute for Balkan Studies; Ex-Library edition, Thessaloniki 1978.

Ristovic, Milan, *A Long Journey Home: Greek Refugee Children in Yugoslavia 1948-1960*, Institute for Balkan Studies, Thessaloniki 2000.

Rodakis, Pericles, *The History of Pontus*, Gordios, Athens 2003.*

Psathas, Dimitris, *The Land of Pontus*, Mares Editions, Athens 1966.*

Salkitzoglou, Takis, *Asia Minor in the Revolution of 1821*, Foundation of the Hellenic World, Athens 2010. *

Samouelides, Christos, *History of Pontian Hellenism*, Alkyon, Athens 1985.*

Soulioti, Baso, *The events of 1955 in Constantinople and my life*, Smyrniotakis, Athens 2010.*

Triandafyllides, Stavros, *The History of Drapetsona*, self-published, Athens 1998.*

Tsaousi, Agathaggelou, *The History of the Pontian village Hopsa and its destruction*, Kyriakides Brothers, Thessaloniki 2002.*

Tsirkinides, Haris, *At Last We Uprooted Them... The Genocide of Greeks of Pontos, Thrace and Asia Minor, based on the French Archives*, Kyriakides Brothers, Thessaloniki 2009. Greek edition: Kyriakides Brothers, Thessaloniki 2002.

*available only in Greek

Index

Theodora Ioannidou was born in 1953 in Athens, where she lives with her family and works as a dentist. She is a third-generation Pontian, two of whose grandparents hailed from the coastal city of Oinoe and the other two from the remote mountain villages of Matsouka and Chaldia. *The Pontian Holocaust still an open wound* is her first book.